Kay Thomas has captured real life experiences and woven them into the eternal truths of Scripture to produce a meaningful tapestry of a faithful Christian life. Her stories are so authentic that the reader catches a glimpse of her soul and lifetime of unwavering faith. What a joy to walk with Kay who obviously walks with God day by day.

Dr. J. Howard Olds—Senior Pastor,
Brentwood United Methodist Church

Poignant, practical, powerful—these devotionals will help you focus on the Lord and deepen your relationship with Him.

Marlene Bagnull—Director, Colorado and Greater
Philadelphia Christian Writers' Conferences

In this book of daily devotionals Kate Thomas has drawn from her years as a Christian, a pastor's wife, a mother and a grandmother to share practical truths from the Bible that will help us all to draw closer to the Lord.

Donna Goodrich—free-lance writer,
editor and leader of Christian writer's seminars

Because Kay Thomas is one of those people I want to be like when I grow up, I'm thankful she's given us these daily, behind-the-scenes reminders of what wisdom on two feet looks like.

Jan Johnson—Author of *Enjoying the Presence of God* and *When the Soul Listens*

NEW EVERY MORNING

A Daily Touch of God's Faithfulness

Kate R. Thomas

ACW Press
Phoenix, Arizona 85013

New Every Morning: A Daily Touch of God's Faithfulness
Copyright ©2001 Kate R. Thomas
All rights reserved

Cover Design by Alpha Advertising
Interior design by Pine Hill Graphics

Packaged by ACW Press
5501 N. 7th Ave., #502
Phoenix, Arizona 85013
www.acwpress.com
The views expressed or implied in this work do not necessarily reflect those of ACW Press. Ultimate design, content, and editorial accuracy of this work is the responsibility of the author(s).

Library of Congress Cataloging-in-Publication Data

Thomas, Kate R.
    New every morning : a daily touch of God's
faithfulness / Kate R. Thomas
        p. cm.
        Includes index.
        ISBN: 1-892525-57-7

        1. Devotional calendars. 2. Prayer-books.
I. Title.

BV4811.T46 2001   242'.2
                             QBI01-200417

Printed in the United States of America.

DEDICATION

This book is dedicated to my wonderful family. Their help and inspiration, along with God's faithful guidance, have given me the courage to begin and complete this book. I am forever grateful to:

- My dear husband, Wally, for his untiring patience and many hours at the computer during the book's preparation;

- Our daughter, Debbie, who has been a constant source of encouragement; her husband, Steve Caswell; and our granddaughter, Katie;

- Our son, David, whose words to me at a "dry" time in my life—"Mom, this is your time to study and write"—inspired me to begin; and his wife, Karen; and our grandson, Luke; and

- David, Karen, and Debbie for their suggestions for the book title and cover design.

FOREWORD

*I*n the few months since the birth of our little boy, Luke, Karen and I have found ourselves becoming baby toy experts. Karen especially has read up on the safety and developmental features of different toys with which Luke now loves to play. We have confidence in these toys because they've been tested and found beneficial for infants.

The truth is, we look for the same reliability in our grown-up world, too. We don't want to be the guinea pig for some FDA drug research project. In a world of virtual reality and artificial ingredients and superficial relationships, we want the real thing. We're looking for truth on which we can build our lives—truth that's been tested and found beneficial for us.

That kind of proven, practical wisdom is what you're holding in your hands. I can vouch for it. Vividly engraved in my memory is the picture of my mom at her desk, every day, anchoring herself in each new morning's touch of God's faithfulness. I have never known anyone with a more authentic and steady devotional life or with a more resilient prayer life than my mother's.

She shares here the simple wisdom I've seen in her life—through the Scripture verses sprinkled in countless conversations and notes she has shared with me throughout her life. What makes these words trustworthy is not just their distillation through a life faithfully lived, but, even more, their source in the Word of God that is true and can be trusted (Revelation 22:6).

I am so proud of my mom for pursuing this dream. And I am honored to recommend her treasury to you.

David R. Thomas
Lexington, Kentucky

ACKNOWLEDGMENTS

$\mathcal{T}$he writing of these daily devotionals has been a long but meaningful part of my spiritual journey. Besides my immediate family, to whom this book is dedicated, I am also thankful for:

- All who have nurtured me in my faith through the years, especially my mother, Vina Cooksey Radford;

- My extended family and all whose lives have touched mine, making possible the experiences shared in this book;

- Reverend Gregory Hatfield, my co-leader on young adult retreats in the1970s, who said to me, "Your personal experience stories should be written down and shared. Have you ever considered writing a devotional book?";

- Judy Radford Branham, my niece, who has been both an encourager and an editor; Betty Whitworth and Donna Goodrich for their help in proofing and editing; My pastor, Reverend Russell East, and our church secretary, Rose Zanone, for their assistance;

- Joyce Joines, my friend, who has shared writing retreats with me over the years;

- Steve Laube, Chuck Dean, and the staff at ACW Press; Fred Renich and the staff at Pine Hill Graphics; and

- Most of all, my heavenly Father, His Son Jesus, and the Holy Spirit—my ever present companion all along the way.

INTRODUCTION

These devotionals cover the span of my lifetime, but I began putting them on paper some seventeen years ago.

Throughout my life I have found God faithful. I have found His provisions for all my needs to be new every morning—and evening! He goes before us. He is present with us. And He will follow after us all our days.

I trust that as you read these meditations each day, you will recall experiences in which God's mercy, love, and faithfulness abounded in your own life.

May the truth in God's Word come alive each day in your heart. I encourage you to read this book through more than once, for the Bible is the *living* Word. Its truths and insights will be new for you each day.

May God bless you abundantly both now and always.

The steadfast love of the Lord never ceases, his mercies never come to an end;
they are new every morning; great is thy faithfulness.
Lamentations 3: 22,23

New Every Morning

The steadfast love of the Lord never ceases; his mercies never come to an end; they are new every morning, great is thy faithfulness.
Lamentations 3:22,23

What a blessed thought to know that our heavenly Father's love and mercy are new *every* new day of *every* new year! Because of His faithfulness, we can claim and proclaim with the psalmist, "This is the day which the Lord has made; let us rejoice and be glad in it" (Psalms 118:24).

On this New Year's Day, we have a new beginning. Resolutions are born on this day. We can resolve today that, because of God's great faithfulness, all troublesome days in this new year can become triumphant days. Each day is a new beginning because:

We can't see tomorrow, but God's faithfulness will see us through all of our tomorrows.

> God's mercies are new;
> His grace is new;
> His comfort is new;
> His protection is new;
> His forgiveness is new; and
> His love is new.

So today we have a fresh start for a new year—and also a new life! Each morning these divine provisions are ours. They are graciously showered upon us. They are like John describes in the prologue of his gospel, "And from his fullness have we all received, grace upon grace" (John 1:16).

To God be all glory for the things He has done *and will do!*

Loving God, thank You for all of Your provisions that are new for us every morning. Thank You especially for sending Your Son, Jesus. In His name. *Amen*

God's Time

He has appointed a time for every matter, and for every work.
Ecclesiastes 3:17b

As we begin a new year, we are conscious of the rapid passing of time. We race against the clock, feeling that our time is so limited. We rush from one appointment to the next. We look for the fastest way to cook, clean, communicate, perform surgical procedures, etc. The writer of Ecclesiastes named the various times: a time to be born, to die, to plant, to harvest, to weep, to laugh, to seek, to lose, to speak, to keep silence. In fact, there's a time, he said, for every matter under heaven.

God's timing may seem delayed, but it's never late.

We use every minute of every hour of every day in one way or another. Sometimes we say that we just don't have the time when asked to accept certain responsibilities. But what do we do about God's time—*kairos* time? When it's God's time to reveal Himself to us, do we allow Him to or are we too busy?

God's time is always right. It's never too early and it's never too late. Sarah was old when she gave birth to Isaac, but God's time was right. Jesus waited forty days and nights in the wilderness for power and peace about His ministry, but God's time was right. We wait for prayers to be answered, and the answer comes in God's time. His time is always right. His *answer* is always right.

Patience is a part of God's plan for our Christian growth and maturity. It would be well to learn to trust God in His timing, and say with the psalmist, "My times are in thy hand" (Psalms 31:15a).

Dear God, help me to wait patiently for Your perfect timing in my life, for I know in my heart that Your will and way are worth the wait. In Jesus' name. *Amen*

Promises to Keep

This is the sign you have from the Lord, that the Lord will do this thing that He has promised.
Isaiah 38:7

Snowfalls are not a common occurrence in Atlanta, Georgia. But on that cold winter evening in the late 1950s, snow seemed appropriate as we walked the tree-lined street to Agnes Scott College. There we would hear America's beloved poet Robert Frost read some of his beautiful works.

The crunchy snow and wooded street made for a perfect prelude to Mr. Frost's "Stopping by Woods on a Snowy Evening." The closing lines are especially meaningful to me:

What promises will I make to the Lord at the beginning of this new year?

> "But I have promises to keep
> And miles to go before I sleep,
> And miles to go before I sleep."[1]

I have replayed these words again and again in my memory over the years. I've often thought of "stopping places" that I've experienced along the road of life. Many of these places were ones where I would have liked to linger longer. The energizing beauty of a full rainbow or the serenity of a sunset, or the majesty of a mountain range can capture our whole being for a moment. But reality nudges us on. We remember our commitments and responsibilities. We have miles to go before we sleep, and we have promises to keep.

Isaiah reminds us that the Lord is faithful; He will do that which He promised. Will we?

Dear God, You have been faithful in all Your promises. Help me to keep my eyes focused on You as I travel the road ahead. In Jesus' name. *Amen*

In His Hands

In the shadow of his hand he hid me.

Isaiah 49:2b

*T*oday's experience will be forever imprinted in my memory. Through the wonder of ultrasound, I saw my first grandchild—a four-inch, three-month fetus. Its parents and grandparents watched in amazement as two little arms and two little legs moved about in our daughter's womb. With the conviction of a grandmother, I'm sure I saw a little head turn in our direction!

We're not only in God's hands—we're in His heart as well.

But what really struck me was that this little new life looked so cradled and protected—almost as though it were lying in the palm of a hand. In fact, I believe it is—in God's hand. God was in the creating process even before this child was conceived. A long time ago God spoke to Jeremiah, "Before I formed you in the womb I knew you, and before you were born I consecrated you" (Jeremiah 1:5a).

Before our grandchild is born, its position in the womb will change many times, but it will never be out of God's hand. Then after its birth and on through the toddler stage of taking the first steps, through that first day of school, through the temptations of youth, and on through all of life's struggles, God's hand will lead and guide. In Isaiah 41:10 God promised that He will uphold us by His right hand. In Isaiah 49:16, God said, "Behold, I have graven you on the palm of my hands." What love and care our Father gives us even before we're born! What a blessed sense of security we can have in knowing that we are hidden in the shadow of His hand.

Loving Father, our lives are in Your hands. Remind us of this so we need never be afraid. In Jesus' name. *Amen*

Encouragement for the Heart

I have sent him to you for this very purpose, that you may know how we are, and that he may encourage your hearts.

Ephesians 6:22

*I*n today's world, hearts often become heavy and need encouragement. The same need was present among the young Christians in the church at Ephesus. So Paul sent Tychicus to them to encourage their hearts.

All of us experience discouragement. Our spirits become drained. Hope diminishes—even vanishes. Disappointment and disillusionment seem to dwell too long in our hearts. Instead of experiencing the joy of the Lord, we become heavy-hearted, weary in well-doing, and sick in the very depths of our soul.

Our loving heavenly Father can heal hurting heavy hearts.

The opening sentence of Scott Peck's book *The Road Less Traveled* says "Life is difficult."[2] Financial setbacks seem to be able to hit even the wisest budget managers. Health can diminish or disappear in an instant. Schedules become overloaded. Communication breaks down. Corporate boardroom tactics find their way into church meetings. Man's inhumanity to man seems almost overwhelming at times. Hearts—good hearts—Christian hearts—become heavy and discouraged and demoralized. Where do we turn for help?

I don't purport to have all the answers. I only know what helps me in times of discouragement. I believe, like Tychicus, we can bring encouragement to a heavy heart. Likewise, we can receive encouragement from a fellow Christian. We can be mutual encouragers. I believe this is a part of our responsibility and privilege as Christians. Paul longed to visit the church at Rome "that we may be mutually encouraged by each other's faith" (Romans 1:12).

I also believe we are to lean heavily on God's truth in His Word. Discouragement is the devil's best tool, but he cannot penetrate God's armor (Ephesians 6:11-20). One of the most important aspects of this armor, I believe, is His Word. We need to have implanted in our minds such verses as, "He who is in you is greater than he who is in the world" (I John 4:4b) and "I can do all things in him who strengthens me" (Philippians 4:13).

Dear God, thank You for those who encourage us along the way. Show us how to encourage others in Your name. *Amen*

Our Times Are in God's Hands

My times are in thy hand.
Psalms 31:15a

*M*y husband Wally and I visited a young baby from our church who was in Kosair Children's Hospital in Louisville. The Down's Syndrome child had just undergone heart surgery that morning. Lying flat on her back with a multitude of wires and tubes connected to her small, fragile body, the baby fought for her life. The young father smiled and said with all confidence, "We believe better times are ahead." It was obvious that he had placed the situation in God's hand.

In God's hand, we don't need to fear.

Later as we left the hospital we began to talk with a young mother who walked alongside us. "You have someone in Kosair?" I asked. Tired eyes met mine. "Yes," she replied, "my baby has been here for three months." She explained that due to a medical error her baby was in a vegetative state and could die at any time.

"We're prepared," the young mother said. "He's already lived longer than the doctors predicted. Yesterday, he even *looked* at me for a brief second!" Then glancing out the window, she said, "I'm prepared—whatever way it goes." Her times were in God's hands.

Our times are in God's hands, too. Hope enabled these young parents to hold together. Faith in God was preparing them for the future. In God's hands, they found comfort and security.

No one can take us out of God's hands except ourselves. John 10: 29b says, "No one is able to snatch them out of the Father's hand." We, like these young parents, can face the future when we know the future is in God's hands.

Loving Lord, we trust You. You are faithful. Continue to lead us and help us to remain always in Your hand. Through Christ. *Amen*

Holding God's Hand

If I take the wings of the morning and dwell in the uttermost parts of the sea, even there thy hand shall lead me, and thy right hand shall hold me.
Psalms 139:9,10

During the summer that our son David turned six, we took him to visit the elementary school where he would begin first grade. The new town and new school were frightening to him. All the way through the empty hallways he held onto my hand. His grip tightened as we walked to the doors of the two first grade rooms. Even today, he says he remembers the courage he felt just from having a hand to hold.

"I am continually with thee; thou dost hold my right hand" (Psalm 73:23).

We moved to another new town as David began his sophomore year. Again, he needed a hand. Only this time it was into God's hand that he slipped his hand. This has continued to be a precious experience for him on many occasions over the years.

As a young adult he faced challenges to his faith during a year's study of theology in Bristol, England. Again, he imagined God by his side. Another time he boarded the wrong train and headed for what was then Communist Bulgaria. Realizing the mistake, he made his way up the crowded aisle and pled with the conductor to let him off. The conductor refused, so David opened the door himself and jumped. He suffered some bruises, but he was in safe territory. Psalms 37:24 was proven true: "Though he fall, he shall not be cast headlong, for the Lord is the stay of his hand."

Later as a young adult beginning a job as research analyst at Banker's Trust Company in Atlanta, he once again faced a challenge. As he stepped off the elevator that first day on the job, he prayed, "God, hold my hand today." God did.

Always when our family is on a long (or even a short) flight, we have a practice of imagining the plane in God's hand, believing Deuteronomy 33:7, "The eternal God is your dwelling place, and underneath are the everlasting arms." The Lord asks in Isaiah 50:2b "Is my hand shortened, that it cannot redeem?" I believe we can trust the hand of God to reach us wherever we are.

Dear God, You formed us by Your mighty hand and that same hand leads us all the way home to You. Thank You for such love and care as this. *Amen*

The Church's Source of Power

The prayer of a righteous man has great power in its effects.

James 5:16b

*W*hen Charles Spurgeon was only nineteen years of age, he became pastor of a dying, tradition-bound church in a large metropolitan area of London. On his first night in a nearby boarding house, the old-timers, who predicted his stay would be short-lived, razzed Spurgeon. The next thirty years proved them wrong.

Have I prayed for my minister and my church to be endowed with power— God's power?

As Spurgeon preached to growing crowds, a tabernacle was built to accommodate them. More than ten thousand came to Christ and united with this church.

People outside the church began to wonder why all this was happening. What was this church's source of power?

London newspapers sent journalists to report on Spurgeon's sermons, attributing his success to his earnestness, zeal, courage, sincerity, and genius for commanding an audience. A group of ministers came to a service and before it began asked Spurgeon a pointed question, "Where does your power come from?" Spurgeon replied, "Come with me." He led the group down some stairs to the basement of the church. As the ministers walked along they began to murmur to each other, "Oh, he's going to show us the electrical power room—we wanted to know the source of *his* power."

In a moment Charles Spurgeon led them to a large room where many parishioners were on their knees, fervently praying for God's blessings to be upon the service. "There," said Spurgeon, "is where the power comes from!"

James said, "The prayers of a righteous man has great power in its effect." He also said, "You do not have, because you do not ask" (James 4:2b). Jesus said, "And I tell you, Ask, and it will be given you" (Luke 11:9a).

Loving God, forgive us when we try to function in our own strength. Give us Your power so that we can truly be Your body on earth. In Jesus' name. *Amen*

Ice Can Melt

A new heart I will give you, and a new spirit I will put within you; and I will take out of your flesh the heart of stone and give you a heart of flesh.

Ezekiel 36:26

A young man in our church was deeply concerned about his father Ed's relationship with the Lord. He spoke to us often about his father's coldness of heart. But one day his face brightened as he said, "You know, my dad's heart is like ice, but ice can melt!" And with that statement of hope our own faith was strengthened. We began to believe this father could and would change.

This icy cold heart *did* melt! It required many years of patience and perseverance and prayers. But it melted—slowly and surely. My husband Wally visited Ed's home many times and was not invited inside. He made many attempts at conversation by telephone only to be cut off curtly and quickly.

As warmth is to ice, so is God's love to hearts of stone.

But one day things changed. Wally went to Ed's door and was warmly invited in. In fact, Ed said he had been looking for Wally.

That day, this father with the icy heart began to open his heart to God. The melting process began. He began to admit his need for the Lord to be a part of his life.

A few months later it happened. Ed was driving down Western Kentucky Parkway and felt that God was nudging him to pull off the road. He did. He turned the car motor off and began to pray. God entered the man with the cold heart that day, removing the icy, stony heart and replacing it with a new one filled with joy.

Ed never lost this joy. He remained a happy and committed Christian until his death.

Perhaps you know someone with an icy cold heart. Just know that God *can* melt icy hearts and replace them with hearts filled with His love.

Dear Jesus, please forgive me for the times my heart is cold. Melt and renew it by the power of the Holy Spirit. *Amen*

The Master Weaver

His master said to him "Well done, good and faithful servant."
Matthew 25:21a

*L*iving out our lives day by day is something like the process of weaving a piece of fabric. Each day we add another thread to the total design, creating our own unique pattern. Some day's thread may appear dark to us, because of the struggles, suffering and disappointments that have come our way. Other days may bring tangles and knots and bobbles in our life's fabric, representing those times when we've felt tied up in the mistakes we've made. Still other happy days may add a bright, cheerful color to the woof of the design. But *all* threads are needed for the overall pattern.

"Well done, good and faithful servant."

We may not always like the design that life weaves for us. But we need to remember that our view is different to God's vantage point. We see from the "under side." God sees the total pattern from the "upper side" and understands why it is as it is. He knows why the dark threads, the knots, the tangles, and the bright threads are a part of the total picture. He knows because He was with us through it all, making something beautiful out of the completed pattern.

I believe when we do our very best, day by day, we'll one day meet Him face to face and hear Him say, "Well done, good and faithful servant." Only then can we understand the total picture—from the upper side!

The Weaver

My life is but a weaving
Between my Lord and me;
I may not choose the colors,
He knows what they should be;
For He can view the pattern
Upon the upper side,
While I can see it only
On this, the under side.
Sometimes He weaveth sorrow,
Which seems strange to me;

But I will trust His judgement,
And work as faithfully;
'Tis He who fills the shuttle,
He knows just what is best,
So I shall weave in earnest
And leave with Him the rest.
Not till the loom is silent
And the shuttles cease to fly
Shall God unroll the canvas
And explain the reason why—
The dark threads are as needful
In the weaver's skillful hand
As the threads of gold and silver
In the pattern He has planned.
                    —Author unknown

Loving Lord, we don't always understand each day's design, but we know in our hearts that You hold the shuttle. Help us to trust our days to You, knowing that You are working everything together for our good. *Amen*

Barrier or Blessing

As for you, you meant evil against me; but God meant it for good.
Genesis 50:20a

One of the most fascinating movies I have seen at the Imax Theater in Louisville was "The Great Barrier Reef." The aerial view of this broken chain of reefs along the coast of Australia was truly breathtaking. Long stretches of coral formation—some 1250 miles in length—form the largest reef of its kind in the world.

Today I want to focus on life's blessings rather than life's barriers.

The reef can be both a barrier and a blessing to those who encounter it. Ships that sail too close to it can be damaged and even become lodged upon the reef. On the other hand, sailors have found that once inside the reef, they are shielded from the dangers of the open sea.

Barriers and blessings. Along the course of a lifetime, we constantly encounter both. Some barriers we create for ourselves. Others we can label circumstantial happenings. Still other barriers may even result from heredity. But I believe all barriers—with God's help—can become blessings used for our good.

Joseph said to his brothers, who had mistreated him, "You meant evil against me, but God meant it for good." Paul said in Romans 8:28, "We know that in everything God works for good with those who love him, who are called according to his purpose."

"In everything." That includes life's obstacles and barriers. Storms may rage in our lives, but we can find safe harbor and peace with our Lord. "In all these things we are more than conquerors through him who loved us" (Romans 8:37). God intends for our lives to be abundant in spite of the barriers.

Loving God, in our storms, setbacks, and rocky glitches, help us to find a safe harbor in You. In Jesus' name. *Amen*

Laundry Without Detergent

Wash me, and I shall be whiter than snow.
Psalms 51:7b

oday I put in a load of laundry, set the dial on "normal," and lowered the washer lid, which set the agitator in motion. Moments later I noticed a different sound coming from the washer—an empty, dissonant swishing. Then it occurred to me. I had forgotten to add the detergent, and I realized that no amount of tossing and turning the clothes in clear water would remove all the soil from them.

This experience reminded me that often in my life I need a cleansing agent, too. I go through the necessary motions and activities of the day. I may even go through the routine of a quiet devotional time with no real change taking place within me. My life continues to feel empty and out of tune with Jesus. I can find neither cleansing nor harmony in my life until I realize the ingredient I've left out.

It's up to me to allow the cleansing power of the Holy Spirit to work in my life today.

I believe all of us need cleansing. Maybe our need to be purified is not as great as the psalmist David when he wrote, "Wash me, and I shall be whiter than snow." But all of us sin and fall short of God's glory. Trying to do laundry without detergent doesn't work, and neither will we know joy and peace without the cleansing power of the Holy Spirit at work in us. Inevitably, life will bring plenty of dirtiness and blemishes, plenty of tossing to and fro. But it is the addition of the cleansing power of the Holy Spirit that will make us clean and whole. No amount of attempts to "clean up" our lives in our own strength will work. Just as detergent emulsifies dirt, allowing it to leave clothing, so does Jesus cleanse our hearts through the purifying power of the Holy Spirit!

Lord Jesus, I want to be pure and whole in Your sight. Cleanse me of all unrighteousness. *Amen*

Daddy, Please Pray

A little child shall lead them.
Isaiah 11:6b

When my husband Wally was young, he often stood beside his daddy's chair at mealtime and asked him to say a blessing. Over and over he repeated, "Daddy, please pray." Finally one day his dad bowed his head and said grace for the first time. Thus began a custom in the family that continued as long as Mr. Thomas was able to come to the table for meals.

Are we delaying setting the right example for our families today?

Many years later, Wally's mother recalled the incident. She remembered that Wally was only nine the summer he accepted Christ in the local revival meeting. He walked from his one-room school to the morning service of the revival. Wally later described his conversion experience as feeling like he had had "a bath inside." This experience expressed itself in his answering the call to ministry. But he knew, even at the tender age of nine, that the decision to become a Christian called for commitment. It called for family prayer, and especially at mealtime. It gave him the courage to stand by his dad's side and nudge him to pray until he got results.

"Daddy, please pray." These were the wise words of a child leading his father to begin a family tradition. Some sixteen years of his parent's marriage had already passed by this time, but it is never too late for Christian mothers and fathers to be the kind of leaders that our homes so desperately need today.

Loving Father, strengthen the homes of our land that we can have the courage and wisdom to give voice to our faith in Christ. *Amen*

What Do You Want To Do?

Jesus said to him, "What do you want me to do for you?"
Mark 10:51a

A student in my young adult Sunday school class said that he saw no need to pray, because God already knows our needs. God does know more about us than we know about ourselves, but He says, "Ask, and it will be given to you" (Matthew 7:7a). Luke 11:9 and John 14:14 record Jesus promising the same. James boldly states "You do not have, because you do not ask" (James 4:2).

God's promises are sure and can be trusted.

Jesus was asking blind Bartimaeus to put into words exactly what he wanted the Lord to do. Bartimaeus answered simply, "Master, let me receive my sight" (Mark 10:51b). He knew precisely what he needed. He acted in faith and received his sight. When we go to Jesus with a deep longing as Bartimaeus did—and with the same kind of faith—things will happen.

Hannah had a deep longing for a child. She went to the temple and cried out to God in her need. God heard her cry and blessed her with Samuel. Hannah said, "For this child I prayed; and the Lord has granted me my petition which I made to him" (I Samuel 1:27).

When we examine our lives, determine our greatest need, and ask God in faith for our miracle, I believe He will hear and answer. The answer may not come in the way and time we want, but God knows best. Jesus stopped what He was doing when Bartimaeus cried out to Him. I believe He will do the same for you and me. Peter said "Truly I perceive that God shows no partiality" (Acts 10:34). For those who pray, there is no limit to God's power and no partiality in His blessings.

Dear God, our needs are many and our faith is often weak. Thank You for hearing the cries of Your children. In Jesus' name. *Amen*

Blinded by Self-Pity

The blind man said to Him, "Master, let me receive my sight."
Mark 10:51b

*I*t was a cold January night as we drove through the Atlanta slum area. Like blind Bartimaeus in the scripture verse, I felt like crying out to the Lord for help. The load of going to seminary felt pretty heavy right then, both financially and emotionally. Our weekend living conditions were poor. Our salary was not adequate to pay our monthly bills. The weekly, 120-mile round trip was taking a heavy toll on our old car. We had purchased it used just before leaving for Atlanta, and the old, retread tires were coming apart. No funds, no free time, and then, on top of everything else, the heater in our car had gone out!

What are the needs of those around me that I need to see today?

The car windows began to fog as I pulled three-year-old Debbie close to me. The thought of another doctor bill was frightening. I had just endured a lengthy illness, because our funds were too low to go to a doctor. Insurance was out of the question. I was having a real pity party!

Wiping the fog from the window beside me, I saw a scene that will be forever etched in my memory. In the shadows of the darkened street, I saw a woman and little girl. *Why would anyone be out on these streets at ten o'clock on a cold night like this*, I wondered. Then I saw that the child was barefoot, not even socks on her feet. Somehow, in that moment, the inside of our car didn't feel so cold.

Like Bartimaeus I realized my deep need to receive my own sight—to be stripped of the self-pity that had blinded me to the needs of others. I had no reason to complain or feel sorry for myself. At least we had a car. We had shoes on our feet, and we would soon be in our warm little apartment. I made a commitment that night. I promised God that I would *try* to always recognize the needs of others and not be blinded by my own self-pity.

Master, help me to receive my sight every day of my life. And, seeing, help me like Bartimaeus to follow You faithfully. Through Christ. *Amen*

Knowing Peace

And the peace of God, which passes all understanding,
will keep your hearts and your minds in Christ Jesus.

Philippians 4:7

A sign in front of a church read "No God, No Peace. Know God, Know Peace." While this may sound like a simplistic statement, it holds truth. There are some situations that call for trained intervention, but I believe that Christian faith is a vital part of integrated treatment for all stress-related problems.

Stress is a part of our lives. It's a universal problem. Yet we are told that 92 percent of what we worry about never happens. Why do we allow ourselves to succumb to worry? Sometimes we may not even be aware that we are stressed. Other times we feel so weighted down that we feel like a rock in water. Regardless of the degree of stress we are feeling, we have to find the route to peace.

My degree of peace is determined by my closeness to God.

People have come up with hundreds of ways to deal with stress. Humans are said to have twelve basic emotions of which only three are pleasant feelings. The other nine generate unpleasant feelings. These unpleasant feelings make for unpleasant memories. Unpleasant memories can guide our behavior and cause painful stress.

I believe that much of our stress can be cast upon the Lord. I Peter 5:7 says "Cast *all* your anxieties on him, for he cares about you" (emphasis mine). The source of perfect peace is God. Paul says that God's peace is beyond our understanding. Jesus offers it freely. In John 14:27, He said, "Peace I leave with you; my peace I give to you; not as the world gives do I give to you. Let not your hearts be troubled, neither let them be afraid." I know from personal experience that these words are true. Knowing Him personally helps me know peace.

God of peace, I praise and thank You for receiving my cares and burdens. Thank You for the comfort found in Your Word and for Your presence that sustains us. In Jesus' name. *Amen*

Set the Example

*Let no one despise your youth, but set the believers an example in
speech and conduct, in love, in faith, in purity.*

I Timothy 4:12

Much is being said and written today about how to raise good children. Family values, moral intelligence, and civility are all hot topics. Paul was giving young Timothy good advice on what exemplary conduct should be. He was saying that verbal defense may not silence critics, but setting an example in speech conduct, love, faith, and purity will.

Jesus has set for us the example. It's up to us to follow.

Parents and grandparents—even uncles and aunts—help shape the conscience of the children. This requires time. Studies show that parents today spend 40 percent less time with their children than parents in the 1950s.

We must decide to *make* the time to be with our children—to truly listen to their pain and fears, dreams and goals. But, beyond this, we need to live out for our children an example in speech and conduct.

God's Word gives us helpful advice for the example we should set. Colossians 4:6b says that our speech should be gracious. Proverbs 10:23 says that our conduct should be wise. Romans 12:9 says our love should be genuine. I Timothy 1:5 says that our faith should be sincere. Philippians 1:10 says that our lives are to be pure and blameless.

Are there harmful habits in our lives that we wouldn't want our child to emulate? Our actions speak more loudly than our words. Our example is caught more than taught. What message about love, faith, and purity is your example sending today?

Dear Lord, we want to live our lives in a way that would be pleasing to You. Help us to be gracious in our speech, wise in our conduct, genuine in our love, and sincere in our faith, so that our lives will be an example to those around us. *Amen*

Eight Important Words

If we say we have no sin, we deceive ourselves.
I John 1:8a

Someone has said that the eight most important words we may ever say are, "I may be wrong—you may be right." Admitting a mistake, a sin, or a wrong judgment is difficult—maybe even impossible—for some people. But a simple "Maybe I *am* wrong" could lead another person to concede the same thing.

Being willing to say and mean these eight words requires strength of character. It requires courage and a healthy self-esteem. All of us make mistakes. We can be misinformed and sincerely believe that we are right. Yet, we can be mistaken. Sometimes we can know clearly that we are wrong, and, because of our stubbornness and foolish pride, refuse to admit it.

We can be sincere, and still be sincerely wrong.

If we feel we are always right, we not only deceive ourselves but also hurt those around us. Only truth can set us free. Jesus said, "And you will know the truth, and the truth will make you free" (John 8:32). He also said, "I am the way, and the truth, and the life" (John 14:6a). When our character and self-esteem are based on who we are in Jesus, we are set free to be whole persons. We can then speak truth and live truth. We can be authentic. We can admit when we are wrong. We can acknowledge our shortcomings and flaws.

When I have hurt or offended someone, I want to be able to say with Paul, "Forgive me this wrong!" (II Corinthians 12:13b). Sometimes it can be extremely difficult to admit a mistake to those nearest and dearest to us, but, by the grace of God, we can!

Loving Lord, thank You for forgiving us when we repent of our mistakes. Help us never to be so proud that we can't see our own faults. Lead us always in the way of truth. In the name of the one who is the Way, the Truth, and the Life. *Amen*

It Takes Time

Be strong, and let your heart take courage,
all you who wait for the Lord!
Psalms 31:24

Fred Wiche, the "weekend gardener" for many years on Louisville's WHAS television and radio, was asked about a certain tree that grows very rapidly. Fred said, "Forget it! Any tree that grows twenty feet a year is not worth much."

Anything in life that is worthwhile will likely require time. It takes time to build good relationships with family and with friends. It takes time to build a relationship with our heavenly Father, too.

Time is a precious gift from God. It's up to us to use it wisely.

Most of us place a premium on time because our lives are geared for the fast lane. Someone reminded me recently that the world says, "Don't just stand there—do something." Jesus says, "Don't just do something—stand there!" He told his disciples, "Come away by yourselves to a lonely place, and rest awhile" (Mark 6:31). It takes time to be apart—to replenish not only our physical strength, but also our spiritual and emotional well being.

We need to remember that delay doesn't mean denial. Time spent waiting on God is never wasted time. The psalmist said, "Be still, and know that I am God" (Psalms 46:10a), and, "For thee I will wait all the day long" (Psalms 25:5b).

Where do you need to spend some quality time today? With a spouse? A child? A parent? Do you need to take time to complete a postponed task? Make a contact? How long has it been since you took the time to be with Jesus? Now's the time to take the time!

Dear God, help us to use our time in ways that honor You. Give us wisdom to make the most of each minute, and patience as we wait upon You. In Jesus' name. *Amen*

A Letter from God

I will write it upon their hearts; and I will be their God,
and they shall be my people.
Jeremiah 31:33b

*A*ll sorts of things have a way of turning up when I pack for a move. When we retired, I came upon a handwritten letter that our daughter Debbie had passed on to me. It was entitled "A Letter from God." Looking more closely, I noticed a few words had been typed. At the top of the page were these typed words, "Dear _____," and at the bottom, "Always remember how much I love you. Your Friend, God."

What is God saying to me today?

The remainder of the letter was to be written to themselves by those attending a retreat. I was touched by the words Debbie had written in the body of the letter. She penned words to herself as though God were writing to her. Here are some lines from Debbie's "letter from God":

> Dear Debbie,
>
> I want you to know how proud I am, and always have been, of you. You are so precious to me. You are a "diamond in the rough." You have always striven to seek my will.
>
> Always remember how much I love you, and that I'm always there for you. This is a difficult time for you now, but I'm making you a stronger person because of it. Keep trusting me and cast your cares on me. I promise I will never let you down no matter what.

As I read "God's letter" to Debbie, the body of which she had written, I thanked Him that He had placed these convictions in her heart over the years. Debbie knows that she belongs to God because of the sacrifice of Jesus and her acceptance of His love.

God confirms His love for us over and over—through Scripture, prayer time with Him, acts of kindness, and countless other ways, maybe even through our own thoughts of what God might say to us in a letter.

Dear God, the greatest word of love You have ever sent us was Your Son, Jesus. His life, death, and resurrection confirm forever Your love for us. I promise to always love You, too. *Amen*

A Cup of Cold Water

And whoever gives to one of these little ones even a cup of cold water because he is a disciple, truly, I say to you, he shall not lose his reward.

Matthew 10:42

Since she was a small child, our daughter, Debbie, has performed a special Christ-like deed. She was twenty-seven years old before it really occurred to me just how much this simple act of love must please our heavenly Father.

Debbie has often given to her family cups of cold water. When her brother was reprimanded and experienced some unhappy moments, Debbie would quickly vanish from the scene only to return with a cup of cold water for David. When her dad and I were sick or burdened or frustrated, it was Debbie who would quietly offer to us cups of ice water. When I suffered the long days of grief after the deaths of my parents, Debbie's thoughtful acts of kindness brought a special kind of comfort.

Cups of cold water bring healing for the moment, but the Living Water brings wholeness for eternity.

As so often happens, deeds of love and mercy go unnoticed. I have too often overlooked the cups of cold water given to me because I have been too focused on my need or problem. But during a recent quiet time, God seemed to imprint a word of wisdom upon my heart. "Do you realize how much like me your daughter's acts of mercy are?" He seemed to say. No, I hadn't noticed, and I was deeply sorry.

When Jesus advised His twelve disciples before sending them out, He said, "And whoever gives one of these little ones even a cup of cold water because he is a disciple, truly, I say to you, he shall not lose his reward." That same advice still holds for His disciples today. I want to always be giving cups of cold water, but I also want to be aware of those given to me—and especially from those dearest to me.

Father, help me to be more sensitive to loving deeds of kindness and mercy all around me, and especially within my own family. *Amen*

Life's Hard, but God Makes It Good

And the people complained in the hearing of the
Lord about their misfortunes.

Numbers 11:1a

At times I'm like the people of Israel in their wilderness wanderings: I complain, and I'm not as grateful as I should be. I take the good things in life for granted.

Many of us at one time or another tend to focus on the negatives in our lives. Maybe it's as simple as the effect a low barometer reading can have on our spirit. For some people a rainy, cloudy day plays havoc with their attitude. I once heard about a man who had been sick, and, when asked how he felt, he replied, "I'm afraid I'm better."

I saw a sign near Brunswick, Georgia, which read, "Life's hard, but God makes it good." Attitude makes all the difference. The attitude of the people of Israel concerning their misfortunes left a bit to be desired. They acknowledged that life was hard, but they forgot that God was good. And this displeased God.

> *Life's hard, but God has said, "I will never fail you nor forsake you" (Hebrews 13:5b).*

God's grace is present in the good times as well as the bad. Sometimes we aren't aware of it in the good times. It's when life is hard that we learn to rely on God's grace.

In his book *A Grace Disguised*, Gerald L. Sittser tells how in a split second he lost three members of his family in a tragic accident. He says, "I lost the world I loved, but I gained a deeper awareness of grace."[3] Life *is* hard, but God's grace is sufficient in the midst of every trial. Claim this promise for your life today. God is trustworthy.

Heavenly Father, when life is hard help me to remember that Your grace is always sufficient. I pray in Jesus' name. *Amen*

Relaxing a Commandment

Whoever then relaxes one of the least of these commandments and teaches men so, so shall he be called least in the kingdom of heaven.

Matthew 5:19a

I saw a bumper sticker recently that read, "How much sin can I get by with and still go to heaven?" Is this a mindset in our country? Is it prevalent and growing? Relaxing a commandment seems to go unnoticed as the world becomes more decadent. As on the day of our Lord's trial, the voice of the multitude is the voice too often heeded. We keep releasing Barabbas and crucifying Jesus over and over, every day.

We aren't called to be popular— just faithful.

Are we ever tempted to relax a commandment and go with the crowd? How loud is our voice when we see insidious sins creep steadily into our lifestyles? Did we voice opposition when stores began to stay open on Sunday afternoon? What about when the opening time became the 11:00 worship hour or earlier? What is our response to premarital and extramarital sex? Have we been duped into believing that being neutral on issues is simply being tolerant? Has belief in God and His commandments become an encumbrance rather than a guide for living?

Some newspapers held back on reporting some atrocities during World War II because Hitler might have been offended. Can we relax commandments in order to avoid confrontation or loss of popularity? I believe not. It *is* easier to stay in the comfort zone than take a stand, but sometimes all we can do is stand. Ephesians 6:13 says, "Therefore take the whole armor of God, that you may be able to withstand in the evil day, and having done all, to stand."

Someone has said that people don't go to football games to see the team stay in a huddle. As Christians, we can't huddle in our churches and expect the world to become a better place. Rather, we need to be the scattered church—empowered to stand against the wrongs in our world.

Dear God, help us to have the courage to be in the world and not of the world. Help us to not only live out Your commandments, but also stand for them. Through Your Son, Jesus. *Amen*

Letting Go of the Clutter

By him every one that believes is freed from everything.
Acts 13:39a

*H*oping I could get rid of some household clutter, I priced the last item for the yard sale. The thought of clearing out some closets and cabinets made all the work worth the effort. My spirits fell a bit when I noticed in our local paper that thirty-eight other yard sales were scheduled on the same day. For a small town, that's a bunch! Yet I knew that yard, basement, and garage sales were the going thing. They seemed to grow every week in number and size—multi-family sales, block sales, and even highway sales stretching across state lines.

Can we learn to be content with less in order to enjoy life more?

This growing trend in our country surely indicates that many households have become too preoccupied with acquiring things. As a result, our homes and lives have become cluttered with non-essentials: closets and cupboards too full and schedules too crowded. We find ourselves working more hours but enjoying life less.

Our lives can become cluttered emotionally, too. We need to identify the extra baggage that loads us down. Could there be grudges and resentments that weigh heavily upon us? These can cause our minds to become muddled and our hearts encrusted. Emotions drain from us as we become desperate for release. But through God's help and the help of a trusted friend, counselor, or mentor, we can begin to rid ourselves of mental clutter. If the need is to give or receive forgiveness, God's grace will be sufficient in this way also. Acts 13:39 reminds us that all who believe are set free from everything!

Lord, help us to care less for material things and care more for things eternal. Empty our lives of clutter so that we can be filled with Your joy. *Amen*

Salvaging Self-Control

For the love of Christ controls us.

II Corinthians 5:14a

In Galatians 5:22, 23, Paul lists the fruit of the Spirit as, "love, joy, peace, patience, kindness, goodness, faithfulness, gentleness, and self-control." Why did Paul place "self-control" last in the list of fruits of the Spirit? Could it be because it's the most difficult to attain? This seems to be true for me. I've prayed and prayed for more of the "ninth fruit," particularly in relationships. Self-control in moral, ethical, and spiritual issues is not a challenge for me. It is in relating to persons whose very personality is a constant challenge that I have the most difficulty.

When the love of Christ controls us, we are set free!

It's a task for me not to respond verbally against phoniness, greed, self-centeredness, derogatory remarks, gossip, lies, and other character flaws that demean and demoralize. It's difficult to salvage self-control when inside I'm boiling. I'm a long way from being an example of self-control, but I have learned an important lesson recently.

Through a devotional in *God Calling*, these words have made a difference in my life, "Leave to Me all the necessary correcting…. Love will break down all difficulties."[4] I realized that it's Christ's love that constrains us. It's His love that is the source of our self-control. It's the Holy Spirit's control of my heart and mind that will enable me to have self-control. I can't manufacture self-control. I can't change a person's personality. Only the love of Christ can do this.

This was a freeing moment in my life. I can leave with God all the correcting of the persons who drive me to distraction. All I need to do is surrender these persons to God, pray for His love to change them, and pray for more of His love to flow through my own heart. My self-control will be salvaged in proportion to my surrender to the Holy Spirit's control of me.

Holy Spirit, help me to surrender to You the persons and circumstances that deplete and destroy Your fruits in my life. Empower me to be controlled today by Christ's love. In His name. *Amen*

Hand in the Hip Pocket

*I stretch out my hands to thee; my soul thirsts
for thee like a parched land.*

Psalms 143:6

Although Wally and I hadn't known each other until we met in college, we have often enjoyed sharing stories of the many childhood experiences we have in common. One of these experiences was "going to town" with a parent, usually on Saturday. Growing up on farms, both of us looked forward to these times—getting a hamburger, an ice cream cone, or, occasionally, a "plate lunch" for a real splurge!

Wally shared recently an especially fond memory from those trips that he and his dad made to Glasgow. As a young boy he held tightly to his dad's hand as they walked the sidewalk leading to the town square. Occasionally, Mr. Thomas met a friend or neighbor and stopped to chat awhile. During these times, Wally slipped his hand into his dad's hip pocket and waited quietly for the conversation to be finished. Often while Mr. Thomas talked, he gently put his hand in his hip pocket to be sure his little boy's hand was still there. It was natural for him to check to see if his son was close—still connected and safe from harm.

I must not allow any experience to distance me from God today.

This story reminds me of our relationship with our heavenly Father. He walks life's roads with us—hand in hand. He stops along the way to give needed attention to other fellow travelers, but He never leaves us nor forsakes us. He never wants to lose touch with one of His children, the ones who are depending on Him for loving care, guidance, and protection. He longs for us to stretch out our hand to Him like the psalmist said.

I want to always stay just that close to my heavenly Father—hip pocket close!

Heavenly Father, I want to always stay close to You. You are my source of life. Thank You for sending Your Spirit to walk with me every day. *Amen*

Looking on the Brighter Side

A glad heart makes a cheerful countenance.

Proverbs 15:13a

As I walked into a discount department store recently, an elderly gentleman greeted me. Offering me a shopping cart, he cheerfully asked, "And how are you today?" I told him I was fine and asked him the same question. Smiling broadly, he answered, "If I was any better, I'd have to take something for it!" Maybe this comment seems a little garish, but I have to admit that his sunny disposition lifted my spirits that day.

The Christ in me can enable me to look on the brighter side today.

A cheerful spirit *is* contagious. All of us can recall times when a simple smile made our day brighter. Someone once said that a smile is a gently curved line that sets a lot of things straight. Our day can be made brighter, or things more straight, when we see a smile across a crowded room, or we are greeted in a grocery aisle, or someone simply says, "I love you."

A smile is always in season. A smile is a gift—requiring little effort, but resulting in great dividends. Romans 12:8 talks about the person "who does acts of mercy, with cheerfulness." But the passage goes on to say that this gift is to be used and we are to be "aglow with the spirit" (Romans 12:11b).

We in our human spirit can't always be "up," but the Christ in us never wavers. His Holy Spirit can constantly shine through us. So, as Christians, a smile can be a natural part of our countenance, because as Paul put it, "It is no longer I who live, but Christ who lives in me" (Galatians 2:20). He *is* the brighter side!

Loving Father, help me always to remember that it is not I who smiles but Christ who smiles through me. *Amen*

Hope Deferred

Hope deferred makes the heart sick, but a desire fulfilled is a tree of life.
Proverbs 13:12

I keep a prayer list before me on my desk. On one side of the page is an ongoing list of needs of both family and friends. On the other side of the page is a list of names of persons who are sick. Both lists seem to continue to grow longer even though many prayers are answered.

What a joy it is to enter a date beside a name when a prayer is answered. I have just written today's date beside the name of a bright young medical student whose brain tumor miraculously disappeared. The surgeon announced to the family just before the scheduled surgery that the tumor could no longer be detected, even though he knew from the records it had been there. The combined prayers of many caring people to our loving God made the difference.

Let us never give up hope, even though the desired results are deferred.

Today as I thanked God for answered prayers, I felt strongly impressed to add my church to the "sick list." It brings deep grief to me to hear of the continued decline in membership, and I keep asking "Why did my church get sick?" I remember as a child my cousin and I proudly posting the number in attendance each Sunday. I remember the joy deep within as we watched the numbers increase.

I want my children and grandchildren to be a part of a healthy, growing church. I long to see a reversal in the trend of membership loss, and, in all honesty, the deferral of this hope has made my heart sick. But thanks be to God, hope deferred is not hope defeated. My hope will remain in the power of the living Lord who can bring not only new life to the dying, but also to the dead! Thanks be to God that nothing can defeat this hope through Christ.

Heavenly Father, forgive us our sins and heal both Your sin-sick church and the world. In Jesus' name. *Amen*

God Is Good

*For the Lord is good; his steadfast love endures forever,
and his faithfulness to all generations.*
Psalms 100:5

*H*elen Keller once said, "I thank God for my handicaps, for through them, I have found myself, my work, and my God."[5] And to this I—at least at times—have to ask, "Did you ever wonder why you have had to suffer?"

All of us have probably asked a "Why?" at one time or another. Why did that little girl walk into the path of the car and get killed? Why are babies born with birth defects? Why does a vibrant twenty-six-year-old woman have to succumb to leukemia? Why does a bride of ten months lose her husband to a heart attack? Why does a bright, young high school student get killed in a hunting accident?

"I consider that the suffering of this present time are not worth comparing with the glory that is to be revealed to us" (Romans 8:18).

All these tragedies—and many others—have occurred among members of our parish over the years. Often the persistent "Why?" gnaws at the very core of our being. We long for answers, not only for these dear families, but for ourselves as well. We don't have the answers to these questions, but from the depths of our souls we can honestly say, "I don't have the answers; I only know that God is good."

I know that His love is steadfast and sure. It is unshakable and endures forever. I know that nothing can separate us from God's love (Romans 8:39). I know that His faithfulness will endure to all generations. When we struggle and find it difficult to affirm God's presence, we can be honest and admit, "I believe, help my unbelief!" (Mark 9:24). This kind of mustard seed faith will enable us to honestly say, "I don't know why this happened—I only know that God is good and He suffers with me."

Loving God, I'm so glad that Calvary wasn't the end of the story. The open tomb confirms Your love and goodness through Jesus Christ our Lord. *Amen*

Go Forward Unafraid

Let your eyes look directly forward, and your gaze be straight before you.
Proverbs 4:25

*E*ach day I read from a devotional book called *God Calling*. A resounding theme in this little book that has spoken to me so many times is "Go forward unafraid."[6] These were the last words of the devotional on July 14, 1986: the day we boarded a plane for Kenya to attend the World Methodist Conference.

In the fall of 1987, I faced needed surgery. Many aspects of the decision to have surgery were not clear. Words from this devotional book spoke to my heart, "When you look to Me for guidance, My hand is laid upon your arm, a gentle touch to point the way." This devotional closed with the words, "So go forward into the future bravely and unafraid."[7]

I can go forward unafraid because I know who will go with me.

There have been other times as well when the message of going forward unafraid has brought courage. Wally was in the decision-making process concerning church staff, and again, advice from *God Calling* was in good timing. He read the May 8 devotional saying, "I lead you. The *way* is clear. Go forward unafraid,"[8] and he knew the route to take.

What a wonderful philosophy to follow! Isn't that what Jesus would say to us each day? *Go forward in faith unafraid!*

We have to keep going and growing and moving, pressing on toward the goal as Paul advised in Philippians 3:14. Each year, each day, each moment that we live calls for courage, and courage comes as we step out in faith.

We don't have to know the results before they occur. Hebrews 11:1 says "Faith is the assurance of things hoped for, the conviction of things not seen." With faith in a loving heavenly Father, we can go forward unafraid—even if we don't know what lies ahead.

Dear God, thank You for sending Your Son to be our Savior and the Holy Spirit to be our Guide. *Amen*

Accountability

Each of us shall give account of himself to God.
Romans 14:12

I'm glad there's a new interest in accountability today. The idea is not a new one for those of us who have roots in Wesleyan theology. John Wesley saw the small group "class meetings" as an opportunity to be accountable in the disciplines of the Christian life.

Can we open our lives to friends and, more importantly, to our best friend Jesus? Luke reminds us that each of us will one day give an account of ourselves to God. But in the meantime, is there anyone to whom we have chosen to be accountable? Charles R. Swindoll in his book *Living Above the Level of Mediocrity* says "Accountability includes opening one's life to a few carefully selected, trusted, loyal confidants who speak the truth—who have the right to examine, to question, to appraise, and to give counsel."[9] Sometimes, though, it's not easy to listen to that carefully selected, trusted, loyal confidant who is speaking the truth.

Wally and I have been in an accountability group. I recall times when it was not easy to receive the questions *or* the advice. But in retrospect, truth was spoken. That spoken truth was freeing as the Scripture promises in John 8:32, "You will know the truth, and the truth will make you free."

Truth is valuable, and it is necessary for human survival. A society breaks down when it is no longer accountable to truth. So does an individual. Facing truth is necessary for accountability, both on earth and when we meet our Lord in heaven—because Jesus is truth (John 14:6a).

Accountability is a healthful and helpful experience when we are willing to deal with the truth, and follow the One who is truth.

Heavenly Father, help me to be willing to give an account for my life. Lead me always in Your path of truth. Through Christ. *Amen*

A Tender Heart

But Jesus said, "Let the children come to me, and do not hinder them;
for to such belongs the kingdom of heaven.
Matthew 19:14

$\mathcal{I}$t seemed unusual for David to resist singing a hymn in a worship service. In the past he held the hymnal and sang even before he could read the words. Now that he was seven, he ordinarily turned quickly to the announced hymn and sang heartily.

But this time he was refusing to sing "The Old Rugged Cross."[1] Maybe this was the first time he understood the meaning of the lyrics. I watched from the corner of my eye as he cradled the heavy hymnal in both hands, but he only looked at the words as I sang along with the congregation.

Is my heart easily touched like that of a child?

Maybe he's not feeling too well, I thought as I bent down to look into his face. Huge tears were welling up in his eyes and overflowing down his freckled cheeks. "Are you okay, son?" I asked. With deep emotion he whispered in my ear, "Mom, I just can't sing that song. It's too sad."

It became more difficult for me to sing, too. I realized how often I had sung the words to this dear old hymn without really hearing their profound and piercing truth. It would be natural for a tender, sensitive heart to ache at the very thought of our Savior's suffering on a cruel cross. And that is the kind of heart—a child's heart—that our Lord said He desired in all of us. I guess that's why He said "Unless you turn and become like children, you will never enter the kingdom of heaven" (Matthew 18:3).

Father, thank you for the wisdom and honesty of children. Help me to be more childlike in my faith. In Jesus' name. *Amen*

"Ro-Fre"

Commit your work to the Lord, and your plans will be established.
Proverbs 16:3

For several years our two children enjoyed a game called "Ro-Fre." Debbie pretended that she was "Rosie" (Ro), and David was "Fred" or "Fre." So the word "Ro-Fre" was coined. The whole activity centered on the preparation for a make-believe journey. Rosie would busy herself bathing and dressing the "children": her dolls. Fred waited patiently, passing the time by watching the Saturday morning cartoons or playing with matchbox cars. In no way would he help with the doll dressing, even if it meant the journey would never begin.

When we are older we are to put away childish ways.

Sometimes, the "trip" never took place. By the time all the dolls were dressed and the suitcase was packed, it was time to eat lunch or do homework. At other times, Rosie and Fred lined up the children on the back seat of the old Chrysler parked by the parsonage. Fred would scoot into the driver's seat, swing the steering wheel from left to right, and off they went on their imaginary trip.

It occurred to me that the game of "Ro-Fre" is much like our own good intentions in the church. We meet to plan and prepare for a project, but sometimes that's as far as it goes. We take too long with details. Some are preoccupied with their matchbox interests. Patience wears thin. Time runs out. We have to move on to other things.

Perhaps if we were committed to the work (or journey) our Lord would have us begin, our plans would be established before the deadline. When we put away our childish ways, we can become the mature and motivating body of Christ. There is no greater joy and fulfillment than is found when we allow God to establish our plans.

Loving Father, forgive us when we play games rather than allow You to establish Your plan for our lives. Help us to daily commit ourselves anew to You. *Amen*

The Everlasting Arms

Underneath are the everlasting arms.
Deuteronomy 33:27

*I*t is said that when a mother eagle nudges the eaglet out of the nest for its first trial flights, she doesn't forsake it. Knowing the young eagle will likely need some assistance, the mother bird stays close by. When the mother eagle sees the eaglet unable to make the flight in its own strength, she flies underneath the eaglet. Then the baby bird can land safely into the feathers on the mother eagle's back and be carried once again to the nest. This act of loving protection is continued over and over until the young eaglet has sufficient strength and skill for flight.

> *We can't fall below the "underneath" of God's everlasting arms.*

We, like the eaglet, struggle at times and need undergirding for life's journeys. Deuteronomy 33:27 says, "Underneath are the everlasting arms" of God. The God who created us empowers us to live victoriously.

It is God's will that each of us reach our full potential. God wants us to mature and develop the needed skills and strength to face each day. But we can falter and fall. Burdens become heavy and our fledgling faith may not carry us far enough. Thanks be to God for His everlasting arms. He watches over us. He sees our struggles. He knows our weaknesses. He makes Himself available through the enabling power of the Holy Spirit the moment we begin to lose our "flight power." This assurance of our loving Father's power and presence should give us sufficient courage for our daily journey.

Father, thank You for Your arms of love and protection that are forever reaching out to us. In Jesus' name. *Amen*

Words Fitly Spoken

A word fitly spoken is like apples of gold in a setting of silver.
Proverbs 25:11

No one had much to say one particular day at the beauty shop. Usually there are four or five conversations going on at the same time.

I was in a quiet mood myself. I didn't care whether or not much conversation took place that day. But my hairdresser peered around at me and asked, "Well, what good things happened in your life since I last saw you?" Camille's question caught me off guard. If I were completely honest, I needed to answer, "Can't think of a thing right now." In fact, I felt plain empty at that moment. A call from a relative earlier that morning drained me emotionally, and a call from a friend seemed curt and cold.

I want my words to be instruments of healing and encouragement.

"What good things are happening in my life?" I repeated, stalling for time. Then a strange thing happened. When I intentionally and honestly thought about this question, many good things in my life came to mind. I began to name some of them, and, as I did this, other people around me began to do the same.

I could hardly believe what happened that day, but I realized that each of us holds the potential for altering the atmosphere around us by our very words. We have all seen this happen when a gloomy word chills and depresses another person or a cheerful word lifts and encourages. Someone has said that a word can mend a heart or break a heart; it can enhance a reputation or ruin a reputation; it can start a friendship or end a friendship.

Being asked to name the good things happening in my life that day was for me a "word fitly spoken." It caused me to concentrate on my blessings and name them one by one. As I left the beauty shop, I was amazed how brightly the sun was shining. I resolved to try harder to remember that my words have the power to hurt or heal.

Heavenly Father, help me to count my blessings and be a blessing to others. In Jesus' name. *Amen*

In Whose Eyes?

You are precious in my eyes, and honored, and I love you.

Isaiah 43:4

A mother felt deep concern over the boy her daughter was dating. Each day she prayed for God to send the right person into her daughter's life. On one particular day, the mother was more specific in her prayer request. She prayed, "Lord, send a nice, good boy to Mary." She reminded God of how "nice and good" Mary had always been, and continued her pleading for a similar mate. Suddenly, deep within her spirit, she heard a loving God say, "In whose eyes?"

I need to have eyes of mercy and acceptance like the Christ I try to serve.

The mother realized she was praying from *her* vantage point—from the way *she* was seeing the young man her daughter was presently dating. She was not seeing him through God's eyes. God saw him as a forgiven sinner, clean and whole. God saw him as precious, honored, and loved.

Abruptly, the mother stopped praying. She sat at her desk in stunned silence, realizing the deep truth she had just been taught. Granted, the young man's past was not admirable, but he had begun a new life, sincere and restored. He lacked nothing in his heavenly Father's eyes—only in the eyes of this mother.

And I must ask myself: How often do I judge blindly? How often do I look upon the outward appearance rather than the heart as God would look? I want to have eyes like my heavenly Father. I want to see all people as precious, honored, and loved by Him.

Father, forgive me for my blindness. Open my eyes to see with Your eyes. In Jesus' name. *Amen*

Walking Securely

He who walks in integrity walks securely.
Proverbs 10:9a

When Wally's grandmother was near death, she took David's hand in hers and pulled him close. In her weakened voice she said, "David, always be a good boy, and you'll be glad when you're ninety like me." That's good advice for living a life of integrity. Mammy Thomas had walked with God, and at the end of her earthly life she was secure.

Will my daily walk be a good model for someone today?

What a rich legacy to leave to an impressionable teenager—and to *all* of us! Trust and obedience were a part of Mammy's daily walk, and at the end of her life, she had no regrets. Mammy left us an "example to imitate" that Paul spoke of in II Thessalonians 3:9b.

At the end of our lives, will we feel that we have lived a life to imitate? Can we admonish those who follow us to walk each day securely in the Lord? I believe, with God's grace, it is possible. Mammy's life is proof of this. Like the psalmist David, she could say, "My steps have held fast to thy paths, my feet have not slipped" (Psalms 17:5).

Loving Father, we thank You for those whose lives model Your Son. Help us to walk each day in trust and obedience, secure because You walk beside us. In Christ's name. *Amen*

Heart Letters

You are a letter from Christ delivered by us, written not with ink but with the Spirit of the living God, not on tablets of stone but on tablets of the human hearts.
II Corinthians 3:3

Through the years I have kept meaningful cards that I have received for special occasions containing sweet verses or loving handwritten notes. I treasure, too, the "heart letters" I've received through the years from my family and friends. Someone has said that a letter delivered by the postal service can carry God's love. I believe it is a wonderful ministry of encouragement to faithfully send little reminders of God's love. Paul says *we* are letters from Christ. So we are to not only write letters, but we are also to deliver in person His message of love that is written on the tablets of our heart.

What kind of letter from Christ will I deliver to the people around me today?

The message of God's love we share by the way we live isn't written with ink, but with the Spirit of the living God. Christ's life of love was His letter to the world. God trusts us who have received this love to share it with the world. "We love because He first loved us" (I John 4:19).

What will my heart letter to the world be today? Will the tablets of my heart have love inscribed on them? What about compassion? Will forgiveness be readable? Or mercy? Will joy, peace, patience, kindness, goodness, faithfulness, and gentleness be visible? Will there be any evidence of self-control? Too often the letters from my heart fall short of what they should be, but by the grace of God, I will determine to be more conscious of my heart's message to the world.

Father, help me to live so others may know that Your loving Spirit dwells within my heart. In Christ's name. *Amen*

Love Makes You Real

*If I have all faith, so as to remove mountains,
but have not love, I am nothing.*

I Corinthians 13:2b

"Turn your head to the left. Lean forward. Don't breathe." The x-ray techni-cian automatically clipped off the routine instructions for my annual mammogram. Feeling a tinge of irritation at her unfeeling, memorized direc-tions I said, "You repeat those words several times throughout the day, don't you?" She responded without once looking into my face, "Yes. Raise your right arm. Don't breathe."

God has loved us for a long, long time, and that makes us real.

I'm not really real to her, I thought. *Just one more woman over forty to process today.* I was one more manila folder among the day's stack. "Keep your robe on. I'll be back in ten minutes," she ordered as she quickly left the room. Still no eye contact.

Wrapped in the pink terry cloth robe I waited in the tiny dressing room. Sitting there in the cold silence I began to recall Margery Williams' story of *The Velveteen Rabbit.* The toy rabbit was just another toy among all the other toys in the nursery. Skin Horse befriended Rabbit. "What is real?" Rabbit asked Skin Horse. Skin Horse wisely replied, "Real isn't how you are made. It's a thing that happens to you. When a child loves you for a long, long time, you become Real." Then Skin Horse added, "Once you're Real, it lasts for always."[2]

Isn't there truth in Skin Horse's reply to Rabbit? Love gives life meaning. Love from our family and friends makes us feel special. And once we realize God loves us unconditionally, we are never the same again. This love lasts for always. Throughout eternity! This love makes all the difference during the times the world makes us feel like a number or a nonentity.

Loving God, thank You for revealing Your love through Jesus. Help me to share Your love so Jesus will be real to others. In His name. *Amen*

Simple Love

Truly, I say to you, whoever does not receive the kingdom of God like a child shall not enter it.
Mark 10:15

I found myself noticing two little boys; one was a preschooler and the other was a first grader. They were wandering freely from room to room in the antique doll shop, while their mother calmly discussed with the shop owner the best doll to purchase for the sister at home.

I kept thinking I would hear a crash as the two little boys continued rough-housing through the shop. The young mother seemed much more interested with the latest Madame Alexander doll than what the boys were up to in the other room.

It's no wonder that Jesus enjoyed so much the refreshing company of children.

Several minutes later I made my small purchase and felt a sense of relief to be leaving the doll shop. Suddenly, the preschooler waved to me and said warmly, "Bye, bye!" Thinking he must be glad to see his "watchdog" leaving, I returned the goodbye and walked on toward the door. I was totally taken aback by what followed. "I sure do love you!" the little boy bellowed out, looking straight up into my eyes. I melted in my tracks, for no longer did I see a potential doll-breaker. Now I saw a precious, innocent child, eager to share his simple, sincere love.

"I love you, too," I responded, wondering if he could sense my feelings of guilt. At that, he made a step in my direction and announced, "Wish I could give you a hug!" He hardly had the time to finish the sentence when my arms opened wide. I was so very glad to receive that day one of the little ones of which the kingdom of God is made, and like which we need to become if we hope to enter this kingdom.

Father, help me never to judge one of Your children—of any age. In Jesus' name. *Amen*

A Double Relationship

We love, because he first loved us.
I John 4:19

*L*ove has a double relationship. It comes from God and it leads us to God. By knowing God, we learn more about love. By learning to love, we know more about God. A good marriage needs a two-way love relationship. Union with Christ requires a double relationship as well.

Who needs God's love channeled to them through me today?

We are never closer to God than when we love, for "God is love" (I John 4:8b). So if we want to become more like God, we need more of His love in us. If we want a better relationship in our family, we need to share more of God's love.

The world needs God's love. God didn't plan to operate His world through law and justice. Our loving and merciful God sent a remedy for sin when He sent us a Savior.

God chose love's way—the "more excellent way" as Paul said in I Corinthians 12:31. In Romans 5:8, Paul reminds us that "God shows his love for us in that while we were yet sinners Christ died for us." God has already done his part in the double relationship of love. It's up to each one of us to do our part.

Love doesn't function well in isolation. Love needs a relationship—a double relationship. This double relationship can then reach out to family, to friends, to neighbors, and to the world. "God so loved the world that he gave his only son, that whoever believes in him should not perish but have eternal life" (John 3:16). Surely, that was the perfect double love relationship!

Dear God, we've received Your love. Grant us the blessing of sharing Your love with someone who needs it today. In Jesus' name. *Amen*

Love Builds Bridges

*This commandment we have from him, that he who loves
God should love his brother also.*

I John 4:21

Reverend Wallace Chappell shared the following story at Lake Junaluska, North Carolina. Helen was getting up in years and had never accepted Christ into her heart. The pastor visited her. Neighbors dropped by to see her, but it seemed that no one could break through Helen's protective shell. That is, until Margaret began to visit Helen. Each time she visited, she took Helen a token of love. She took a chocolate pie, a passage of Scripture that had spoken to her own heart, or an encouraging article from a magazine.

As God replenishes our love, we should give it away to others.

Slowly, but surely, Margaret won Helen's friendship. Eventually, she was able to share her faith with Helen. Helen became a happy Christian and joined the local church. The folks who tried to befriend Helen wondered what Margaret did that they had not done. Finally, someone got up the nerve to ask Helen, and she replied, "Margaret simply built a bridge from her heart to mine, and Jesus walked right across it!"

Love builds bridges. The world needs bridges built by love. We must never underestimate the power of unconditional love. We must never forget that as a Christian, loving is a requirement. It's not a suggestion. It's a commandment from our Lord. Jesus said, "This is my commandment, that you love one another as I have loved you" (John 15:12).

Where does the Lord need you and me to build bridges of love today?

Dear God, help me to build bridges of love so that You can walk right across from my heart to another person's heart. In Jesus' name. *Amen*

Out of the Heart

Out of the abundance of the heart the mouth speaks.
Matthew 12:34b

There is nothing so revealing of a person's heart as words. Words can be good or they can be evil. They can bless and build up or they can curse and tear down. Jesus said that we will give an account for the idle or careless words we speak (Matthew 12:36). Careless words are spoken when the conventional restraints are gone and the real feelings of the heart surface.

What kind of words will my mouth speak today?

There are many uplifting and encouraging words that come out of the heart. But there are also many—too many—that are unkind, bitter, envious, or angry words. If we speak gossip, tell a dirty joke, say unkind words, or curse, then we need to do a heart check.

A careless tongue reflects a serious heart problem. Our hearts need cleansing. In Matthew 12:35, Jesus described an evil person as one who stores an evil treasure; likewise, the good person stores in his or her heart good treasures. It's up to us what we store in our hearts. For me, it's a matter of prayer each day to ask God to help me "bridle my tongue " (James 1:26).

If our hearts are filled to overflowing with an abundance of good things, then good words will come out. If we hold the fruits of the spirit—love, joy, peace, patience, kindness, goodness, faithfulness, gentleness, and self-control—in our heart, then these will affect our speech. But for this to happen we need a daily walk that is close to Jesus. We must allow the Spirit to guide us and protect us from the evil one. We must ask God for forgiveness and cleansing. Then, and only then, will words that build up come out of the treasures of our heart.

"Let the words of my mouth and the meditation of my heart be acceptable in thy sight, O Lord, my rock and my redeemer" (Psalm 19:14). *Amen*

A Cheerful Heart

A cheerful heart is a good medicine.
Proverbs 17:22a

*H*aven't you experienced a good laugh and then felt much better deep down inside? I have, but not until recently did I learn that researchers have proven that certain hormones, such as endorphins and enkephalins, are activated by pleasant experiences.[3]

Much is being written today about how a happy heart restores energy. Cheerfulness, both experienced and observed, makes a positive difference like good medicine. Norman Cousins says, "Ten minutes of solid belly laughter would give me two hours of pain free sleep."[4]

A glad heart helps the body in which it beats, and also lifts the spirit of those in the circle of its influence.

A cheerful heart *is* good medicine. It's simple and practical advice, but putting it into practice requires cultivation and determination. It requires a deliberate act of the will for many of us. When circumstances are such that we feel gloomy and heavy in heart, we may think that it's just not possible to be cheerful. Yet, a cheerful heart comes from a deep faith in a God who can and does work things together for our good if we love Him and cooperate with Him. It grows from a faith that God *is* in control of our lives—even when we don't see the evidence of it.

So what can I do to be cheerful? I can make a conscious effort to count my blessings each day. I can remind myself that Jesus came to make my joy full. I can remember the healing art of laughter and try to laugh more every day of my life.

Father, You sent Jesus to earth that we might know abundant and eternal life. Help us to experience Your full joy today. *Amen*

Heart Messages

Where you go I will go, and where you lodge I will lodge;
your people shall be my people, and your God my God.
Ruth 1:16b

For a St. Valentine's Day gift one year I gave Wally a small red satin box in the shape of a heart. I carefully prepared fifty-two special "heart messages" and placed them in the box. Each Monday morning Wally read his heart message for the week.

Have you received God's ultimate heart message sent through His Son, Jesus?

One message in particular seemed timed and inspired by God during our struggle in deciding if we should move to another church. One Monday morning Wally drew the heart message with this verse of Scripture from the book of Ruth, "Where you go I will go, and where your lodge I will lodge; your people shall be my people, and your God my God" (Ruth 1:16b). Later he said that little message was the confirmation he needed to accept a new challenge in a new church.

All of us enjoy "heart messages." They mean a lot when they come from family and friends. But none mean more than the heart messages from our heavenly Father and his Son. Here are some of my favorite heart messages from God's Word:

- Isaiah 43:4a "Because you are precious in my eyes and honored, and I love you."
- John 14:27 "Peace I leave with you; my peace I give to you; not as the world gives do I give you. Let not your hearts be troubled, neither let them be afraid."
- John 3:16 "For God so loved the world that he gave his only Son, that whoever believes in him should not perish but have eternal life."
- Galatians 6:9 "And let us not grow weary in well doing, for in due season we shall reap, if we do not lose heart."
- I Peter 5:7 "Cast all your anxieties on him, for he cares about you."
- Philippians 4:13 "I can do all things in him who strengthens me."

Dear Lord, thank You for Your message of love sent to us by way of Calvary. Forgive us when we fail to hear and respond to You. *Amen*

Hope in the Midst of Gloom

And now, Lord, for what do I wait? My hope is in thee.
Psalms 39:7

*I*t was a gloomy January day as I waited by the hospital bedside of my mother-in-law. At eighty-two years of age she was struggling with the discouragement of a broken hip—her second one—and a fractured shoulder. Like the psalmist David, we wondered about what was ahead. How would we arrange the proper care when she was dismissed from the hospital? How would we care for her disabled husband as well? Many questions loomed before us.

Are you in the midst of a struggle today? God's grace will see you through.

Beyond the gloom of the weather and the hospital room were the foreboding shadows of this day in history. It was January 15, 1991, the deadline set by the United Nations for Saddam Hussein to withdraw his troops from Kuwait. At midnight the clock would run out of waiting time. The likelihood of war was the topic of every conversation. But no one—doctors, nurses, aids, janitors, waitresses in the hospital restaurant, or newscasters—could seem to muster any hope that the war would be averted.

Then into the hospital room came the faint yet distinct sound of church chimes. My heart quickened as I listened carefully to such a welcome sound piercing the somber grayness of the day. Above the hum of the floor polisher in the hallway, I began to recognize the tune and recalled the words of "America the Beautiful" by Katherine Lee Bates.[5]

The waiting somehow seemed easier as I concentrated on the church chimes. What a ray of hope in the midst of the gloom of the hour! Again I was reminded that our hope for healing to come to a broken hip, broken spirit, and broken world is rooted in our faith in God. God has truly shed His grace on us, and this is my hope in the midst of life's gloom.

Father, You are our creator, redeemer, and sustainer—not just a ray but a whole spectrum of hope. Thank You for Your grace and for sending daily reminders of it. *Amen*

Heart Peace

Let the peace of Christ rule in your hearts.
Colossians 3:15a

*P*eace is rare. Peace among nations has existed only for short periods of time. Heart peace was the kind of peace Jesus was talking about. Heart peace is much more than a cessation of hostilities between countries or factions. It's much more than a halt in war. It's an experience within the heart. It's an experience to be desired more than all the world's riches. In fact, no person or thing can give this gift except Jesus.

Today I want to experience and share this wonderful gift of peace.

Life can cave in on us. Our hearts can be burdened, even broken, from misunderstanding, betrayal, illness, death, handicaps, discord, and disappointment. And the *only* source of peace—complete perfect peace—is in Christ Jesus.

Job suffered a series of terrible setbacks and calamities. He lost his possessions and, much worse, his children. His body was covered with disease. In the midst of all of this, his friends offered sound advice, "Agree with God and be at peace" (Job 22:21a). Isaiah promised, "Thou dost keep him in perfect peace, whose mind is stayed on thee" (Isaiah 26:3a). Paul, writing to the Ephesians, reminded them "For he is our peace, who has made us both one, and has broken down the dividing wall of hostility" (Ephesians 2:14).

Studies show that in homes where Christ abides and rules, fewer words of hostility exist. I believe there can be no lasting peace in our world, nation, community, home, or heart until we come to know and follow the Prince of Peace—the One who left for us His gift of perfect peace.

Gracious Lord, thank You for bringing to our troubled world and troubled hearts this blessed, priceless gift of peace. Help me to keep my mind stayed on You today and always. *Amen*

Breaking Down Dividing Walls

For he is our peace, who has made us both one,
and has broken down the dividing wall of hostility.

Ephesians 2:14

During the long months of caregiving before Daddy died, there were times when it seemed that roles were reversed. For his own good, those who cared for him had to be firm, in love, like a parent. Sometimes I wondered if my patience had extended quite far enough.

I visited Daddy in a Glasgow, Kentucky, hospital on February 16, 1984. Our son David drove up from Vanderbilt University that day. During our evening meal together, I shared some of my concerns. I'll never forget the wisdom of David's response. He said, "Mom, if there's any apologizing that needs to be done, it's probably Grandpa who needs to apologize. But you'd better check it out. You'll be glad you did."

Are there walls of hostility dividing your family today? Let God break them down.

So we prayed together and I asked for God's guidance. I asked that if this were something I should do, the opportunity would come for me to have a few minutes alone with Daddy.

As God always does, He made the way easy. The room totally cleared as I was leaving to go home. I knew what I had to do. I bent over close to Daddy and asked him to listen carefully. I began, "Daddy, there have been times when I've been a little irritable with you. I just want you to know that if I've done or said anything to hurt you, I'm sorry. I love you, Daddy." Such a tender expression came over his face as he said, "I love you, too. I love all you children, and I guess if anybody ought to apologize, it would be me."

No walls—no hostility. Just God's peace as I hugged him and we said our goodbyes. How extremely grateful I'll always be for those precious moments. The next morning the call came that Daddy had just died. He was hoping to go home to Burkesville that day, but instead he went home to heaven.

Heavenly Father, thank You for sending Your beloved Son whose love breaks down all barriers. In Jesus' name. *Amen*

Roll Call

They have labored side by side with me in the gospel together with Clement and the rest of my fellow workers, whose names are in the book of life.

Philippians 4:3b

*M*y dad couldn't carry a tune, but he loved to bellow out the old hymn "When the Roll Is Called Up Yonder."[6] It seemed appropriate for David to sing this song about God's "roll call" in heaven at Daddy's funeral.

Roll call in heaven is an interesting thought. Paul talks about names in the book of life, as does the author of Revelation (Revelation 21:27; 20:12; 13:8). He was concerned about some quarrels going on in the church at Thessalonica. He wanted healing to take place among the Christians there. Paul knew that there is no room for unforgiveness and arguing when the roll is called in heaven.

Through the sacrifice of the Lamb of God our names can be placed in the Lamb's Book of Life.

Our names are recorded in so many places—in our county, state and nation. Vital statistics are fixed firmly through our Social Security numbers. An offer came to me by mail recently to receive free of charge—the all-important information on my credit rating. My first thought was, *What's the catch? What rights have you to access information on my credit rating? Is there no such thing as private records anymore?*

Since that incident, I have thought about how much less important it is for my name to be on earthly documents than in the Lamb's Book of Life. When the roll is called in heaven, I want to be there. Don't you?

Dear God, help me to labor faithfully for You now, and look forward to roll call in heaven later. Thank You for providing the way through Christ. *Amen*

Trapped in the Snowstorm

And the Lord will guide you continually...
Isaiah 58:11a

$\mathcal{T}$he weather forecast on that February morning was for snow flurries. But by the end of the day, south central Kentucky was in one of the worst blizzards in its history. Our daughter, Debbie, was engulfed in this blustery blanket of snow.

Her grandparents had watched warily as the clouds rolled in only minutes after she left to return to her apartment in western Kentucky. They began to call us, describing the severity of the storm. Calls to state police in that area brought no encouragement. Their replies were, "It's bad," "We've never seen anything quite like this," or, "We hope your daughter will pull off the road until she can be located." Between all the telephone calls we prayed constantly.

From God's vantage point we are never lost.

The words "until she can be located" haunted us the remainder of the afternoon. Hours passed, and, after what seemed like an eternity, the call from Debbie came. She had managed to follow the rear lights of a state policeman until she came to an exit off the interstate, and finally into the parking lot of a service station. The normal thirty-minute drive to this point had taken her three hours.

Our hearts overflowed with thanksgiving that she was all right. Even the question of where she would spend the night hadn't seemed so big until now. The town's only motel had been filled for hours. We prayed again. Then the name of a woman I had known some twenty-five years earlier flashed across my mind. A quick phone call assured us that this dear lady would gladly host our daughter until someone could come for her. I can still feel the deep gratitude that permeated my very being as I hung up the telephone that night. Truly, God had directed Debbie's path—and her very life.

Loving God, thank You for watching over Your children. Help us to stay sensitive to Your presence and guidance. In Jesus' name. *Amen*

Bind Us Together, Lord

And above all these, put on love, which binds everything together in perfect harmony.
Colossians 3:14a

*D*uring our flight to Kenya to attend the World Methodist Conference in 1986, we were assigned those dreaded inside seats of the plane's center section. For me to get up required that I disturb a young woman named Beatrice from Nigeria, with whom I had found it very difficult to communicate. More than once I tried to initiate conversation, but she always avoided looking at me. Language was not the problem, because I noticed she spoke fluent English with the flight attendants.

A clear sign of my faith is the presence of God's love.

Finally, after our takeoff from Dakar, Senegal, Beatrice looked directly at me (for the first time) and asked where I was going. When I explained that my husband and I were delegates to the World Methodist Conference in Nairobi, her eyes brightened. "You believe in Jesus?" she asked. From that moment on, the ice was broken and we shared our common faith for the next two hours.

Beatrice told how her husband felt a call to practice medicine in South America only to be deeply disillusioned with working conditions there. She was returning from a visit with him. My heart ached as she shared about her husband's meager income and poor diet.

Before deplaning in Logos, Nigeria, Beatrice turned to me with open arms and we embraced. She kissed my cheek before walking down the aisle. I have often wondered what has happened to Beatrice and her family with all the strife in her country, and I will always remember the kinship we felt once we discovered we shared the Christian faith. I have also realized this fellowship might have been enjoyed for the entire flight had I found a way to share my faith sooner with Beatrice. And even though we may never meet again in this life, we are eternally bound together in God's love.

Thank You, dear Father, that Your love transcends all circumstances. We pray that this bond of love will continue to spread throughout the world. In Jesus' name. *Amen*

One Stripe for Katie

With his stripes we are healed.

Isaiah 53:5b

Soon after we learned of Katie's autism problem, I heard someone speak on the above passage from Isaiah. I remember the comfort it brought to my heart to listen to this message on the suffering servant. I remember the new hope that welled up within me, as this truth was impressed on my mind: One of the stripes that Jesus bore was for Katie! The whole passage from Isaiah 53:4,5 took on new meaning that morning.

Regardless of your need today, one stripe is for you.

"Surely he has borne our griefs and carried our sorrows; yet we esteemed him stricken, smitten by God, and afflicted.

But he was wounded for our transgressions; he was bruised for our iniquities; upon him was the chastisement that made us whole, and with his stripes we are healed."

One stripe for *our* Katie! One stripe for all the Marys and Joes in our world! I claimed these verses that day, and I continue to claim them now! Because our Lord—the suffering servant Son of God—was willing to take upon Himself the sins of the whole world, I can make this claim. His chastisement has made wholeness possible—wholeness for the suffering and sorrowful, the hostile and the helpless, and a little girl with autism. Believing this makes all the difference in holding on to hope. Thanks be to our Savior!

Precious Lord, I can never fully understand Your example of sacrificial love, but I am eternally grateful for it. Thank You for including all of us in Your redemptive plan. *Amen*

Pedestrian Grace

They shall walk and not faint.
Isaiah 40:31b

*A*t what speed do you feel your life is moving today? If you're like me, the day's pace depends on many things: schedules, circumstances, health, and even attitude. Isaiah talked about different speeds for the Israelites: mounting up like an eagle, running and not becoming weary, and walking and not fainting. I have some days when I feel motivated and energized, when I can work hard all day and not become weary. But more of my days fit the walking or plodding along speed.

No matter what pace I travel today, God's grace is new every morning.

I came upon a phrase recently that spoke to my need for patience and grace for those "plodding along days." Pedestrian grace—that phrase rang a clear note in my soul. It's what I need. Life has a way of slowing us down, even bogging us down. Old age, illness, grief, disappointment, and discouragement are inevitable. During these times life can be a struggle. But it's a comfort to know that God provides for our needs during each phase of our journey. He gives the exact grace we need for each day. He allows enough "mounting up" times and days of excitement to make life enjoyable and fulfilling. But I believe it is during the plodding days that we are most likely to call upon the Holy Spirit for power and strength.

Jesus promised that He would never leave us nor forsake us. He said He would be with us even to the end of the age, and that's what really matters anyway. We don't need to dread the plodding days, for His grace is sufficient for the entire journey!

Dear Father, I praise You for Your abiding grace that greets us at the dawn of each new day. Help me to remember that regardless of what the day may bring, You are with us all the way. In Jesus' name. *Amen*

Lift Each Other Up

*Woe to him who is alone when he falls
and has not another to lift him up.*
Ecclesiastes 4:10b

*A*t the close of a worship service in our church, an elderly man whom we had never seen before knelt at the altar. Wally prayed with him and dismissed the service. Imagine the surprise when Wally got to the door of the sanctuary and found the man receiving a collection of money. But the greater surprise came when we learned the man had "collected" at several other churches in town. Later this person was incarcerated in the Jefferson County Jail.

How can I be near to the brokenhearted and crushed in spirit today?

The story doesn't stop there. Wally visited the man in jail, prayed again with him, and the man surrendered his life to the Lord. Wally helped lift him up. Wouldn't it be wonderful if more lifting up occurred in our society and in our churches instead of tearing down?

God requires of us to "love kindness" (Micah 6:8b). Yet, too often wounded people are cut down by unkindness. Too often people are trampled while trying to lift themselves up of their own accord. Psalms 34:18 says, "The Lord is near to the broken-hearted, and saves the crushed in spirit." People need people—the fallen especially need people. Ecclesiastes 4:12b says "A threefold cord is not quickly broken." We gain strength from fellow Christians.

There are those all around us who are experiencing spiritual, mental, and physical exhaustion. There are those who are tempted to throw in the towel and quit. Some of these may be faithful pastors and parishioners. Let's be sensitive to people around us and form "threefold" cords to lift up the fallen.

Dear God, help us to have hearts of compassion for both the falling and the fallen all around us. In Jesus' name. *Amen*

Faith Talk in the Family

*You shall teach them to your children, talking of them when you are
sitting in your house, and when you are walking by the way,
and when you lie down, and when you rise.*
Deuteronomy 11:19

Is faith talk happening at your house? You may be thinking, *we don't have
time to talk about our problems, let alone our faith.* I believe we must find the
time. God instructed Moses about the necessity for faith talk in the family. He
said it should happen all day long: sitting in your house, walking by the way,
when you lie down, and when you rise. That's a pretty
big order!

*Jesus always took
time for children.
Do I?*

We know that families who do manage to discuss
their faith together reflect healthy and positive traits.
Royce Money in his book *Building Stronger Families*
says that families who openly discuss faith are more
likely to have these qualities: a sense of purpose and
meaning, positive attitudes, common morally-based values, trust and respect,
and a strong sense of family.[7]

Faith discussions aren't easy to come by in today's busy households. They
require time, energy, patience, and perseverance, but I believe they reap great
dividends. I can recall many times that Wally and I have had faith discussions
with our children. Many times these were at inopportune moments—maybe late
in the evening after a date or by long distance from a college dorm. I remember
a faith discussion around 4:00 A.M. after working our way through the clutter
from a break-in, and another time in a hospital storage room as David struggled
with his grandmother's death.

There are so many opportunities to discuss our Christian convictions with
our children, if we will only take advantage of the opportunity. Some of these
opportunities may come our way only once. The time we give our children in
faith talk is one of the most precious gifts we can ever give them.

Loving God, thank You for the privilege of sharing faith with
children. Help us to always make faith talk a priority in our
homes. *Amen*

Stay Focused

Take heed to the path of your feet, then all your ways will be sure.
Proverbs 4:26

*T*he nurse practitioner carefully guided the young man away from the Habitat for Humanity work site. It was obvious that he had sustained an eye injury. Ironically, on the back of his T-shirt were these words: "Stay Focused."

After witnessing that incident I've asked myself, *how focused is my life*? As I attend to the daily demands of living, on what do I concentrate? Is the center of my attention meeting a deadline? Is it a career, housework, the next commitment, or a dozen other activities? On what do I bring all my energies to bear? Do my present priorities deserve the time they require? Is the path of my daily walk with the Lord clearly defined, or is it a bit blurred and out of focus? Proverbs 3:6 says, "In all your way acknowledge him, and he will make straight your paths."

On whom or what will my focus be today?

The psalmist David said, "My heart is fixed O God, my heart is fixed: I will sing and give praise" (Psalms 57:7 KJV). On what do we fix our hearts? What is really important to us? Jesus said, "Where your treasure is, there will your heart be also" (Matthew 6:21).

If a faithful daily walk with the Lord is our focus, then our steps will be sure. We may meet up with obstacles along the way. We may need to allow a friend or family member to put an arm around us and guide us. We may need to guard against selfish desires that can unsettle us. Circumstances beyond our control can circumvent our good intentions. The devil can discourage us, but discourage is all he can do when our focus is fixed soundly on the One who is the Way.

Dear God, I pray that You will keep my feet securely in the path of Your will so my way will be sure. In Jesus' name. *Amen*

Reflecting His Presence

Now when they saw the boldness of Peter and John,
and perceived that they were uneducated, common men, they wondered;
and they recognized that they had been with Jesus.
Acts 4:13

*B*abies love mirrors. They are fascinated by the reflection of their face in a mirror. Our lives are like mirrors, reflecting to the world an image of some kind.

Jesus reflected the image of God. His life mirrored God. Jesus said, "He who has seen me has seen the Father" (John 14:9a). Jesus reflected the presence and likeness of God to the world.

Who will the world see reflected in my life today?

Peter and John reflected the presence of Jesus to their world. The Sanhedrin knew them to be uneducated, common men. Yet, they seemed different. Their boldness was out of character, so the conclusion was simply that "they had been with Jesus."

Does the world see anything in my life that would suggest I have been with Jesus? Is His presence mirrored in me? Can my friends, neighbors, and family see Christ in me? I hope so. But to be honest, I'm sure His image is dimmed in my life at times.

I want my heavenly Father to be pleased with the reflection He sees in my life. I want my life to resemble His Son's. I know that for this to happen I must spend quality time with Him. I need to remember that I can't reflect the presence of Christ unless I spend time in His presence.

Dear Lord, You have modeled for us our Creator God. Help me to spend time with You so that my life will be a testimony of Your nature and character today. *Amen*

Practice Hospitality

Practice hospitality ungrudgingly to one another.
I Peter 4:9

*W*hen our children were young and saw me baking a pie, they would usually ask, "Who is that one for, Mom?" The desserts I made were usually to take to a sick or shut-in person or a potluck supper.

Though I trust my efforts blessed some people, I don't think this is what our Scripture was speaking of. Jesus said in Matthew 25:35,36, "I was hungry and you gave me food, I was thirsty and you gave me drink, I was a stranger and you welcomed me, I was naked and you clothed me, I was sick and you visited me, I was in prison and you came to me." Hebrews 13:2 says, "Do not neglect to show hospitality to strangers, for thereby some have entertained angels unawares."

We need to remember that when we practice hospitality with the "least of these" (Matthew 25:40), Christ is present with us.

In today's world we are hesitant to allow a stranger into our home. Though we encourage hospitality, we need to warn our children to be cautious with adults they have never met before. Yet, we need to find ways to help the less fortunate

Jesus talked about inviting "the poor, the maimed, the lame, the blind," and added, "You will be blessed, because they cannot repay you" (Luke 14:14a)

Some of our most memorable and rewarding attempts to be hospitable were when we've had people in need in our home: a couple of transients stranded in a snowstorm in our town, four hungry and needy children in our community, an elderly man who lived alone. We are blessed by being a blessing to others. I want to look for ways to practice hospitality ungrudgingly—beyond our family and friends.

Gracious God, help us to be willing to share with Your people in need. Forgive us for the times we have failed to offer Your love and compassion. In Jesus' name. *Amen*

A Patient Encourager

Encourage the faint-hearted, help the weak, be patient with them all.
I Thessalonians 5:14b

"Are you crying?" the older lady asked the little boy beside her on the plane. Nodding his head, quiet sobs began to shake his body. I was sitting directly behind him—next to the window—and could see a small, pale hand waving goodbye to the disappearing city below.

Will anyone recognize Christ's compassion through me today?

As we became airborne, the kind lady continued to try to piece together his story: a dad living in Louisville and a mother in Chicago to whom he was returning. Caught in the middle was a little boy torn by grief over his broken family.

A flight attendant walked by and with little feeling asked how the child was doing. Then almost before the answer came, she glanced toward me and said, "We see this every day." What a sad commentary on our society—families falling apart and the children bearing the deepest wounds of all.

This dialogue between the grandmotherly woman and the sad little boy continued during the entire flight from Louisville to Chicago. She looked deeply into the little boy's eyes and said, "That's really hard, isn't it?" Once the lady glanced back at me, and rolled her eyes in a feeling of helplessness. I complimented the job she was doing in her conversation with the child and told her that I wished I could do more. I prayed that the Holy Spirit would counsel this kindhearted woman as she brought comfort to the child.

We deplaned in Chicago and each went our separate ways. But I was left with a haunting question: How willing would I have been to patiently encourage a hurting heart that happened to sit by me? I hope that I will remember that as I try to minister to one of the least of these, I minister to my Lord.

Dear Father, You know the hurts of Your children. Help me to be more sensitive to the needs about me and give me the courage to reach out in Your love. *Amen*

An Angel Inside

*Thy eyes behold my unformed substance; in thy book
were written, every one of them, the days that were formed for me,
when as yet there was none of them.*

Psalms 139:16

The story is told that one day as Michaelangelo chiseled away on one of his sculpted masterpieces, an observer commented that his work looked futile. He could not see any possible potential in that unsightly hunk of marble. Michaelangelo continued patiently, determinedly forming his work of art. Again the observer commented on the seemingly useless endeavor. The artist is said to have replied that he knew there was an angel inside the piece of marble— it only waited to be found.

Today, I will strive to see the good in every person.

Michaelangelo saw the potential inside a cold, hard block of marble. How good it would be if you and I could see a person's potential and not just the faults. It's so comforting to know that God has the eyes to do just that. He even sees the unformed substance of our very being.

I believe that within every person is an unformed, unfulfilled possibility for purpose. There is that God-spot that will remain void unless occupied and filled by God Himself. I believe He sees, even in the embryo, the capacity which each life holds. Sadly, though, so many persons never have the opportunity to experience life itself, let alone the opportunity to reach their full potential.

In Matthew's gospel, the story is told of two blind men sitting by the roadside. They cried out to Jesus as he passed their way, "Lord, let our eyes be opened" (Matthew 20:33). This plea could well be ours, too. For so often we look blindly upon God's creation. We see only outward appearances, never looking at the potential—the unformed potential—of a possible angel inside.

Loving Creator, help me to remember that within the coldest, hardest heart is the potential for something beautiful. Through Your Son, I pray. *Amen*

Offer Always Good

The free gift of God is eternal life in Christ Jesus our Lord.
Romans 6:23b

*O*ffer good from May 27, 1998, to July 30, 1998." The cut-off date caught my attention as I prepared to tuck the refund slip in an envelope. But it was too late to receive the one-dollar refund—three months late, in fact.

As I pitched the small pink slip of paper in the trash can, I thanked God that His offer of eternal life is not like that refund slip. His offer is for always in this life—no cut-off date! His offer requires no "net proof of purchase." It's a free gift. All God asks of us is our sincere repentance of sin as we allow Him to be Lord.

Jesus gave His life to offer us eternal life.

In order to receive this free gift of eternal life we need to leave the *net weight* of our sins at His feet. The real proof of purchase of our free gift of salvation is the cross where our Lord paid the price.

We don't have to wait for the request to be processed and returned. His forgiveness is available at any time—no waiting.

The offer is always good, and the gift is so good that God wishes for all to receive it. "The Lord is not slow about his promise as some count slowness, but is forbearing toward you, not wishing that any should perish, but all should reach repentance" (II Peter 3:9).

Loving Father, how grateful we are of Your gift of eternal life through Your Son Jesus. Help us never to forget the price He paid on Calvary. In Jesus' name. *Amen*

Stranger in Our Midst

Their eyes were kept from recognizing him.
Luke 24:16

*D*uring breakfast at the Universal Studios Hotel in Los Angeles, we noticed a steady stream of people walking up to a table near us. Two men sat at the table, and one—the husky, bald-headed fellow—appeared to be signing his autograph. I whispered to Wally, "I don't know who that man is, but he must be a star—I'm going over to ask for his autograph, too." The man graciously signed the paper place mat, and neither Wally nor I recognized the name.

I want the Holy Spirit to place a permanent signature upon my heart.

Later at home, I remembered to show the autograph to our children. "Mother," David burst out, "How did you *ever* get Telly Savalas's autograph?" And my naïve reply was, "Who is Telly….what's his name?" Both our children groaned and said, "I don't believe you sat next to Kojak and didn't know who he was!" A television star had been in our midst and we didn't recognize him. And in the eyes of our two children, we were quickly relegated to the company of the uninformed.

In reflecting on this experience, I've thought about another person who is often a stranger in our midst. He's not a Hollywood star—He happens to be the King of kings, and Lord of the universe! But like the disciples on the road to Emmaus, our eyes are blinded to Him, because we are too caught up in our own self and daily living.

I want to recognize the presence and power of my precious Lord *every* day in my life. For He is no stranger—He's my friend. Through the mystery of the Holy Spirit, He's my counselor, my comforter, my enabler, my guide, and my strength. He will even abide in my heart forever if I allow Him.

Loving God, thank You for not only giving us a Savior, but also His presence all along life's road. May I never be blinded to Him. In Jesus' name. *Amen*

The Unwritten Chapter

Now we see in a mirror dimly, but then face to face.
Now I know in part; then I shall understand fully.

I Corinthians 13:12

Many times over the years I have told our children to be patient with life, that the final chapter hasn't been written yet. This statement might have come at a time when they wondered about life's fairness. It might have been when a classmate cheated on an exam and made a high score because of it. It might have come when they were asking why the life of a young friend was not spared, especially after scores of people prayed for her healing. Or it might have been when a young college student was harassed because of his Christian principles.

Can't we trust the author and finisher of our faith?

Life does seem to have many chapters, and I believe that when the final chapter of life's story is written, we'll see meaning and purpose in the events along the way. For the moment we may feel like Paul: we only understand a part of it all. But one day we will understand fully.

One day we'll realize that God was with us, working all along the way. Often it is in retrospect that events have meaning, and what we label as coincidences are really "God-incidents." Jesus promised in John 14:18, "I will not leave you desolate; I will come to you." Through the presence of the Holy Spirit, even the unwritten chapters of our lives need not be feared. And those chapters we've already lived out can be entrusted to God as He works everything together for our good. Both trials and triumphs are encompassed in the plot of our lives, and our struggles become God's opportunities to write a new chapter.

Loving Father, give us Your wisdom as we search for meaning and purpose through every chapter of our life. In Jesus' name. *Amen*

Sewing, Waiting, Reaping

For here the saying holds true, "One sows and another reaps."
John 4:37

I gave each kindergartner a special seed to place in a paper cup filled with soil. With a little luck I knew that in a few days the seed would sprout and break through the soil. I always felt a little apprehensive, though, that one of the cups would never produce a plant and be a disappointment to the child.

Some seeds we plant in life don't produce a harvest at the time we expect it. Some seeds may never produce a harvest in our lifetime, but no seeds are wasted. Even seeds that never sprout make a difference in the soil. They decay and enrich the soil, making it easier for sprouts from future seeds to appear and grow.

If we don't see the results of our labors, we can rest in the faith that someone will someday.

Some of us are to be sowers. Some are to reap the harvest. Sometimes a long wait occurs between the sowing and the harvest. Many worthwhile ministries grow and flourish—not because of one person's merit, but often by seeds planted by others. Many people may never see the results of their labor, but the seeds planted make the soil fertile for a rich harvest later.

The sowing is never in vain, even though, like the kindergarten child, we feel disappointment when the seed doesn't sprout. No seeds are wasted! God doesn't allow anything we do for Him to be wasted (I Corinthians 15:58 TLB).

Seeds of love planted will ultimately bear fruit. Love never fails (I Corinthians 13:8 NIV). We may not see the results in our lifetime, but remember, even Jesus didn't see all the results of His love during His life on earth. God brings the harvest in His time. We aren't responsible for the harvest—just the planting and the willingness to wait. The result—the reaping—is in God's hands, and He's always on time!

Dear God, help us to never become discouraged in serving You. Give us the assurance that You are the Lord of the harvest. In Jesus' name. *Amen*

Go On Singing

Come into his presence with singing!
Psalms 100:2

*O*ne of the great blessings that has come to our family is that of knowing Tony Fontane. Tony was a popular radio, television, and recording star. After a serious automobile accident, he accepted Christ and spent the remaining years of his life serving Him.

Can my heart go on singing during the tough times?

Tony recorded a number of albums and performed Christian concerts throughout the world. He traveled some 250,000 miles annually and made numerous appearances before servicemen overseas. He sang for Presidents Eisenhower, Kennedy, Johnson, and Nixon. One of the highlights of his singing career was a command performance before the heads of state in England.

As a result of giving up his show business career after his conversion, Tony's agent brought suit against him. Tony and his wife, Kerry, also a former movie star, lost all of their material wealth. But their ministry reaped a rich harvest of souls.

Wally had the privilege of participating in Tony's funeral. Stuart Hamblin sang one of the songs he had written—a favorite of Tony's—entitled "Until Then." On the last stanza, Mr. Hamblin was deeply moved. He began the chorus, "But until then my heart will go on singing," then he stopped. Looking heavenward, he bellowed out in his own unique cowboy drawl, "Go on singing, boy!"

Later that evening, Mr. Hamblin explained the inspiration for this song. He and his wife were worshiping at the Hollywood Presbyterian Church when some ladies told him that he sang a little too loudly. In fact, they said he was distracting them from the worship service. Mr. Hamblin couldn't seem to shake their comments, until Mrs. Hamblin wisely advised him, "Stu, now don't you pay any attention to those ladies. You sing from the heart, and that's what's important. So, you just go on singing!" Later that same day, Mr. Hamblin penned the words to the song that has inspired millions in the years hence.

Dear Father, thank You for the spiritual giants that touch our lives. Help us to serve You with joy until You call us home. *Amen*

It Is No Secret

*The secrets of his heart are disclosed; and so, falling on his face,
he will worship God and declare that God is really among you.*

I Corinthians 14:25

*I*t was almost midnight when we said our goodnight to Stuart and Suzy Hamblin, and what a wonderful evening it had been in their home. We shared how our lives had been enriched over the years by our mutual friend, Tony Fontane. Somehow this seemed an appropriate way to close the painful day of Tony's funeral.

The Hamblins offered such warm hospitality in their beautiful Los Angeles home. Mrs. Hamblin slipped into the kitchen around 10 P.M., and it was not until she served the hot peach cobbler that we realized what she had been doing. "Nobody can make a peach cobbler like my Suzy," Mr. Hamblin proudly admitted.

The world needs to know about the transforming power of God.

Before leaving, we paused momentarily at their entrance door just as the old grandfather clock struck midnight. Mr. Hamblin looked toward the clock and recalled, "That's the inspiration for my song 'It Is No Secret.'" He went on to tell of the time many years earlier when he and Mrs. Hamblin had hosted a party for some Hollywood friends, among them John Wayne. As Mr. Wayne prepared to leave that evening, he congratulated Mr. Hamblin on his recent conversion in a Billy Graham crusade. To this Mr. Hamblin replied, "You know, Duke, it's really no secret what God can do." Just at that moment the same clock had struck midnight. Thus, the the song begins, "The chimes of time ring out the news another day is through."

Suzy Hamblin went on with the story. She said that at that very moment, John Wayne looked at Stuart Hamblin and wisely advised, "Stu, you should write a song about that." Before Mr. Hamblin went to bed that night, he penned the lyrics to "It Is No Secret." And today, it is still no secret what God can do if we will only allow Him to work in our lives!

Loving Father, I pray that our home can be a place where we can welcome old friends and new, and where we are always found faithful telling others about what You mean to our lives. In Jesus' name. *Amen*

By the Side of the Suffering

Even though I walk through the valley of the shadow of death,
I fear no evil; for thou art with me.

Psalms 23:4

When David was in seminary in Atlanta, one of his courses required that he spend four hours per week in a homeless shelter there. Among the group of children he came to know was a little boy with bad burns all over his body. He was an obvious victim of child abuse. His feet were so badly burned that he could not walk. The palms of his hands were so badly burned that he could not use them for crawling. So he bent his hands back, and using the tops of his hands and his knees, he crawled about, whimpering barely above a whisper.

We bless the Lord when we bless one of His children.

David made many efforts to console him and talk to him, but the little boy would only cry. Finally, David got down on the floor on his stomach beside the little boy in order to look into his eyes. It was only then that the little boy finally smiled and spoke a few words. When David finished telling this story to his dad, he said, "One of these days I will be a preacher. And I know there will be a certain amount of paper work I'll have to shuffle across my desk. But, Dad, I will never let a week go by without going to people who are hurting."

This little abused boy knew what it was like to be in the valley of the shadow of death. It was when someone was willing to be by his side—down where *he* was—that he could find it in his heart to smile. He, at least for a few fleeting moments, feared no evil.

Do we see the hurting all about us? Are we willing to be by their side in order to look into the pain of their hearts? What valley might God be calling me into today in order to be by the side of the suffering?

Merciful God, forgive us when we fail to be by the side of the suffering. Help us to be Your instruments of healing for the hurting of this world. Through Christ we pray. *Amen*

Making Our Steps Secure

*Though we stumble, we shall not fall headlong,
for the Lord holds us by the hand.*

Psalm 37:24 (NRSV)

Recently I observed two persons walking with some insecurity. One was a toddler taking her first steps in learning to walk. The other was an older person learning to walk again after an illness. Each one faltered at times. The child, learning to coordinate her leg muscles, would sometimes lift her feet too high. The elderly person, weakened by disease, was struggling to lift his feet at all.

I need never walk alone.

As a child, I walked to the elementary school in our rural community. I remember on one cold, snowy morning my dad walked beside me. At times I would drag my feet in order to make my steps more secure, and then Daddy would ask me, "Can't you pick up your feet a little?" I would chuckle because I knew he wasn't as afraid of my falling as he was of my wearing out my shoe soles. He *knew* that my steps were secure, because he was holding my hand over the dangerous spots.

We all can use a helping hand at whatever our age or stage in life may be. But most important of all, our Heavenly Father is ever by our side. He makes our steps secure and holds our hands as we travel over the dangerous places.

Our Father, we thank You that You are ever by our side through the Holy Spirit. Help us, in turn, to be willing to extend a helping hand to others. *Amen*

A Place to Call Home

*If a man loves me, he will keep my word, and my Father will love him,
and we will come to him and make our home with him.*

John 14:23

Riding down a street in Atlanta, my eyes caught a glimpse of what looked like a body hanging on a cross on a rooftop. Underneath the cross were these words of ridicule: "Vagrant Christ." I stared in disbelief. Our son David saw my troubled expression and asked, "What's wrong, Mom?" I pointed to the porch roof, somehow hoping he would tell me I had misinterpreted the scene. "I know," he said soberly, "I was hoping you wouldn't notice."

Does Christ have a home in your heart today?

How could anyone label our Lord a vagrant? My *Webster's New World Dictionary* describes vagrant as "rover," "wanderer," "vagabond," "beggar," "tramp," "prostitute," "bum," and "hobo."[1] Such mockery pierced my heart. I prayed silently, *Father, forgive them; for they know not what they do* (Luke 23:34a).

Jesus did say, "Foxes have holes, and birds of the air have nests; but the Son of man has nowhere to lay his head" (Matthew 8:20), but to label Christ a vagrant was to me outright heresy. Yet the whole incident made me think seriously of Christ's true place of residence. That place is in a loving, forgiving heart if we will allow Him entrance. In fact, our Scripture today says, "*We* will come to him, and make our *home* with him" (emphasis mine). Our God and our Lord will reside in our heart through the Holy Spirit.

We can't prevent the labels that evil in our world may place on our Lord. But we can be sure that He is always welcome and at home in our hearts.

Dear Jesus, I pray for forgiveness for those who would mock You and say all manner of evil against You falsely. Forgive me, Lord, for the times I have failed to give You Your rightful place in my heart. *Amen*

A Dark Night in Nairobi

When I am afraid, I put my trust in thee.
Psalms 56:3

*M*ost of us, at some point in our lives, have experienced long, dark nights, feelings of lostness, and deep fears. All of these feelings came together at once for us during our first night in Nairobi, Kenya.

Wally and I, along with several other delegates and visitors to the World Methodist Conference, arrived at the Nairobi airport around midnight. Having been assured that someone would be waiting to transport us from the airport to our dorm or hotel room, our group climbed into the first available van. After an hour we began to ask each other how long it should take to reach our rooms. No one knew. Attempts to communicate with our driver were not successful. Two hours passed, then three. Fear began to well up within me. The streets were dark. Armed guards could be seen in the shadows everywhere. The old van's creaking and groaning seemed to worsen with every pothole.

God's presence knows no boundaries.

After four hours of wandering the Nairobi streets, the stark reality hit us: we were lost. I prayed and recalled John 14:28b: "Let not your hearts be troubled, neither let them be afraid." All of us were edgy by then, including our driver. Finally, he stopped at an American hotel to once again ask directions. I could see the fear in his eyes. In broken English he confessed that he was lost and would be fined over this episode. He was out of gas and had no funds to purchase any.

We gladly pooled our resources, filled the gas tank, and continued our search. Just as the first streaks of light broke over the African horizon, our driver seemed to get a clear direction for finding our dorm.

I have reflected many times on our wandering in that dark wilderness. I've recalled those deep feelings of fear and the parable of life we experienced that night: How often do we wander aimlessly through the darkness and dangers of life? We feel afraid. We run out of energy. And, finally, we are able to confess our lostness and accept help from those close to us. But most important, it's when we allow the light of God's presence to break through that we begin to see our way clearly again.

Loving God, thank You for leading us through the dark times in life. Let Your light shine through me today. *Amen*

Believe in the Dawn

Then shall your light break forth like the dawn.
Isaiah 58:8

*H*ave you ever heard a bird start singing even before the first streaks of daylight appear? This experience always inspires me, because it reminds me that birds really believe in the dawn!

It's so important for us to believe in the dawn, too. Isaiah was reminding a weary people that their light would soon break forth like the dawn. That's good for us to hear. We can somehow persevere through the darkest hours in life when we can hold on to the faith that these, too, will pass.

Because God is trustworthy, we can believe in the dawn.

All of us have had—or will have—some dark hours, but Psalms 30:5b promises, "Weeping may tarry for the night, but joy comes with the morning." Problems always seem a little worse at night. Learning to believe in the dawn helps us make it through the dark nights of the soul.

If you are experiencing a dark time in your life, just know that there *will* be a brighter day. Faith grows this way. Hebrews 11:1 says "Faith is the assurance of things hoped for, the conviction of things not seen."

Birds sense the assurance of the dawn. Even before they see it, they have the faith to announce it's coming. Jesus said in Matthew 6:26, "Look at the birds of the air: they neither sow nor reap nor gather into barns, and yet your heavenly Father feeds them. Are you not of more value than they?"

So we surely can trust each new day to Him. We can voice our praise to Him even before we see the first streaks of dawn breaking into our darkness.

Loving Father, Your mercies are new every morning! Help us to trust You during the dark times as well as the dawn. *Amen*

"Sir, We Would See Jesus"

*So these came to Philip, who was from Bethsaida in Galilee,
and said to him, "Sir, we wish to see Jesus."*
John 12:21

J was granted permission to place a small brass plaque behind the new pulpit in our church. The engraved words, "Sir, we wish to see Jesus," seemed to be the right directive for the messages to this newly merged congregation. In retrospect, perhaps the "Sir" should have been omitted, because, undoubtedly, the pulpit will be open to female pastors as well.

I do believe that the clarion call of lay persons throughout the church is to experience Jesus lifted up from the pulpit. We wish to see Jesus through the Word and the works of our church's leaders. We wish to see Jesus in attitudes and actions, in the spirit and love of Christ, lived out daily. I believe that authentic Christian witness can be perceived in us only as our walk is congruent with our talk—only as Christ is exemplified in our lifestyles.

We must never allow anything or anyone to distract us from focusing on Jesus.

So, the Scripture's charge is not just to clergy but to laypersons. It's to each of us who claim to be the body of Christ. The challenge is clear. Jesus said, "I demand that you love each other as much as I love you" (John 15:12 TLB). He said, "For I have given you an example, that you also should do as I have done to you" (John 13:15). The words and works of Jesus were the same. Later, Paul advised Timothy, "Set the believers an example in speech and conduct, in love, in faith, in purity" (I Timothy 4:12b)

Whether we serve as leaders or followers in the church, we are called to be examples of Christ. For we are the only way Christ can be seen in our world.

Oh Divine Master, grant us the willingness to seek You and Your kingdom first so that the world can see that You are first in our lives. Through Jesus, our Lord, we pray. *Amen*

Accepted or Excepted

We know that the Son of God has come and has given us understanding.

I John 5:20a

I recently saw a teenage boy standing by a curb in front of a service station holding a sign which read, "CAR WASH—DONATIONS EXCEPTED." Obviously the boy intended to say, "Donations Accepted." But if the passers-by had taken him literally, his youth group might have come up short in donations that day.

A heart heard is a heart helped— maybe even healed.

Trying to understand each other is a tough assignment. Our choice of words may be wrong. The spelling of a word can completely change its meaning. It's often difficult to communicate to another what one feels in the heart. Yet communication and understanding are vitally important in every aspect of life.

We would do well to follow the Kenyan motto: "Let us sit down and talk about our problems." But in today's busy households there seems to be no time to sit down and talk. Few families have meals together any more. Schedules can take family members in a dozen directions in one day. Too often family members can feel *excepted* rather than *accepted*.

Is there someone in your family who needs your understanding today, someone who needs to feel accepted rather than excepted? Let's take the time and make the emotional investment needed for communication and understanding. I believe God can enable this to happen through parents as well as children. The Kenyan families have a handle on how it's done—sitting down and talking about their problems together. Communication is the glue that holds families together, making each member feel accepted. May God help us in our understanding of each other.

Loving God, forgive me when I fail to understand as I should. Give me Your spirit of understanding. I pray in Jesus' name. *Amen*

Handling Emergencies

Be strong, and let your heart take courage,
all you who wait for the Lord!
Psalms 31:24

Recently I fell behind an older station wagon in the midst of heavy traffic. A young woman was driving, and behind her sat eight children. All of them looked to be of elementary school age. When I was close enough to read their bumper sticker, I saw these words clearly emblazoned: "I can handle any emergency. I have children." My heart immediately responded, "Hats off to all young mothers!" What patience, fortitude, ingenuity, and grace they must have to be successful mothers in today's world!

I can handle the emergencies in my life because God is with me.

After the station wagon exited the expressway, I continued to think about the bumper sticker. How do I handle emergencies? How do I respond in a crisis situation? Suddenly I remembered the Chinese character for crisis. It means both trouble and opportunity. I can always recognize the "trouble" part of a crisis, but seeing it as an opportunity is not as easy.

Yet, how many of us would ever reach any sort of maturity in our faith if we never faced emergencies or times of pain and suffering?

Regardless of our age and stage in life, we will experience emergency situations. We will know suffering. Trouble is inevitable; we live in an imperfect world. But like the young mother behind the wheel of that station wagon, we can have confidence. We can be strong and courageous for we know God's "grace is sufficient," and His "power is made perfect in weakness" (II Corinthians 12:9). Thanks be to God who supplies all our needs!

Loving Father, thank You for the power and strength that comes from Your presence with us in every situation. Help me to live daily in this confidence. *Amen*

Outward Appearances

Do not judge by appearances, but judge with right judgment.
John 7:24

I once heard a parable of human experience. It's a story about the two streams which flow into the mighty Colorado River. One of the streams is a beautiful, clear, sparkling brook that is a joy to travelers who pause to view it. It is rightly named "Bright Angel Creek." The other stream is a muddy and ugly stream, bearing silt and debris. No one stops to look at it. In fact, it's rather repulsive and appropriately called "Dirty Devil Creek."

How often do I look on a person's appearance without attempting to see his or her heart?

Now suppose that Bright Angel Creek should suddenly find voice and say to its neighbor, "Aren't you ashamed of being so dirty and muddy and ugly? Don't you wish you could be clean and fresh and beautiful like me?" At that, Dirty Devil Creek seems to slow up a bit and in a somber voice replies, "Bright Angel Creek, if you had been through what I've been through, you'd be dirty and ugly, too."

Too often we judge before we make any effort to understand the circumstances. I believe God intends for each of us to be a part of the clean, pure, and useful stream of life. But, somehow, the flood of circumstances in life leave many persons swept over by the silt of hate, hunger, disease, and despair.

We must be careful not to judge by outward appearance. I Samuel 16:7b, says "Man looks on the outward appearance, but the Lord looks on the heart." In fact, we are not to judge at all. Jesus taught this in the Sermon on the Mount when he said, "Judge not, that you be not judged. For with the judgment you pronounce you will be judged, and the measure you give will be the measure you get" (Matthew 7:1,2).

Loving Father, please forgive me for the times I've made up my mind about a person or a situation before I tried to understand the circumstances. In Jesus' name. *Amen*

Patience

But if we have hope for what we do not see, we wait for it with patience.

Romans 8:25

A child once asked me, "Why are rose buds ugly when I try to help them open, but pretty when God does it?" What would your answer be to this question? God's way is the best way? Nature has its own timetable?

I just tried to talk about patience. Patience is the needed component for the perfect opening of a rose. It's not meant to be hurried. Everything—each flower, each tree, each person—reaches full potential and beauty in God's perfect timing and not by our rushing and nudging.

In what areas of my life am I in most need of patience?

Patience. It's such an important virtue. Most of us desire it, but few of us want the discipline required to experience it. Yet, patience is that spirit that never knows defeat. It's the power to bear, to suffer, to sacrifice, to endure, to wait, and to hope—even when we see no evidence of the desired result or answer in sight. It's that kind of love that knows no limit.

We see so many examples of patience in the Bible: The father waiting patiently for the prodigal son's return (Luke 15:11-32); the good shepherd searching diligently for the lost sheep (Luke 15:3-7); the woman sweeping the floor for a lost coin (Luke 15:8,9); and the weary disciples fishing all night (Luke 5:5).

Patience is a quality that grows through tribulation. Paul spoke from experience when he said, "Be patient in tribulation" (Romans 12:12). During the years that followed his Damascus Road experience, Paul faced all kinds of tribulation: shipwreck, beatings, imprisonment, and even starvation. But Paul patiently endured, and wrote from a prison cell, "I have learned, in whatsoever state I am, to be content" (Philippians 4:11).

Weather, insects, disease, even people can thwart the natural beauty of an opening rose bud. Evil forces, disease, trouble, and various other circumstances can thwart our plans and our development. God's patience—His orderly plan for our lives—will bring not only beauty, but ultimate victory, if we have hope for what we do not see.

Loving Father, enable me to be strong during the difficult days knowing that patience is being processed in me. *Amen*

Calling in Help

My help comes from the Lord, who made heaven and earth.
Psalms 121:2

A prominent businessman was being interviewed one day. The reporter said, "Sir, I understand you are a self-made millionaire." The man thought for a moment, then replied, "Well, I guess you could say that…. But I can tell you that if I had my life to live over, I'd call in help along the way." In gaining success by the world's standards, this man had lost the more necessary components of the happy life. His family was estranged, and his life and faith were in disarray.

We can call in God's help at any point of need.

Recently, Wally preached the funeral of a ninety-four-year-old friend. This person was a successful leader in his community and church. His faith had never wavered, and his family remained a strong, supportive unit over the years. The difference: This man, Mr. Harlan Landrum, had called in God's help all through his long life. His many friends in the community called him the salt of the earth and a pillar of the church.

After the funeral that day, we went to the home of Mr. Landrum's daughter. After some time of fellowship and a delicious meal, we prepared to leave. I struggled for a word of comfort for his dear, devoted wife of some seventy years. Taking her hand in mine, I bent over close to her and said, "Mrs. Landrum, just always remember, 'My grace…'" and before I could complete the verse from II Corinthians 12:9, she smiled and in total confidence, completed the sentence "…is sufficient."

Mrs. Landrum knew about calling in help. She knew, as did her beloved husband, that their help had always come from the Lord who made heaven and earth. Time and circumstances can never change this fact.

Loving Father, You are present with us all day long and all life long. Thank You so much for this blessed assurance. *Amen*

God Shows Us the Way

Even though I walk through the valley of the shadow of death,
I fear no evil; for thou art with me.
Psalm 23:4a

I came upon a letter the other day from a dear friend who is now in heaven. Betty Bratton's letter was dated August 30, 1980. In it she shared how her strength was rapidly leaving, and how she was making preparation for her home-going. She didn't sound the least bit sad, but was making plans for her funeral as one would plan for a trip.

She wrote, "Now, Wallace, you know that you will be preaching my funeral. It will be at 2:00 P.M., but the date is still up in the air." Then she closed the letter with these words from a poem:

It's not necessary for us to know the way, but only to know the One who lights the way.

> Not for a single day can I discern the way,
> But this I know,
> Who gives this day will show the way,
> So I securely go.
> —Author unknown

Betty Bratton lived each day in that spirit of security in the God she served. She knew that in the valley of the shadow of death ahead, there would be light to guide her. If there were to be no light the psalmist would not have mentioned a shadow. Without a source of light a shadow would be impossible.

With the light of God's presence showing the way, Mrs Bratton could "securely go." She did, and so can we.

Our current valleys may not involve facing death immediately. But there are other kinds of valleys—valleys of discouragement, disillusionment, suffering, sadness, and other struggles. None of us can discern the way for a single day without knowing the One who assured us in Matthew 28:20b, "Lo, I am with you always, to the close of the age."

Gracious and loving Father, thank You for showing us the way and giving us Your Son who *is* the Way. *Amen*

The Everlasting Rock

Trust in the Lord forever, for the Lord God is an everlasting rock.

Isaiah 26:4

I have a precious memory of my mother and father-in-law which took place in a hospital room in Glasgow, Kentucky. Mrs. Thomas, sitting in a wheelchair by the bedside of Mr. Thomas, was enjoying the visit of a young girl from their church. She looked into the girl's face and lovingly asked, "Would you all come out to our house when Kenneth gets home and sing for us?" The young friend assured her that she and others from the church would come out and sing for them soon.

In whatever circumstances we find ourselves right now, God knows, and we can trust Him.

The church friends did come and sing. They sang about an anchor that holds during the tough times of life. It holds because it is attached to a firm Rock, the Rock that Isaiah talked about in today's Scripture.

We, too, can recognize our constant need for an anchor, and we can be very sure who that anchor is. We may struggle, we may stumble, and we may have doubts and fears. We may face sickness and death. But our personal faith in Jesus Christ is the sure anchor because it's fastened to the everlasting Rock.

Father, thank You for giving us a sure anchor through Your Son, Jesus. In His name. *Amen*

A Close Shave

I will be glad and rejoice in your mercy,
for you have considered my trouble.
Psalm 32:7a (NKJV)

*A*s I opened our apartment door to urgent knocking, the stranger blurted out, "Are you driving a green Chrysler?" Wally answered, puzzled by the inquiry, "Yes, I have one borrowed while my car is being repaired." "Well," the stranger responded, " It's inside that barber shop at the bottom of the hill!" "It *can't* be," Wally insisted, "I've just parked it—and I turned the wheels toward the curb!"

The reality of what the man was saying sent sudden chills up our spines. Remembering how steep 15th Street was and the busy Center Street traffic at the foot of the hill, we could hardly utter the next question. "Was anyone hurt?" we stammered in unison. "No," came the stoic reply. "But it has to be some kind of miracle."

God's promises made are promises kept.

We raced to the bottom of the hill and found that the news media had already arrived. There it was: the old Chrysler, covered in shattered glass, wedged between two barber chairs. The stunned barber said quietly, "A little boy had just gotten out of the chair next to the front window." Thankfully, it was late afternoon and the last customer had left.

The next morning's paper had the story emblazoned across the front page, complete with a large picture and headline reading "A Close Shave!" We will forever be grateful to God for His mercy in our trouble.

Loving Father, Your Word teaches us that You extend mercy in considering our troubles. I am so thankful for Your promises kept. *Amen*

Inspected by No. 7

The Lord will not forsake his people.
Psalms 94:14

J sorted the laundry into the usual three groupings and started the first load. There was a comfortable feeling of routine in the familiar hum of the washer and smell of my favorite detergent. Doing the usual pocket check turned up a broken toothpick, a parking stub, a stray coin, and that little scrap of paper that always

How often do we overlook persons for whom we should pray?

seems to irritate me a little. "Inspected by No. 7," it read. In every garment with a pocket, that little rectangular piece of paper inevitably shows up. Sometimes, it will show through in a shirt pocket. At other times, the garment is washed with the inspector slip still in place.

As I crumpled one more inspector slip and aimed it toward a waste can, an important truth occurred to me: The little piece of paper—the *number*—represents a person. More than that, it represents a soul created in the image of God. How could I so irritably crumple and discard that paper without thinking of the person? Who knows? Inspector No. 7, laboring somewhere in a factory, might be having a difficult day. He or she might be working under stressful conditions or might have a home burdened with problems.

So, that day in my laundry room in Louisville, Kentucky, I stopped what I was doing and prayed for Inspector No. 7. Since then, I have continued to pray for those persons represented by inspector slips. We are told that some 85,000,000 Christians worship in this country every Sunday. The thought occurred to me of the dramatic difference it would make if all of these people prayed for our nation's work force each time we found a little white inspection slip in a pocket. I will never forget the day when an inspection number became a person. I trust that somewhere in this world a few inspectors' lives have been a little more pleasant because of my prayers. I know my life has been enriched by the lesson God taught me that day in the laundry room.

Dear Father, help me to always remember that every person is precious and important in Your eyes. In Jesus' name. *Amen*

Who Said So?

By what authority are you doing these things?
Mark 11:28a

One of my kindergarten students said to me as she walked in the classroom, "Mrs. Thomas, I've got a growing pain this morning." "How do you know?" I asked. She quickly replied, "'Cause my Mama said so!" She could count on her mama telling the truth, and she didn't want anyone to question it.

Have you ever shared something with a person who in turn replied, "Are you sure?" or "How do *you* know?" I have and, at times, felt a bit irritated like my kindergarten student. A quick retort can cause us to feel that our truthfulness is being questioned.

Our attitude toward truth indicates our relationship with Christ.

The cunning questions of the chief priest, scribes, and elders were intentionally placing Jesus in a dilemma. They asked Him by what authority He was "doing these things," and Jesus answered them with a question they could not answer. They could not answer because they could not face truth.

Jesus faced truth. He, being Truth personified, "taught them as one who had authority" (Matthew 7:29). Our own integrity depends on our truthfulness. When truth breaks down, so do trust, morality, and meaning in life.

Our guide to truth is God's Word. Jesus said, "If you continue in my word, you will truly be my disciples, and you will know the truth and the truth will make you free" (John 8:31b,32). Paul encouraged Timothy to be a person who is approved by God, "a workman who has no need to be ashamed, rightly handling the word of truth" (II Timothy 2:15).

Are we trusting and testifying to the truth in God's Word as completely as my kindergarten student trusted and testified to her mother's word of truth?

Dear God, help us to know truth, speak truth, and live truth. In the name of the One who is Truth. *Amen*

Shock Absorbers

The uneven ground shall become level, and the rough places a plain.
Isaiah 40:4b

*M*ost of us have ridden in vehicles with bad shocks. A sudden bump in the road can thrust our bodies upward while it seems the bottom falls out of the vehicle.

Car springs need special equipment to avoid the jerking and jarring caused by rough spots in the road. Sometimes our lives need shock absorbers, too. Worn out shocks on our vehicles need repair at times, and so do our bodies and spirits. Our capacity to absorb any more of life's bumps can become so depleted that a way to smooth out the rough spots has to be found.

I can travel life's rough road because of the One who travels it with me.

In his book *On the Anvil*, Max Lucado refers to life's rough spots as times when we're "thumped." He says our day-to-day living can become "thump-packed." Mr. Lucado adds, "The true character of a person is not seen in momentary heroics, but in the thump-packed humdrum of day-to-day living."[2]

Isaiah was talking about making the uneven ground level and the rough places a plain in preparation for Christ's coming. This is how a courier in Isaiah's day prepared for the king's visit. We, too, must make ready for Christ's entry into our lives afresh each day. But it is because He has already come to earth that we can cope with life's rough spots and tough times. Only God can repair us. Only He can renew our thump-packed, worn-out, shock-absorbed spirits. Only God could send a Savior to carry our burdens for us.

Do you feel weary today because of life's uneven ground and rough places? Do you feel you have absorbed all the bumps and thumps you can take? Then "cast all your anxieties on him, for he cares about you" (I Peter 5:7). His grace is sufficient to absorb all of life's shocks.

Dear God, as rough spots come into my path today, help me to come to You for needed repair and restoration. In Jesus' name. *Amen*

The Robin's Example

*Look at the birds of the air: they neither sew nor reap nor
gather into barns, and yet your heavenly Father feeds them.
Are you not of more value than they?*
Matthew 6:26

Robins enjoy being near people and often build their nests near homes. Recently we watched the activity of a beautiful robin family just outside our kitchen door. A mother robin built her nest on a low limb over the deck, and each day we saw her put together the intricate work of straw, slowly adding each tiny piece, then adding clay for the inside of her nest.

One by one she laid her beautiful turquoise eggs—three in all. Then she sat patiently as the days of incubation rolled by. Seldom did she fly away when we were near her on the deck.

Since God cares for the birds of the air and the fish of the sea, how much more He must care for me!

One morning we noticed the mother robin was using her beak to throw particles from the nest. The eggs had hatched, and now mother robin was doing her spring cleaning. What a joyous experience! Nature's best sign of spring's arrival had come, and a favorite songbird had endeared herself to us in a fresh way.

The robin offers us an example: the robin seems at peace with the world. "They neither sew nor reap nor gather into barns," they just live each day in God's loving care. The robin family cooperates with each other. The mother birds prepare for the birth of the baby robins and then cares for them until they leave the nest. Father robins provide the necessary food and protection for the babies. Both mother and father robin bring cheer to those within hearing distance with their rich and clear voices. Their song rises and falls, seeming to say, "Cheer-up! Cheer-up!"

Jesus used the analogy about "birds of the air" in His Sermon on the Mount. He talked about being anxious over such things as "what you shall eat or what you shall drink, nor about your body, what you shall put on" (Matthew 6:25).

We don't need to be anxious; we are of ultimate value to our heavenly Father. Look to the robin for the example of trust in God's providential care.

Father, You are such a good and loving Creator. Help us each day to entrust our lives to You. *Amen*

The Dependable Daffodil

Blessed are the meek, for they shall inherit the earth.
Matthew 5:5

When the daffodils bloom each spring, I am reminded of this verse of Scripture on meekness and its meaning. I'm fascinated by the numbers of these bright, cheerful blossoms that appear each year where homes once stood but have long since deteriorated and disappeared. Along the roadside I see the remains of a chimney, a tree stump, or possibly an old, leaning outbuilding. All other shrubs and flowers are absent, but the dependable daffodil faithfully returns and graces a once-bustling yard with its beauty. Sprouting, growing, blooming, dying—only to return once again when the March winds begin to blow.

I want to be dependent upon God to supply my need today and every day of my life.

In our world today the adjective "meek" is hardly admirable. Too often the idea of meekness connotes spinelessness, submission, or lack of courage. But the word in Greek holds positive meaning: It means self-control. To Aristotle it meant a balance, a happy medium between too much and too little. Jesus said it is the meek who will inherit the earth. Those who surrender to God's control will have qualities of balance, self-control and humility.

Families are formed. They blossom and bloom, grow old and die. Houses withstand the harsh elements of nature for a time, then fall down and decay.

The daffodil is surrendered to God's control, completely dependent on nature to supply its needs of sunshine, water, and nutrients from the soil. The dependable daffodil really *does* seem to inherit the earth!

Loving God, thank You for the ways You remind us of Your faithfulness and providence. Help me to reflect the attributes of meekness that Your Son Jesus taught us. In His name. *Amen*

Desires of the Heart

Take delight in the Lord, and he will give you the desires of your heart.
Psalm 37:4

Two of our daughter's deepest desires were to meet the right person to be her husband and one day to have children. During one of her times of soul searching, we discussed this verse from Psalms. We talked about the action required of us to "take delight in the Lord." We have to intentionally allow God to inspect our desires and invite Him to grant us those things that are pleasing to Him. We have to believe that the Lord is trustworthy and know that He desires our joy to be full.

When God's desires become our desires, our hearts will be full and fulfilled.

Trusting this promise, we began a "wedding folder" when Debbie was still a young girl. Each time I came upon an idea that might be useful for her wedding one day, into the folder it would go. Debbie often added to the folder as well—wedding programs, napkins, invitations, and other ideas from friends' weddings.

When Debbie and Steve became engaged, we looked through the wedding folder, planning to use some of the ideas and eliminating others.

Then after a few years of marriage, they began to plan for their first child. In faith, and remembering Psalm 37:4, I began another file. This one was labeled "Grandchildren," and it soon began to bulge with ideas and helpful suggestions for grandparenting.

On February 18, 1991, Debbie and Steve were told they would become parents. On September 28 of that year, beautiful Katherine Elizabeth Caswell was born. Katie is a joy and a delight, even with her special needs. One of the deep desires of our hearts is that she will continue to improve. We know that God is still working! He is good, and He continues to work for our good. Thanks be to God.

Loving Father, help us to take joy in knowing that You want the best for us. Through Your Son Jesus. *Amen*

God's Delivery System

Then they cried to the Lord in their trouble, and
He delivered them from their distress.

Psalms 107:6

*R*ecently I heard a Vietnam veteran tell of his experience on the battlefield. He told how, during the suffering and death all about him, he kept hearing cries for "Medic! Medic!" In sharing this experience, he used the analogy of the battle scene of the world in which we live. Trouble and distress, suffering and death are all about us. As Christians we are the medics—in our homes, our neighborhoods, our churches. We are the ones called to offer Christ, the great physician, wherever life's battles rage.

We not only receive God's help, but we need to share it as well.

Who are the wounded and suffering who need help around us? Where are the battle zones? Within the past few weeks I've heard cries coming from many wounded persons. A friend struggling in the balance between life and death following his second heart surgery. A young mother trying to pick up the pieces after the emotional and physical wounds of her husband's abuse. A family wondering how they would be able to pay their utility bill. A young minister aching to help teenagers in his youth group whose minds are polluted by fallacies of fun and freedom. An elderly couple trying desperately to maintain a meager portion of quality in life. The young, "upwardly mobile" executive searching his heart as he sees Christian ethics eroding all about him. These are only some of the wounded crying for "medic" in my small world.

How will we answer these cries? The psalmist reminds us in Psalms 46:1, "God is our refuge and strength, a very present help in trouble." But He's not an escape hatch. He's not a panacea. He doesn't push a magic button and wipe all the tears away. He is our help. He is *with* us during our cries of distress and hurt. He walks the rough roads with us. He supplies our needs. He is our "safe place." He is our enabler. He is a comfort through His Holy Spirit. And we are His extensions—His medics—as we allow ourselves to be a part of His delivery system of help.

Father God, You have heard our cries of suffering. Help us to reach out to others with Your love. In Jesus' name. *Amen*

Instant Access

While they are yet speaking I will hear.
Isaiah 65:24b

*I*f anybody can hear me please take this call!" came our son David's voice over the telephone speaker. An extremely busy day—complicated by illness in the family—had required the answering machine to work overtime. Though we think we need them, at times they can be a real source of frustration.

Reflecting on David's plea for someone to answer the phone caused me to think about our instant access to God. God doesn't use an answering machine. Thank goodness!

"Then you shall call and the Lord will answer; you shall cry, and he will say 'Here I am'" (Isaiah 58:9).

One of my kindergarten students said to me one day, "Every time I call Mamma, her line is dizzy!" None of us like "dizzy" phone lines. It is so good to know that I can get through to God anytime. I don't have to be put on hold. I don't have to leave a message for Him to return my call at His convenience. When I call my heavenly Father, there are no instructions like, "Press 1 for prayer requests," "Press 2 for emergencies," or "Press 3 if you want to return to the original menu." God hears me as I speak, and He knows my heart even before I say a word.

The book of Psalms is filled with assurances of God's instant accessibility. Psalms 86:7 (NIV) says, "In the day of my trouble I will call to you, for you will answer me." The psalmist also said, "I sought the Lord and he answered me, and delivered me from my fears" (Psalms 34:4).

Not only do we have instant access to God, we also have unlimited time at no cost. Jesus said to simply "ask, and it will be given to you" (Matthew 7:7). Paul wrote, "Let your requests be made known to God" (Philippians 4:6b), and, "Pray constantly" (I Thessalonians 5:17). Paul didn't say to them, "Pray constantly to God during regular calling hours." He was teaching them about their instant and unlimited access to God—anytime, anywhere, for all eternity.

O God, we praise and thank You that we can reach You anytime, all the time. Because of this, we can go forward unafraid. *Amen*

A Return Visit

I will give them a heart to know that I am the Lord;
and they shall be my people and I will be their God, for they
shall return to me with their whole heart.
Jeremiah 24:7

*T*he decision we faced weighed heavily upon us that day in March 1989. Wally had been offered the responsibility of pastoring a large church in a large city with an even larger challenge. Returning home after visiting his parents, we came in sight of the little rural church where he, as a nine-year-old boy, accepted the Lord. It occurred to me that it would be good for us to return to the altar where his faith walk started some forty-six years earlier.

Big decisions are easier to make when we commit our whole heart to God.

So he pulled into the graveled parking lot and turned off the car engine. We sat quietly for a few minutes, totally engulfed in the serene stillness of that rural setting. Memories began to flood our minds as each of us recalled our similar experiences of conversion—mine in Cumberland County and his in Barren County. Every fall we walked with our teacher and classmates to the morning revival service in our community. Each of us accepted Christ during one of these revival services.

The door to the church was unlocked, so we went inside and walked down to the altar. There on our knees, we recommitted our lives and our ministry. We returned to God that day with our whole hearts. Our covenant was renewed. We would be His people and He would be our God, regardless of where we were sent to serve.

What heavy decisions are you facing today? Whatever they are, just know that "He who began a good work in you will bring it to completion" (Philippians 1:6). We need to make return visits to God. We need to get back in touch with those special moments in our lives when we surrendered our will to His. God's faithfulness is new every morning. He will go with us into every new challenge!

Dear God, thank You for being our God, and for letting us be Your people through Jesus. Help us to be faithful in returning to You every day. In Jesus' name. *Amen*

The Everlasting Arms

He took them in his arms and blessed them, laying his hands upon them.
Mark 10:16

*A*s the pastor concluded the morning prayer, I noticed the stained glass window above him. The scene of Jesus, the Good Shepherd, holding a lamb on His arm had never meant more than it did that morning.

We had just learned that Katie, our only grandchild, was mildly autistic. I remember looking up at the window that morning and praying, "Jesus, won't you please hold Katie in Your arms? Katie needs Your everlasting arms to lean on." Tears ran down my cheeks. I envisioned Katie in the place of the lamb on the window, wrapped in the arms of Jesus. Months and years have passed now, but I can still envision Katie in the arms of the Good Shepherd.

Someone may cross my path today who needs to be held in God's loving arms. Will I have the courage to lead them to Him?

While on earth, Jesus took the children in His arms and blessed them. We are called, I believe, to be His arms and hearts. He needs us to be sensitive to the hurting and needy in our world—maybe even in our own families. We are called to be God's everlasting arms extended to hurting people everywhere.

As I go about my daily chores, I often sing the old hymn that my mother sang, "Leaning On the Everlasting Arms."[3] What a blessed comfort to know that our Good Shepherd cares for us and opens His arms to us always.

Loving Father, help us to look to You for comfort and support and extend Your arms of love to others. In Jesus' name. *Amen*

In Full View

Would not God discover this? For he knows the secrets of the heart.

Psalms 44:21

Most of us have stood in front of a full-length mirror and looked at the framed reflection. We may or may not like what we see when we do this. We all stand in full view of God. I Samuel 16:7b says, "Man looks on the outward appearance, but the Lord looks on the heart." Nothing is hidden from God.

What does God see

in my heart today?

He knows us well, because He made us. Isaiah 44:2 says, "Thus says the Lord who made you, who formed you from the womb and will help you." We live in a society that puts emphasis on looking young and beautiful. Americans spend millions on diets, fitness programs, and beauty aids. But in time, beauty —if we ever had it!— fades. Our strength fails us. Our minds become dull. Our sight becomes dim. It is only our inner strength and beauty that lasts, and these are the parts of us that God sees.

The sin that Jesus condemned most was hypocrisy. He saw the Pharisees in full view. No cover up. To the people, they appeared holy and good, but Jesus denounced them by calling them "whitewashed tombs" (Matthew 23:27).

William Barclay calls this attempt to cover up our real person by altering our outward appearance a condition of "disguised decay."[4] We can look in a mirror and see our outward reflection, but God discovers the secrets of our heart—the decay as well as goodness.

Dear God, create in me a pure heart and a right spirit. Fill my innermost being with Your love. Through Christ I pray. *Amen*

Pinkie in the Dark

If we confess our sins, he is faithful and just, and will forgive our sins and cleanse us from all unrighteousness
1 John 1:9

The clock struck 11:45. I lay in bed thinking that this was the first time David had gone to sleep without saying "I'm sorry." As a little boy he seemed to understand and take seriously the Scripture, "Be angry, but do not sin; do not let the sun go down on your anger" (Ephesians 4:26). There were days when it was not easy to apologize, but David worked out his own system. He asked if he could raise his pinkie finger as a symbol of saying he was sorry. I agreed.

Our forgiveness was completed on Calvary, and we have only to ask for it.

Disappointment came over me as I lay there thinking that for the first time David had "let the sun go down." It seemed that he was ignoring my teaching. A few more minutes passed, and then, ever so faintly, I heard a voice from David's room, "Mom? Mom, can you come in here?"

I jumped out of bed and rushed to his room. Opening his door quietly, the light filtering in from the street allowed me to see a small pinkie finger courageously lifted upward. Joy filled my heart. David had not committed any big sin. It was not his nature to be rude. But I knew that when he became a man, and relationships hung in the balance awaiting an apology, this simple teaching would make a difference. "You're forgiven, son, and I'm so glad you didn't let the sun go down," I whispered. He turned over, snuggled comfortably under the covers, and said, "Me, too!"

As I made my way back to bed, I recalled how Jesus taught that we should become like children in our faith. I better understood that night what He meant, and I committed myself anew to keep a forgiving spirit in my life.

Lord, help me to be more childlike in my faith so that I will be more ready for Your kingdom. In Jesus' name. *Amen*

A Living Sacrifice

*He has appeared once for all at the end of the age to put
away sin by the sacrifice of himself.*
Hebrews 9:26b

*O*ur friend Tony Fontane told an interesting and moving story of an experience during a mission trip to South America. The pastor of the church in
which Tony was speaking suggested that they observe how local farmers trans-
fer cattle across the Amazon River.

*Because of His
sacrifice on the cross,
we don't have to fear
crossing the rivers
ahead.*

Knowing that the Amazon was crowded with car-
nivorous fish, Tony could not imagine how the cattle
could survive the swim across the river. So he watched
carefully as an old farmer led his treasured herd of
cattle to the river bank, and then drove one of the
cows into the river.

Immediately, the beautiful "lead" cow disappeared under the water and a red circle formed over
it. As blood from the sacrificed cow surfaced, the
farmer knew that it was safe for the remainder of the
herd to swim across. One life was given in order that
the remainder of the cattle could cross the Amazon safely.

That's just what our Lord did for us. We couldn't make it safely to the shores
of heaven in our own power—there are too many snares along the way. God saw
this and knew what He had to do. He directed His beloved Son to move out into
the deep—even take on the sins of the whole world—so that we may have eternal life.

Loving heavenly Father, thank You for providing a way
for our safe passage through the sacrifice of Your beloved Son,
Jesus Christ, our Lord. *Amen*

Meet Me on the Hill

He said to all, "If any man would come after me, let him deny himself and take up his cross daily and follow me."
Luke 9:23

Someone has said that if our prayer life is sincere, we will pray daily, "Lord, I want to live Your way today." Then Jesus will reply, "I will help you. Just meet me on the hill."

Where is the hill? Where do we go to take up our cross daily to live His way? I believe "the hill" is that place of total commitment where our wills become His will. For Jesus, "the hill" was a place of surrender, of suffering, of loneliness— even a place where God seemed to have forsaken Him for a time.

Today will I make my way toward the hill?

Jesus modeled forgiveness in the midst of excruciating pain while on "the hill." Yet we find forgiveness difficult to come by even when life is free of pain. "The hill" for Jesus was where man's inhumanity to man was pinnacled.

When we say we want to walk His way, have we thought about where we will meet Him? "The hill" for us may be in the corporate office where we observe another's character subtly but maliciously undermined—maybe destroyed— while we listen silently. "The hill" may be the bridge club where we laugh at the off-colored joke, or even worse—add a line to the juicy gossip. "The hill" might be on the street where we hear the appeal for food and clothing for the needy and pass it off thinking that if they would work they wouldn't be begging.

"The hill" has to be our meeting place with Christ if we expect to walk in His way. It's not the popular spot. It requires a commitment, so there's no standing in line for it. There are neither cash bonuses nor potted plants as rewards. But it was on the hill that God met all humankind to pour out love, peace, joy— and all the fruits of His presence. And He patiently waits for us there if we want to walk in His way.

Loving God, I do want Your presence and power in my life daily. Help me to have the courage to take up my cross. *Amen*

God's Plan for Hope

Love bears all things, believes all things,
hopes all things, endures all things.
I Corinthians 13:7

I have on my desk a little saying: "To cope is to hope." Hope is a powerful motivating force, and I believe it is a part of God's plan. Jeremiah 29:11 says, "For I know the plans I have for you, says the Lord, plans for welfare and not for evil, to give you a future and a hope."

God has a plan to give us hope today. Will we receive it?

When our granddaughter, Katie, was first diagnosed as being autistic, I was desperate to find a ray of hope. I knew very little about the disease, so I could hardly wait to go to our local library. I checked out the only books I could find on autism. I even turned to the last pages of one autistic child's case history to see if the story offered hope. I was determined to find out if there was a future and a hope for Katie.

I found the answer. There *was* hope for our precious Katie. How that blessed my heart. With hope we could cope. With hope we could dream a new dream for Katie!

But hope is so elusive. It can be strong for a day or so, then becomes weak for a time. Circumstances can alter hope. Negative words can almost destroy hope. Doubt takes its toll on hope. But we must maintain at least a thread of hope if we are to cope with disease and despair and doubt.

The source of hope is Jesus. He wills for all His children to have a future and a hope. We as Christians have every reason to be people of hope. We know our Lord has overcome the world and all things are possible with Him. I'm so grateful for the hope I found for Katie, and I will never let it go!

Father, thank You for Your plan of hope for Your children. Help us to never lose this precious gift. In Jesus' name. *Amen*

The Church–Christ's Body

Now you are the body of Christ and individually members of it.
I Corinthians 12:27

I wonder how often we as the church think of ourselves as the body of Jesus Christ. It's a sobering thought to realize that we are individual members of His physical presence in this world. We embody His arms, His legs, His hands, His feet, His voice, and His heart. What a responsibility! What an opportunity as Christians!

As Christ's body, the Scripture gives direction in how we are to epitomize Him. We are to serve one another (Galatians 5:13), speak truth to one another (Ephesians 4:25), comfort one another (I Thessalonians 4:18), bear one another's burdens (Galatians 6:2), pray for one another (James 5:16), be hospitable to one another (Romans 15:7), and stir one another up to love and good works (Hebrews 10:24).

Does the world see Christ in me?

So, with all that I am, I must typify Christ. I must serve, speak truth, comfort, bear another's burdens, be hospitable, pray, and love as a part of the collective body of Christ. I must try to do all of this in harmony with other believers. Romans 12:16 admonishes us to "live in harmony with one another." As a choir loses its effectiveness if various parts aren't in harmony, so do we lose our effectiveness as Christians when we aren't working in harmony. Discordant notes need to be changed if our witness as His body is to be strong and effective.

We need help if we are to work together harmoniously as Christ's body on earth. I believe that our help comes from the Holy Spirit. He can equip us to be Jesus' arms, reaching out to enfold those in need. He can enable us to be His legs, ministering to the multitudes. He can empower us to be His voice, sharing the good news of Easter. He can permit us to be His heart, channeling His compassion throughout the world.

May His Spirit permeate us and bind us together in unity, so that the world might believe that the church is truly Christ's body on earth.

Come, Holy Spirit, empower us to be all we're called to be as Christ's body on earth. In Jesus' name. *Amen*

Sin's Invasion

*Be sober, be watchful. Your adversary the devil prowls
around...seeking someone to devour.*

I Peter 5:8

I wish I'd had a camera to catch the scene in the cove behind the parsonage. The muddy water from the previous night's rain quietly flowed into the clear water of the city lake. Ever so slowly the rusty brown water inched along, devouring the pristine beauty below it.

When our faith is firm, Satan is stripped of his power.

I could see the irregular line defining the "invasion," and something in me wanted to warn the lake of what was coming. I began to think about the subtle, insidious nature of sin as it creeps into our lives. Peter knew about the shrewdness of Satan. Evil had made entry into his life when he denied Jesus, and he wanted to warn the Christians in Asia Minor to be aware of the devious ways of the devil.

Sometimes I wonder: Does God observe our daily living and see a similar picture of sin's invasion? Does He see a life that He created to be pure and clean begin to become soiled and sinful? Does he look down from the windows of heaven and wish to protect us from evil's inroads to our hearts?

Like the muddy stream, we were created to move in freedom. God gave us the ability to make responsible choices. We are warned to be watchful and sober concerning the devil's ploys. Sin is subtle, but God is faithful in His protection:

- "When you pass through the waters I will be with you" Isaiah 43:2a.
- "The Lord your God who goes before you will himself fight for you" Deuteronomy 1:30a.
- "But the Lord is faithful; he will strengthen you and guard you from evil" II Thessalonians 3:3.
- "For thou art my refuge, a strong tower against the enemy" Psalms 61:3.
- "For he will give his angels charge of you to guard you in all your ways" Psalms 91:11.

Dear God, help us to be aware of Satan's subtle attempts to invade our lives. Protect us and keep our hearts and lives pure—for Your glory. Through Christ our Lord I pray. *Amen*

The Print of the Nail

Unless I see in his hands the print of the nails, and place my finger in the mark of the nails, and place my hand in his side, I will not believe.
John 20:25

A little boy drove a nail in the hardwood floor of his home. He knew that he shouldn't do it, but it was such fun pounding on the nail and watching it disappear. He then realized he needed to pull the nail out quickly before his parents saw it, but was unable to do this in his own strength. With tears streaming down his cheeks, he admitted his wrong-doing and humbly asked his father for help. The father promptly removed the nail, but the little boy would not stop crying. "Now, stop your crying, son," the father said, "You've learned your lesson." "But," sobbed the little boy, "The hole is still in the floor!"

Christ's nail-scarred hands extend to us the invitation to salvation.

What an opportunity to teach the lesson that sin leaves its scars! There were scars—left by the world's sin—in the hands and side of our resurrected Lord, but Jesus used these scars to help a doubter believe. The scars left by sin became salvation for the doubting disciple, Thomas. When he touched the scars in the hands and side of Jesus, Thomas no longer doubted who Jesus was.

Sufferings come to all of us at one time or another and many times they may leave scars. But these experiences can also lead the way to a deeper faith. These times, if we allow them, can cause us to depend more on a strength greater than our own. These times can cause us to rely on a wisdom beyond our own. As Paul said in Romans 5:3,4, "More than that, we rejoice in our sufferings, knowing that suffering produces endurance, and endurance produces character, and character produces hope." He goes on to say that hope does not disappoint us. The end results of "life's nails" can be hope, and this hope is in Jesus Christ.

Loving Father, thank You for giving Jesus for our redemption. Help us, by our very lives, to say, "My Lord and my God!" *Amen*

Were You There?

Indeed I count everything as loss because of the surpassing worth of knowing Christ Jesus my Lord. For his sake I have suffered the loss of all things...that I may know him and the power of the resurrection.

Philippians 3:8,10a

I once heard Bill Mann, choir member of an Alabama church, share an interesting experience. In the service one Sunday morning was Helen Keller and her "miracle worker" friend, Ann Sullivan. Following the service Miss Keller requested that Bill sing for her "Were You There?"[1] Miss Sullivan told him that since Helen Keller could neither hear nor see, she might need to touch his neck or feel his lips. The challenge nearly petrified Bill, but he began singing.

God can speak to the heart regardless of our circumstances.

As Bill sang, Miss Keller began to move her lips to form the words. He continued the song, "Were you there when he rose up from the grave?" At this point, Helen Keller declared, though sightless and deaf, "Yes! Yes! I was there!"

She knew about this Christ. She knew He had died for her, too. She felt the pain of her Lord being nailed to the tree. She knew the sadness of His being laid in the grave. She knew how it felt for the sun to refuse to shine. But most important of all, she knew about our Lord's resurrection from the grave! She felt the joy of His resurrection so deeply that she had to put words to her feelings by exclaiming, "Yes! I was there!"

All of us who have experienced the Lord's resurrection power in our hearts know what Helen Keller was saying. I want to be willing to give voice to that which I've experienced in my heart.

Loving Father, give me courage to declare what I know to be true about You. Through the power of the resurrected Lord I pray. *Amen*

Do We, Like Judas, Sell Out?

*They paid him thirty pieces of silver. And from that moment
he sought an opportunity to betray him.*
Matthew 26:15b,16

Why did Judas sell out? It must have been greed that got the best of him. Was he trustworthy at one time? The other eleven disciples must have trusted Judas, for they named him the group's treasurer.

Why did Judas sell out? Judas loved money more than life—even the life of our Lord. Luke suggests that Judas *became* a traitor (Luke 6:16), so he evidently was not born one. What happens to a person to cause such a change in their moral character? Judas may have become bitter that Jesus didn't turn out to be the kind of ruler he had wished him to be. He may have been shattered when Jesus refused to set up the kind of kingdom Judas wanted.

There is no place for compromise in our commitment to Christ.

Greed. Bitterness. Deception. Disappointment. The bottom line was that Judas thought he knew more about running things than Jesus. Do we ever think and act this way? Is Christ's way always our way? Do we ever sell out? Do we ever betray Jesus? John 13:27 says that Satan entered Judas. Do we ever allow Satan to influence us? Do we ever allow greed and bitterness to linger in our lives?

If we are totally honest with ourselves, most of us would have to admit that at times, we, too, have compromised our convictions. May we always remember that nothing is worth the loss from selling out to the devil.

Dear God, we ask for Your forgiveness for the times we have compromised and sold out in our convictions. Cleanse us, we pray, of all unrighteousness, and protect us from the evil one. In Jesus' name. *Amen*

The Hidden Cross

For we walk by faith, not by sight.

II Corinthians 5:7

*S*itting in a restaurant in Elizabethton, Tennessee, my eyes fell on a large sign on a distant hill. Emblazoned on a white background were these words in red print, "Jesus is Lord!" To the left of the sign were three crosses.

Assuming that this was the scene of an Easter sunrise service for the town, I pictured in my mind the townspeople gathered by the red and white sign at the foot of the crosses.

Our clouds of doubt cannot alter the fact of the resurrection.

Later during the meal I glanced once again toward the hilltop, but to my surprise there were no crosses in sight. Had I really seen three crosses or just imagined it? I strained to discern exactly what I thought I had seen.

Just then the clouds moved slowly toward the east, and three crosses once again came into view. This time the clear, blue backdrop of the sky made the scene even more beautiful, and I began to ponder just how visible the cross is in my life. I asked myself: Is the victory of the empty cross real to me on those dark, dismal days? Do I take for granted what God has done for me through Jesus when things are going well—when the sun shines and no shadows cross the blue sky?

I want to know and experience the resurrection power of Christ in my heart *every* day—come sunshine or clouds. I want to walk every day by faith and not by sight.

Dear God, I'm so grateful to know that Your presence is with me even when I see no visible evidence. Help me to always remember this. *Amen*

Shortcuts

Each man's work will become manifest.
I Corinthians 3:13a

*W*ally and his sister, Helen, helped their dad replant corn one spring day. For several hours they carefully dropped the correct number of seeds into the spots where no corn had sprouted.

As the morning wore on, both became tired and hungry. The idea of burying the remaining seeds all at one time sounded like a great idea! So a hole was dug, and the seeds were covered, with little evidence of their shortcut.

However, a few days later a huge clump of green corn sprouts gave away their secret. Their dad came in for lunch one day and soberly announced, "You know, for the life of me, I can't remember that corn planter breaking down. But I noticed at the end of one of the rows a great big bunch of corn coming up in one spot."

Taking shortcuts on the road of life is not the best route to travel.

At that both children confessed, and won't forget the admonishment that followed, "Let this be a lesson to you. If you try to take shortcuts, they catch up with you sooner or later."

And I ask myself about the shortcuts I take or have been tempted to take. Do I take the easy road out of a situation? Or rush a delicate project? Or fail to do a thorough job? Or let my priorities get out of order? When my body is weary and my spirit becomes weak, what feeling or attitude kicks in? Do I look for ways to take shortcuts in order to finish early?

Paul reminds us that each person's work will be clear and evident. In Galatians 6:7b he says, "For whatever a man sows, that he will also reap." I want my life to reap a good harvest. I want it to bless and encourage others along the way. I pray that my life will honor my heavenly Father whose Son never took shortcuts.

Loving Creator, help me to live each day so that I won't be ashamed when the results of my labor are seen. Through Your Son, Jesus, I pray. *Amen*

Never Forsaken

I will never fail you nor forsake you.
Hebrews 13:5b

A recent newscast told of ten children who were left abandoned in a house near the Boardwalk in Atlantic City. In Louisville, a thirty-year-old retarded girl was locked in her room with no bathroom facility. She was given little to eat or drink during her last year of life.

Is this the day I need to tell someone how much God cares about them?

What a sad commentary on our hardened and sin-stained society that these innocent persons suffered such pain and rejection. I wonder if anyone ever told them about Jesus. Did they know that, even though their parents neglected them, they were never alone? I hope so. I'd like to think that, at some point during the lives of these eleven persons, someone shared about God's love with them. I trust that someone told them that God will never fail nor forsake His precious creation.

I wonder how many hungry, neglected, and even abandoned children are living in my own community today. Who will go to them, care for them, and tell them that Jesus loves them? Who will feed and clothe them? Could it be that this is my opportunity to find these people and let them know that God has not forsaken them? We are the extension of Christ on this earth; we must tell people that God is faithful and His mercies are new every morning.

Loving Father, thank You for Your promise that You will never leave us nor forsake us. Give us the courage and commitment to be faithful to You and Your children in need today. In Jesus' name. *Amen*

Love: Full Circle

We love, because he first loved us.
1 John 4:19

A lady from Indiana was visiting a mission project in Eastern Kentucky. Upon entering the small rural church, she was overcome with a feeling that something seemed strangely familiar. Hundreds of miles from home and in a strange environment, it didn't seem possible for anything to be familiar. Yet her eyes kept going to the church pews on the right side of the sanctuary. They were totally unlike the painted pews across the aisle. "If I didn't know better, I'd think those pews came out of my home church," she said to herself.

The supply of God's wonderful love is boundless.

She walked on toward the front of the church near the altar and paused abruptly.

Stopping in her tracks, she pointed to a certain section of the altar rail and exclaimed in absolute awe and joy, "That's the very spot where I was baptized!" And, sure enough, those were the actual pews from her home church in Indiana. There before her was the spot where she had met the Lord many years before!

Love had come full circle. She had been prompted by love to come to this church in Appalachia. Why? Because a long time ago she had experienced God's love at the altar of her church. And in a place so remote and unfamiliar, she had rediscovered this place so dear to her heart. Once again she knelt at her spot at the altar. Once again she experienced the overflowing love of her Lord. She was so grateful in that moment that her church back home had loved the world enough to send some pews and an altar to a needy people in Eastern Kentucky. But most of all that day she was grateful for a Savior who had given His all on Calvary and made this kind of love possible.

Loving Father, You have blessed us so abundantly. We thank You for the greatest gift of all: the love from Your Son, Jesus. Help us to be faithful in sharing that love with others. *Amen*

The Little White Cross

*So it is not the will of my Father who is in heaven that one
of these little ones should perish.*
Matthew 18:14

During a recent visit with friends we were enjoying a tour of the area in which they had grown up. Shortly, we drove past a cemetery near the state university. Our hostess pointed to a small white cross on a hill and said, "See the little white cross over there?" We noticed the cross and the freshly dug grave. Our hostess went on to explain that the cross marks the grave of a newborn baby.

*How does the way
I live reflect the
sanctity of life?*

The full-term baby had been found in a trash can in the basement of a nearby women's dormitory. The child was dead and no one claimed its body. Local townspeople collected enough funds to give the baby a decent funeral and burial. A large crowd attended the baby's funeral, sharing together in the sad tragedy of the loss of this innocent life.

As I reflected on this haunting experience, I had to ask myself: Do I always respect life? What about those times I've failed to take an active stand against abortion? Or what about those times I may exceed the speed limit just a little and put my own life and the lives of others at risk? What about the careless, sharp words that can destroy someone's spirit and self-respect? Do I care for my own body in a way that models respect for health and life?

Jesus, referring to the lost sheep, said that it is not the will of God that *one* of these little ones should perish. How it must grieve Him as the lives of His precious little lambs are destroyed daily. Jesus came that we might have life in all its fullness. He proved this by a cross on a hill—not a white one—but one stained with the sins of the whole world. I dare not forget that cross, nor the little white one on a hill near a college campus in a southern city.

Creator God, You loved all of us so much that You gave Your only begotten Son for us. Help me to live each day in a way that pleases You. In Jesus' name. *Amen*

Weary in Well-Doing

*Let us not grow weary in well-doing, for in due season we shall reap,
if we do not lose heart.*

Galatians 6:9

Haven't we all at one time or another felt a bit "weary in well-doing" and felt tempted to "lose heart"? We sometimes feel like Isaiah's description of "weak hands" and "feeble knees" (Isaiah 35:13): We've become tired of serving and even a bit weary or discouraged in our praying. We feel that we've given all we can give, and our hearts feel heavy-laden. Yet, we know we must go on. So, we pray with the psalmist, "O God...put a new and right spirit within me" (Psalms 51:10).

Today I will remember that after Friday's Calvary came Sunday's empty tomb—and victory!

I don't have all the answers for renewing strength and spirit, but these things have been helpful to me.

1. Look at the situation objectively. Ask yourself honestly: Have I overextended my energy and have I become discouraged or depressed for no justifiable reason?
2. Dwell on my blessings. Look at the positives in life.
3. Change what I can, and accept what I cannot change.
4. Ask God for wisdom and strength. Be willing to wait upon Him.
5. Trust in God's providence and power—and persevere.

Often the problem in our becoming weary in well-doing is our wanting to rush the "due season." We want to see results—as we think they should happen—in *our* timing. But the reaping, the results, must be surrendered to God's perfect timing and will for us. God's timing is perfect.

It's good for me to remember that nothing I will experience will be as painful as the cross. It's good for me to remember that Christ understands my heart and my struggle, because He's been there. And it's good for me to remember that He will never forsake me; He will come to me at my point of deepest need.

Loving God, I find comfort in knowing that You understand my feeling weary in well-doing. Help me to focus always on Your promises rather than my problems. *Amen*

Where Is Our Somewhere?

For God so loved the world that He gave His only Son, that whoever believes in him should not perish but have eternal life

John 3:16

I recently saw a message on a billboard that read, "Every Person Will Live Forever…Somewhere." The truth in this statement is obvious, but the question remains, "Where is our somewhere?" It is beyond my understanding and ability to explain the exact location of heaven or hell, but I am convinced of their reality.

Each of us has the freedom to decide where we will spend eternity.

William Barclay refers to John 3:16 as "everybody's text."[2] Certainly, it is one of the passages of Scripture that most of us have memorized at one time or another. But I believe the promise of eternal life in this verse is only for those who believe in Jesus and accept His promises. Jesus said elsewhere in the gospel of John, "I am the way, and the truth, and the life; no one comes to the Father, but by me" (John 14:6).

This may feel like a hard statement for those who rely on "universal salvation"—that a loving and just God would not turn anyone away. Certainly it was the *whole* world that God loved so much that He gave His only Son. Augustine put it this way, "God loves each one of us as if there were only one of us to love."[3] I believe that His will is for all persons—lovable and unlovable—to spend eternity's "somewhere" with Him. But because of His gift of our free will, this choice of acceptance or rejection is ours to make.

Bishop C.P. Minnick, Jr. tells of a little lady in a church he once served who often interrupted his sermon by asking, "But Dr. Minnick, what about John 3:16?" Isn't this the question that every person must answer? In light of our eternity's "somewhere," what about John 3:16?

Loving God, thank You for making a way, through Your only Son, Jesus, for us to live forever with You in heaven. *Amen*

A Sacrificial Lamb

The next day he saw Jesus coming toward him, and said, "Behold, the Lamb of God, who takes away the sin of the world!"

John 1:29

Dr. Roy Webster, a United Methodist minister now deceased, once shared this story in his church newsletter: "Over the portals of a church in Germany there is cut in the stone a beautiful lamb. This is how the lamb happened to be there. A man at work on the steeple of the church lost his footing and plunged to the ground below. A flock of sheep chanced to be grazing in the churchyard, and a lamb broke the fall of the man. The lamb was killed, but the man's life was saved. In his gratitude he cut into the stone over the doors of the church the figure of the lamb that saved his life."

How can I show my gratitude today for what Christ has done for me?

All of us have been spared the penalty of sin by the death of Christ—the Lamb of God. No sacrifice was ever made like the one on Calvary. Many have died for their faith—and still do today. But no one has borne the sins of the world, as did our Savior. In order to spare our lives from the crushing power of sin, Jesus, the Lamb of God, was sacrificed.

What is our response in gratitude? We can't place an engraving over the cross at Golgotha. But the indelible mark of that cross can be set upon our hearts. His infinite love can be imaged in our lives. A little lamb spared the life of a worker in Germany. The Lamb of God spared the world from sin and death for eternity. I want His mark on my life to be recognizable.

Dear God, I owe my all to You for the sacrifice You made for me through Christ. *Amen*

God's Mercy and Tree Bark

Surely goodness and mercy shall follow me all the days of my life.
Psalms 23:6a

When I was a young toddler, I somehow managed to reach an open salt dish on the kitchen table. My mother was unaware of the amount of salt I had swallowed, but it became evident shortly thereafter. I'm told that I hemorrhaged for several days, and no doctor in the area could come up with a helpful treatment. Several suggestions for "home remedies" were tried to no avail.

What a comfort to know that God's goodness and mercy are new every morning!

I grew weaker and my family grew more concerned. Finally, my dad recalled hearing about a certain tree bark that had curative qualities. He found some of the bark, my mother boiled it carefully, and the liquid became for me exactly what I needed. I've always been grateful to my parents for not giving up on finding a couteractant to the salt's damage to my intestines.

I've thought of this story many times in relation to God's goodness and mercy. He saw a world in need of redemption and restoration. Nothing He had done up to the time of Christ had seemed to bring the needed healing. He sent the prophets one by one, but their message wasn't sufficient for the sin sick world. The Scripture tells us, "But last of all he sent unto them his son, saying, They will reverence my son" (Matthew 21:37 KJV).

God's mercy was given to us as a free gift through His Son, Jesus. Christ's death and resurrection is only a part of the remedy; the second part is something we must do. We must receive Him. All we have to do to be healed and restored is to receive Him.

As with the tree bark, that availability was not the total answer to my need. I had to receive the healing liquid into my body for it to be effective. So do we have to receive into our hearts the healing love of our Lord.

God is merciful to provide in nature so many remedies for our medical needs, but the greatest of all gifts is His provision for the healing of our souls.

Dear God, You are so good. You truly supply our needs. Help me to be faithful in sharing this good news of Your mercy and love. Through Jesus, our Savior. *Amen*

Everlasting Love

I have loved you with an everlasting love.

Jeremiah 31:3

When my mother gave me a birthday card in April of 1982, little did I realize that this would be the last one I would ever receive from her. In less than a month from that time she passed away.

I've looked at the signature on the card many times and wondered if Mother might have had a premonition that the end was near. She signed the card as usual, "Lots of love, Mother and Daddy"—with one exception. This time she added another word, "always." This additional word obviously had been written at a different time. The color of the ink was a lighter shade of blue, and her penmanship was a little more shaky.

A loving parent can point us to the eternal love of our heavenly Father.

Later I learned that Mother bought the birthday cards early in the year for each of the five children. Jewel's would be mailed in May, Allen's in July, Geneva's in September, and Windell's in October. My birthday happened to fall in April, so I received mine prior to her May 7 death.

I had the blessing of mailing the other four birthday cards to my two sisters and two brothers. I signed them as Mother would have signed them that year, "Lots of love always," but with a sad footnote of explanation.

I've often thought of the parallel between God's love and my mother's love. Jeremiah described God's love as being an everlasting love: It's for always. From the beginning of creation He has always manifested His love to humankind. But it was through His beloved Son that he sent the "lots of love…always." Christ's life, death, and resurrection sealed God's love for us—for eternity. Our real birthday is when we accept His wonderful gift of everlasting love.

Father, our hearts fill up with gratitude at the thought of Your everlasting love for us. May our lives be letters sent to a world who hungers to receive Your "lots of love…always." In Jesus' name. *Amen*

Called by Name

I have called you by name, you are mine.
Isaiah 43:1b

I am constantly asked, "Is your name Kay or Kate?" The truth is I answer to both names and sign letters both ways. When Wally and I first met, I introduced myself as "Kate Radford." He thought I said "Kay Radford," and the name stuck. Over the years his family and people in our churches have called me Kay. My family and many of my friends call me Kate. Sometimes in a crowd when I hear the word "okay," I look to see who is calling me.

> *It isn't important what we are called on earth, but it is important that our name be recorded in heaven.*

The meaning of the names Kay and Kate are the same. But more important than the name we bear or its meaning is the image our life portrays. Proverbs 22:1 says, "A good name is to be chosen rather than great riches." I believe the writer of this verse was saying a good name or good image is established through not only *who* we are but also *whose* we are.

God made us in His image. He knows us by name. He knows who He created us to be. Isaiah says that our names are on the palms of God's hands. "Behold, I have graven you on the palms of my hands" (Isaiah 49:16). We belong to God!

We were created by God to return to Him. Our names are written in the Book of Life if we accept His Son and faithfully serve Him. Paul talks about the names of fellow workers who labored by his side "…whose names are in the book of life" (Philippians 4:3b).

Regardless of what I'm called on earth, I believe that God knows what to write in the Book of Life.

Dear Father, I'm humbled that You know my name, that You claim me as Your child. Help me to live out my life in a way that is pleasing to You. In Jesus' name. *Amen*

Lost and Found

*It was fitting to make merry and be glad, for this your brother was dead,
and is alive; he was lost, and is found.*

Luke 15:32

I recall a time when I got lost, separated from my mother in my hometown of Burkesville, Kentucky. Those few minutes seemed like an eternity to me. The Saturday crowd in town that day seemed like a massive throng of people. I remember looking up again and again into strange faces—fighting fear and stifling sobs. I will never forget the joy and relief as I finally looked up into the face of my mother.

Jesus told some parables of lost things, such as a lost coin and a lost sheep. When each of these was found, there was great joy. I have lost many items over the years, but the relief in finding these pales in comparison to the joy of being found by my mother.

Our soul, created by God, is at home only when it returns to Him.

I believe that God planned for our earthly homes to be places of nurture and care—places where love and forgiveness abound. I believe He desires that the family stay intact, and when one member wanders away into lostness, the family will receive that person with open arms upon their return.

At the portals of heaven, I believe our Father God is watching and waiting for a lost world to come home to Him. It's there that we will be truly alive—truly found, once and for all, where rejoicing lasts forevermore.

Loving Father, You created us. You provide daily for us, and You await our return to You. Thank You for sending Your Son, Jesus, to earth to show us the way home. In His name. *Amen*

What Day Is It?

And He will be raised on the third day.

Matthew 20:19b

*H*ave you ever awakened and asked yourself what day it is? Our schedules become so full and changes in our lives occur so rapidly, it's sometimes difficult to keep up with what day of the week we are experiencing.

It seems that much of life can be compared to one of the three days of an Easter weekend. Friday was a dark day when Jesus suffered the shame and degradation of taking upon Himself the sins of the whole world and the pain of a cruel cross. Saturday was a day of waiting. But Sunday came and with it came all the joy of the resurrected Lord!

Because He lives I can face today and all the tomorrows.

We will never know the suffering our Lord endured; only Jesus has borne the sins of the world. But most of us know about some dark days. We have our own sort of Fridays, filled with pain and struggle, discouragement and depression. You may be experiencing a Friday now. Or, it may be Saturday for you, a time of waiting. Maybe a time of hopelessness like the disciples experienced. If you are in a Friday or Saturday, remember as Tony Compolo says, "Sunday's coming!"[4] Thank God for the day of resurrection! Thank God for victory over sin and death. Thank God that after our days of darkness and waiting, we can experience renewal as life and joy are restored! Our spirits are revived! Evil knows defeat! Death loses its sting! The grave opens to victory on the Sundays of our life.

What day is today in your life? Regardless of your circumstances, just remember that our Lord lives! His Spirit will not leave or forsake us—no matter how dark the day or how long the wait. Thanks be to God that He knows our days, and extends His sufficient grace for all of them.

Gracious God, You know our days. Thank You for walking right beside us through Your Holy Spirit. Thank You for the victory we can experience because of Your Son, Jesus. *Amen*

Scars and Stripes

*He was wounded for our transgressions, he was bruised for our
iniquities; upon him was the chastisement that made us whole,
and with his stripes we are healed.*

Isaiah 53:5

Wounds. Bruises. Chastisement. Stripes. Scars. These are familiar words to us. Most of us have experienced wounds and bruises. Some of us have scars from accidents and disease such as chicken pox or possibly acne. But what about chastisement and stripes? What about the cross—with the sins of the whole world upon us? Not many of us can comprehend this, but *all* of us can be recipients of the wholeness and healing resulting from our Savior's suffering and sacrificial death.

*A scar is evidence
that we are healed.*

Jesus had scars to prove to Thomas that He truly was the Christ. These were visible, believable scars. Few of us would be willing to die for someone or for our faith. Yet, we're told that, even today, multitudes of persons are martyred for being confessing Christians. Nearly two-thirds of the world's population still live under regimes that persecute Christians.[5] Am I willing to suffer, even die, for my faith? What will faithfully serving my Master ultimately require of me?

Lord, help me to be faithful even if it means to suffer or die for You, because I know it's because of Your scars and stripes that I am made whole. *Amen*

Nothing Can Separate Us

Whither shall I go from thy Spirit?
Or whither shall I flee from thy presence?
Psalms 139:7

Friendships are important to all of us, especially, I believe, to children. As a kindergarten teacher, I saw friendship bud and blossom. Questions that I heard often were "Will you be my friend?" or, "Can you and I be best buddies?" As children become youth, terms like "blood brothers" and "forever friends" promise that nothing can separate them.

I would not want to live one minute outside the loving presence of the Lord.

All of us can have a Friend from whom we will never be separated. The psalmist David declared, "If I ascend to heaven, thou art there! If I make my bed in Sheol, thou art there!" (Psalms 139:8). That's a long stretch—from heaven to hell—but our omnipotent heavenly Father can span it!

Paul talked about the omnipresence of God in Romans 8:35-39. He first asked "Who shall separate us from the love of Christ?" Then he went on to say that neither tribulation, nakedness, peril, sword, death, life, angels, principalities, things present, things to come, powers, heights, depth, nor anything in all creation will be able to separate us from the love of God in Christ Jesus our Lord.

Those of us who have been loved sacrificially know something of the love of Christ that binds us to Him. This kind of love never fails. It conquers any obstacle. It penetrates the hardest of hearts. It endures. It abides. It's unconditional. It outlasts everything. It is the more excellent way.

God loved us so much that He wouldn't even spare His own Son. God wouldn't let a cruel cross become a chasm. He saw to it that no circumstance could cancel Christ's sacrifice.

The world needs this kind of love. It's priceless, yet free. It's tough, yet tender. It gives, yet receives. Once we come to experience it in our hearts, nothing can ever separate us from it.

Dear Jesus, through Your sacrifice on the cross we've come to know about the Father's love. Because of Your sending Your Holy Spirit, we have You with us forever. Praise be to God. *Amen*

Painful Parts of Life

*For the sake of Christ, then, I am content with weaknesses, insults, hard-
ships, persecution, and calamities; for when I am weak, then I am strong.*

II Corinthians 12:10

*I*n the verses preceding this Scripture, Paul talked about his thorn in the
flesh. God's answer to him was, "My grace is sufficient for you, for my
power is made perfect in weakness" (II Corinthians 12:9a). Now he is boldly and
gladly boasting of God's bringing blessing out of his brokenness.

When hardships and suffering come into our
lives, we may be tempted to ask, "Why?" or, "Why
me?" or, "Why my family?" But as I look back on my
life, it has been during these times of struggle that I've
grown in my faith. It has been during these valley
times that the soil has been most fertile for growth.
Like Paul, I've asked many times for thorns to be

*Our extremity is
God's opportunity to
give us more grace.*

removed from life. But when they weren't, I have always found His grace to be
sufficient.

Dealing with thorns and brokenness often reminds me of the oyster's suffering when sand gets into its shell. The sand acts as an irritant to the oyster and
causes a wound. The oyster's internal response is to send resources to surround
the irritant, beginning the process that ultimately results in a precious creation.
The oyster's times of suffering forms within it a treasure of great value: a pearl.
I believe our times of suffering form within us a beautiful creation, too: that of
the character of Jesus. How will I react to the irritants in my life today?

Merciful Father, through all the struggles and trials of life,
You are always with us. Help us to remember that, through our
pain, we can show forth the beauty of Your character in our
lives. In Jesus' name. *Amen*

What's a Feather Anyway?

You then who teach others, will you not teach yourself?
While you preach against stealing, do you steal?

Romans 2:21

Most of us can recall a "life defining" moment. One of those experiences for me happened when I was around six years of age. I stopped to look at a small rack of greeting cards while my mother browsed elsewhere in the department store. One card in particular caught my eye: the one with the bright red, *real* feather.

Do I ever try to rationalize giving in to temptation?

I can still remember touching the beautiful, silky-smooth feather. Since it appeared to be loose, I slipped it from the card. *I'll just hold it in my hand a minute,* I thought. But oh, how I wanted to take it home with me. No one would see me and no one would miss it. The card from which it came still looked pretty.

What's a little old red feather anyway? I asked myself. Then I knew deep in my heart that it would be stealing if I took the feather. I tried to put it back on the card, but I couldn't. My hands were probably trembling too much by now. So I carefully laid it where a clerk would see it and replace it.

To this day I can remember the temptation to take the feather home with me.

While I shouldn't have bothered the feather at all, I'm still glad I didn't steal. Since that time I've come to realize that whether our temptation is feather-like or weighty, God can provide a way out. He has promised in I Corinthians 10:13b, "God is faithful, and he will not let you be tempted beyond your strength, but with the temptation will also provide a way of escape, that you may be able to endure it."

More than likely each of us will face a temptation of one kind or another every day of our lives. Let's remember that we have a source of strength that will provide a way of escape for us.

Father, help our lives be an example of that which we teach and preach. Thank You for providing a way of escape when we face temptation. In Jesus' name. *Amen*

Jesus Is the Way

No one comes to the Father, but by me.
John 14:6b

"Is Jesus the only way to God?" was the question posed in the Sunday school class. Various answers came forth, but no one offered a satisfactory one. I was new in the church and was making the rounds of visiting all the adult classes. My heart pounded, yet I remained silent. I was stymied by fear that the deep conviction of my heart wouldn't come out right. I couldn't even remember the chapter in John's gospel where Jesus Himself settled the question: "I am the *way,* and the truth, and the life; no one comes to the Father, but by me" (John 14:6, emphasis mine).

There is only one path to God.

I never did speak up, and I will always regret it. I vowed that day, to God and myself, that I would never be silent again when this question is asked.

One of the troubling trends I see in our society today is to water down truth—or, worse, be totally silent—as I was, when the basic tenets of our faith are challenged. I respect the right of all people to their own convictions, but as a Christian I must remain faithful to God's Word. Paul warned Timothy that "the time is coming when people will not endure sound teaching, but having itching ears they will accumulate for themselves teachers to suit their own likings" (II Timothy 4:3).

In this day of "open-mindedness," we want our faith to be tailor-made to suit our lifestyle. I don't believe that there are multiple paths to heaven. God provided for all people one way: through belief in His Son, Jesus Christ. We can be totally sincere in our beliefs and be totally wrong, but I'll stake my life on Jesus as the Way.

> Last of all God sent His Son
> This work He finished—the battle won,
> He is the Way through heaven's door,
> For now 'til then—I'll need no more.

Loving God, forgive me when I have failed You. Give me Your wisdom and boldness to stand for my faith in Your Son, our Savior. *Amen*

The Imperishable Jewel

Let it be the hidden person of the heart with the imperishable jewel of the gentle and quiet spirit, which in God's sight is very precious.
I Peter 3:4

I gazed at the breathtakingly beautiful Hope diamond at the Smithsonian Institution in Washington D.C. The longer I looked at it, the more of its beauty and colorful light seemed to be reflected. The value of this huge 44½-carat gem was beyond my comprehension.

The gentle, quiet spirit pleases the Lord always.

Diamonds are precious gems. But they are also valuable in industry for cutting, grinding, and boring holes. Paul talked about a precious jewel of the kingdom of God—the gentle and quiet spirit. I believe there are some similarities with the diamond and the jewel of the gentle, quiet spirit:

- Diamonds are formed by heat and pressure. A person who has endured trials and suffering—the heat and pressures of life—often possesses a rock-like faith.
- Diamonds are durable; they withstand the "toughness test" in industry. In the same way, the strength of the person with rock-like faith is evidenced wherever he or she is: in the classroom, the basketball court, on the battlefield, or on a date.
- Diamonds have great potential for reflecting light. So does the Christian with a gentle, quiet spirit. There is a presence about this person that reflects the light of God's love to the world.
- Diamonds are very precious to their owner. The person with a gentle and quiet spirit is very precious to God. Isaiah 43:4 says, "Because you are precious in my eyes, and honored, and I love you."

There is a point at which the comparison stops. A severe blow can destroy a diamond. The gentle, quiet spirit can be bruised but it can never be destroyed. It's everlasting. It was created by God to live eternally with Him.

Our Father, help us to be rock-like in our faith, always reflecting Your light to the world. In Jesus' name. *Amen*

A Pillow on the Pavement

Show me a sign of thy favor...because thou, Lord,
hast helped me and comforted me.

Psalms 86:17

I came around a bend in the road, and there it was—a beautiful pink pillow lying on the yellow line. It looked as though it had been ever so carefully positioned there. Even the ruffles lay perfectly in place. I didn't stop, but I continued to wonder about the incident as I continued my journey.

How in the world did a pillow get placed in the middle of the road? Maybe a child let it fall from a car window. Maybe it had slipped from a load of household items being moved. I'll never know the whole story, but I'll long remember the meaning it held for me that day.

Today, I want to remember that the Holy Spirit will meet me at my point of greatest need.

My heart was heavy, and the hour's drive to babysit our granddaughter had seemed much longer than usual. I somehow needed a reminder that God was with me. I needed a sign of His faithfulness. Strange as it may sound, that beautiful pillow lying on the dark, hard, cold pavement reminded me that the Holy Spirit travels life's lonely roads with us. He meets weary travelers along the way to help and comfort.

The psalmist, David, knew about the need to have a sign from God—a sign of His help and comfort along life's journey. He used these words—"Show me a sign of thy favor...for thou, Lord, hast helped me and comforted me"—as a traditional ending for his prayer of petition. And we, too, can be sure that when our aching hearts cry out for help and comfort, He will place in our paths a sign of His abiding presence.

Loving Lord, I am so glad that You sent the Comforter to travel life's roads with us. Help me never to fail to recognize Him. *Amen*

The Power of Praise

Let heaven and earth praise him, the seas and everything that moves therein.

Psalms 69:34

My mother was in the hospital for tests on her lungs. She was first told she might have a cancerous tumor. Added to that was the possibility of tuberculosis. As I tried to pray in the hospital chapel, I kept getting a strong impression: "Praise, don't pray." It didn't make sense to me. I really didn't feel that I had a lot to praise about at that moment. Still, the thought kept returning: "Praise, don't pray."

In the midst of trouble, we can be cheerful. Our Lord has overcome the world!

I'll never forget trying to sing when my heart was so heavy I could hardly breathe, but I managed to begin. I didn't feel the words, but I sang them anyway. Not many days later, the surgeon came into mother's room shaking his head and said, "Mrs. Radford, we really can't pinpoint anything wrong with you." Mother quickly replied, "Doctor, I think the Lord has touched me." He walked out of the room saying, "He just may have!"

The power of praise! Someone has said that when we praise, we release the God-power within us. That power cannot be operative as long as we imprison it through fretting and doubting. It's not always easy to praise, but it is possible. We have to make praise an act of the will, and look beyond the present problem to God's power.

Philippians 4:4 says, "Rejoice in the Lord always; again I will say, Rejoice." Praise always, not just when things are going well, when we feel good, or when the sun is shining. The psalmist knew about praise. Even though about half of the book of Psalms is devoted to prayers of faith in time of trouble, some forty chapters are of praise.

Today, let's release the God-power in us through praise, regardless of our circumstances. Then we'll feel stronger and full of joy. Nehemiah 8:10b says, "The joy of the Lord is your strength."

Father, thank You for the power of praise. Help me to be able to praise You in all circumstances. Through Christ our Lord. *Amen*

Strength for Today

As your days, so shall your strength be.

Deuteronomy 33:25b

The basement was dark and musty. It somehow matched my mood that day. As a family we were combining all our energies to help our precious Katie move along in her language development. We had found good speech and music therapists to work with her. We were convinced of her intelligence, and were secure in God's power to intervene. Yet, we seemed to still be struggling with how we, as a family, could best bring together all these healing forces. And, to be honest, my faith had become a little stale and musty—like the basement.

God's strength is new every morning!

Somewhere I read that a tambourine would be helpful in Katie's music therapy. So I continued to search dusty boxes in the basement for our children's tambourine. No luck. *Why didn't I label the boxes better?* I wondered. I opened still another "wrong" box when a small brown book caught my eye. It was *In Green Pastures* by J. R. Miller.

Realizing this was a daily devotional guide which was used by Wally's parents for many years, I opened its yellowed pages. Turning to the message for the day I read the title, "As Thy Days." The opening line said, "There is in the Bible no promise of grace in advance of the need…when the conflict is at hand the strength will be given."[1]

The truth in those words penetrated my dim spirit that day. I'll never forget it. Yes, I'd like to know the outcome of Katie's therapies. And, it would be nice to find the tambourine. But there was one thing I could be sure of: the One who knows the future can *and will* provide the strength for each day. We don't really need it in advance anyway!

Dear Lord, You speak to our hearts in unusual ways and in unusual places. Thank You for providing the strength we need for today, and help us not to worry about tomorrow. *Amen*

God Sees Our Potential

*Then Jesus looked at them and said to them,
"With men this is impossible, but with God all things are possible."*
Matthew 19:26

*H*ave you ever noticed that seed companies never show the picture of actual seeds in their catalogs or on seed packages? Rather, the full-grown product is pictured. The vegetable is ready for harvest. The full-blossomed flower is ready to be cut. There's an obvious reason for this: the seed company wants the customer to envision the potential of the seed, not the seed itself. Not many actual seeds are inspiring anyway!

Man can make a replica of a seed, but only God can create a seed that will grow.

I believe God views His children in something of the same way. He knew us even before we were conceived. In fact, the Lord told Jeremiah, "Before I formed you in the womb I knew you, and before you were born I consecrated you" (Jeremiah 1:5). But even more important, God sees what we can become. He sees our potential.

None of us were born fully developed. Our minds were yet unexplored at birth. Our spirits were yet unattuned to God's Spirit. But the potential was there, and God could see it.

He could see in our souls the potential for us to appreciate beautiful music. He planted in our dreams the possibility of writing beautiful poetry. Ideas, goals, plans, and purpose for living were all seeds—with potential—planted deep within us when we came into this world. Left to us, these seeds might never sprout or blossom. But through God's infinite wisdom and power, we can experience the joy and fulfillment of maturing in His purpose for our lives.

Dear God, it's so good to know that you see us not just as we are, but as we can become. Help us to reach the potential You see for our lives. *Amen*

From Whom All Blessings Flow

All the people were praising God for what had happened.
Acts 4:21b (NIV)

*I*n 1988, Orel Hershiser was a guest on the Johnny Carson television show. After several minutes of conversation about the unusual success of this sports giant, Johnny asked Orel how it had all come about. And into millions of homes across America came the words of the "Doxology," which is a chorus of praise to God.[2]

This bold witness moved me. It seemed to me that Johnny Carson was moved a little bit as well. Since that time I've often asked myself: Do I praise God for my blessings? Orel Hershiser gave God credit—simply and unashamedly. The setting wasn't in a Sunday school class or a camp meeting; it was on a nationwide, secular television program.

How easy is it for me to share my faith, regardless of the circumstances?

In our Scripture from Acts, Peter and John gave God the praise and credit for what had happened in their lives. It was a threatening setting. They had to explain to the rulers and elders by what power the lame man had been healed. This testimony required boldness—a boldness that is too often missing in my own life.

Peter and John said they had no choice "but speak of what we have seen and heard" (Acts 4:20). They were set free! Truth was recognizable, and set them free. We, too, need to give God the praise and credit at all times, even when this is not the easy or the acceptable answer. All blessings are from God, and He deserves all praise!

Dear Lord, forgive me for the times when I'm timid in giving You due praise. Help me to be bold in my faith. In Jesus' name. *Amen*

Remember the Sabbath Day

Remember the Sabbath day, to keep it holy.
Exodus 20:8

Before the 1991 Kentucky Derby, large billboards at various entry points to Louisville carried this slogan: "Take Time for Sunday Silence." Sunday Silence was the name of the thoroughbred horse that won the Kentucky Derby in 1989, as well as the Preakness, the Breeders' Cup Classic, and several other important races that year. Though the clever slogan was really an advertisement to visit the Kentucky Derby Museum, the truth of the motto has lingered in my mind.

We can serve Christ better when we've rested on the Sabbath.

Perhaps "Take Time for Sunday Silence" should be the proverb that permeates our weekly schedules. As a child I recall memorizing, "Remember the Sabbath day, to keep it holy." But in the frenzied schedules of our society it seems that we are ignoring this commandment more and more.

My grandmother prepared Sunday's noon meal on Saturday, and this was before the days of refrigeration. She stored the food in cool spring water near her home. My mother didn't always prepare Sunday's food ahead of time, but she was very careful to never "work" beyond the preparation and clean-up of the meal. I never recall my father working on the farm on Sunday either.

Keeping the Sabbath holy is a practical commandment. We need quiet, restful time in our lives—as well as a time for worship. As He created the world, God knew that we would need physical rest and spiritual renewal after a busy workweek.

There are professions such as nurses, doctors, law enforcement, and firemen, whose responsibilities require Sunday work hours. But do highway medians need mowing on Sunday? Do sports events need to be scheduled on Sunday? Do all places of business need to be open on Sundays?

The billboards advertising the racehorse Sunday Silence were later changed, but the profound truth of remembering to keep the Sabbath holy should be an ongoing guide for Christian lives.

Heavenly Father, thank You for instructing us to set aside a day of rest and worship. Help us to be faithful and disciplined in remembering the Sabbath day. *Amen*

It's All in the State of Mind

Let every one be fully convinced in his own mind.
Romans 14:5b

During my elementary school years I entered the county spelling bee three times. Before each contest, my mother recited to me this poem:

If you think you are beaten, you are,
If you think you dare not, you don't.
If you like to win, but think you can't,
It's almost certain you won't.
If you think you'll lose, you've lost
For out of the world we find,
Success begins with a fellow's will—
It's all in the state of mind.
If you think you are outdressed, you are,
You've got to think high to rise,
You've got to be sure of yourself before
You can ever win a prize.
Life's battles don't always go
To the stronger or faster man,
But sooner or later the man who wins
Is the man who thinks he can.
—Anonymous

We have to temper our goals with realism, but it's so important to believe in our potential.

I didn't win the spelling bees. I was never fully convinced that I could win. But this poem from my mother is imbedded deeply in my heart today. Its truth is eternal: success does begin in our mind and in our will. Even though I knew I was a reasonably good speller, I was never convinced that I was the county's best speller.

My teacher and my mother thought I could be the winner in each of the spelling bees, but I wasn't convinced. Yet I do know that I've tackled challenges during my adult years because of this early lesson that success is in the state of mind.

Dear Father, help me to remember that You are with me— in my winning times and in my losing times. Help me to always be fully convinced of what You can do through me. *Amen*

Parents: Friends or Enemies?

Honor your father and mother…do not provoke your children to anger.
Ephesians 6:2a,4a

Recently a youth director was speaking on the twenty-third Psalm to the junior and senior high school students in his church. When he came to the verse, "Thou preparest a table before me in the presence of my enemies" (Psalms 23:5a), he paused. He asked the question, "Who are our enemies anyway?" Their answers were shocking: Every young person in the group answered, "Parents."

Christian parenting should result in homes where friends, not enemies, dwell.

It's difficult for me to believe that these youth meant what they said, especially since they came from supposedly Christian homes. Certainly, peer pressure had played a part in the consensus. But if half—or even one—of the group meant what they said, it is a sad commentary on family life in our churches today.

Surely there must be a word for parent-child relationships in these two verses from Ephesians 6. The practical wisdom of each verse seems interchangeable. Children, honor your father and mother. Parents, don't provoke your children to anger. Or, parents, honor your children, and children, don't provoke your parents to anger. How our society needs to hear and heed this advice!

As the bombardment of temptation and confusion increases with today's youth, so does the need for responsible Christian parenting. We as parents must become our children's friends. I believe this kind of relationship is possible, but not without a price. The price requires an unswerving commitment to patience, perseverance, and sacrifice. Our love will have to be both tough and unconditional. We will have to take the time—that means *make* the time—to listen and listen and then listen some more to our children. We'll have to truly hear our children not only with our ears but also with our hearts.

I believe a relationship of mutual friendship and respect can prevail in our homes if we, as parents, are willing to pay the price. Then our lives will not only be "long on the earth," as Paul described it in Ephesians 6:3, but happier as well.

Loving God, help us as Your children to be so filled with Your love that all our relationships are molded by it. *Amen*

Dwell on Good Things

Finally, brethren, whatever is true, whatever is honorable, whatever is just, whatever is pure, whatever is lovely, whatever is gracious, if there is any excellence, if there is anything worthy of praise, think on these things.
Philippians 4:8

My mother's philosophy was, "You never know what good things are ahead." What a positive affirmation of life! Instead of expecting the bad to happen, she expected good things to happen. She concentrated on the good. Seldom did a negative thought enter into her conversation, and she taught those close to her likewise. Like Paul said in the Scripture above, she thought about those things worthy of praise.

Our mind is like a garden—whatever we plant in it is likely to grow.

This attitude, I believe, is not a "bury your head in the sand" lifestyle, nor is it an unrealistic one. It's an attitude that can enable a person to avoid being overwhelmed by crises and tragedy. It's a conviction exemplified in Romans 8:28: "We know that in everything God works for good with those who love him, who are called according to his purpose."

This kind of attitude helps maintain a balanced perspective. It helps prevent depression. It gives hope to an otherwise seemingly hopeless situation. It nurtures a deep and abiding faith.

I believe that with this kind of faith, circumstances cannot be a factor in determining our attitude. Paul wrote the letter to the Philippians from prison. Yet the dominant themes throughout this letter were joy and encouragement. He wanted the new Christians whom he loved dearly to get beyond self, to remember that to live is Christ, to forget what lies behind, and to have no anxiety. He knew about contentment—even in prison. He dwelled on good things, and encouraged others to do the same.

My mother, like Paul, believed that God would supply her needs, and that's why she was able to dwell on the good things—regardless of circumstances.

Dear Father, help me to center my mind and heart on the good things in life, because in so doing I center on You. *Amen*

Safe Lodging

I will strengthen you, I will help you, I will uphold you
with my victorious right hand.
Isaiah 41:10b

I recently drove by a church with a large wooden cross on its front facade. There's nothing unusual about that, except something caught my eye. Resting securely on the right arm of the cross's horizontal beam was a little bird nest. Driving by the church a few days later, I fully expected to find the nest missing, blown away by the summer storms. But there it was, still in place, and for me it was a statement of God's secure protection.

In whom or what will I place my trust today?

Reflecting later on this scene, I recalled the many times when I have felt shored up or held by God's strength. I'm sure there have been those times when I needed a reminder that I was not alone. But feeling forsaken for a moment never changed the fact of His presence and support through all of my life's stormy times.

When our Lord stretched out His arms on those horizontal beams of the cross, His love was extended to the whole world—forever. In Isaiah 41:10b God promised, "I will uphold you with my victorious right hand." Deuteronomy says it this way: "The eternal God is our dwelling place, and underneath are the everlasting arms" (Deuteronomy 33:27a).

I want to have the faith, as the little bird did, that I can always trust in and rest upon the loving, outstretched arms of Jesus. It is there that I will always find safe lodging.

Loving Father, I'm so grateful that You have provided safety from life's storms. Help me to rest upon Your promises today. In Your Son's name. *Amen*

God Is Love

He who does not love does not know God; for God is love.
I John 4:8

For many years a small night light burned in my kitchen. It was inscribed with these words: "God is Love." We let this little light burn all the time because our home needs this constant reminder. Day and night the words glowed from a socket near our telephone. They've been a staying power when a call has come about the illness or death of a loved one. They've been a staying power when we've tried to counsel or maybe just listen to someone struggling with life. The truth in these three words, I believe, is the most profound truth ever to be revealed to human kind.

I want to know more of God so that I can know more of His love.

God's love is the one constant that we can be sure of in this hectic, chaotic world. It's a fact that can never be tempered or changed by circumstances. It's the same yesterday, today, and forever. It's new every morning!

We were searching for this kind of truth as our family chose the epitaph for Mother's grave stone. So many quotes and proverbs were possible like "Earth has no sorrows that heaven cannot bear," or, "Rest in peace." But none seemed to sum up the life of our mother as well as "God is love." God's love had always sustained her during illness, sorrow, and trouble. God's love filled mother's life with joy, regardless of the circumstances.

It was Goethe who said, "We are shaped and fashioned by what we love."[3] Mother was fashioned by Whom she loved. What better message can our life proclaim than the fact that God is love?

Heavenly Father, thank You for revealing the depth of Your love through giving us your Son on the cross. Help us to grow more nearly into Your likeness each day. *Amen*

Not As the World Gives

My peace I give to you; not as the world gives do I give to you.
John 14:27a

*M*y forty-year-old nephew Doug Davis fought a long and brave battle to live. One complication after another developed. Surgery after surgery was performed. Prayer chains everywhere were activated. But in spite of all that was done, it became obvious that Doug's healing would only happen in heaven.

Never once did this faithful husband and father of two young girls complain or give up hope. His patience never faltered. During a tribute to Doug at our family Christmas gathering following his death, we realized Doug embodied all of the fruits of the spirit, not just patience.

God's peace is beyond our understanding, but not beyond our experiencing it.

We wanted so much for Doug's life to be spared. During a brief moment alone by his bedside the day before he died, I called out to God. I pled for God to spare Doug—to "bring him back." In our hearts we knew his life was slipping away and moving closer to heaven. Yet, even after the doctor's explained the severity of his condition, we found it so difficult to release him to God.

One morning near the end, I got a call from my sister Jewell, Doug's mother. I wondered what was going on for her voice sounded different—so at peace. She said, "Well, Kate, I've released Doug to God this morning. It was the hardest thing I've ever done. You know, it's so strange. I have total peace now."

Total peace. Only God can give us this kind of peace. God's peace is not like the peace the world gives. The world's peace is temporary, fleeting. God's peace will never leave us. It still abides with Jewell today. It will be with all of us when we surrender our wills to His. Thanks be to God for His blessed peace that is new every morning!

Gracious and loving God, thank You for leading us through the valley of death and giving us Your peace. *Amen*

Formed in the Furnace

*For the slight momentary affliction is preparing for us an
eternal weight of glory beyond comparison.*
II Corinthians 4:17

*I*t's hard to believe that sand can be heated in a furnace to a certain degree and come out a beautiful piece of glass. But seeing is believing. I recently watched two brothers slowly move through the steps to make this happen. This generations-old method of making glass objects of incomparable beauty still works.

With fiery furnaces roaring, these skilled artisans take a nucleus of molten sand crystals and eventually form it into designs of paperweights, doorstops, animals, vases, candleholders, and various other items. Their finishing touch is to engrave their signature and date on each item.

I can face the forming furnaces in life knowing I don't have to face them alone.

Watching this process reminded me of some of life's struggles. Paul wrote the words in our Scripture to encourage the Christians at Corinth in their faith struggle. A friend brought this same verse to my mother when she was battling cancer. Mother patiently faced her "momentary affliction," knowing full well that ultimate and complete healing awaited her after this furnace of suffering.

I truly believe that the wholeness my mother, my nephew Doug, and other loved ones have now experienced in heaven is an "eternal weight of glory beyond comparison." I believe that God, the master Creator, put His signature indelibly on their hearts. At their home-going, He places His final seal of approval on their faithfulness.

Are you experiencing a furnace of suffering and struggles today? If so, just know you won't always be there—only long enough for the forming. I Timothy 4:10a reminds us, "To this end we toil and strive, because we have our hope set on the living God." In light of eternity, these experiences will seem slight and momentary. Like the glass artisans, God knows what we can become: a creation of ultimate beauty and worth. And He will be with us through every step of the process.

Loving Father, through our daily trials we learn more of Your endless love. Help us to share Your love with others who are struggling. Through Christ our Lord. *Amen*

Angels—A Part of Our Home-Going

The poor man died and was carried by the angels to Abraham's bosom.
Luke 16:22a

*L*ike with Lazarus, angels can be a part of our home-going. I know this was the experience of my grandmother. When I was around eleven years old, Grandma Cooksey died. My mother was by Grandma Cooksey's bedside at the time of her death, attending to her during her last moments on earth.

Angels can enable us not only in life but also in death.

Grandma had lived a good and long life. She had been sick for many months, but was completely lucid when she announced to her family in her dying moment, "There they come!" When Mother asked her who was coming, Grandma pointed heavenward and replied, "The angels—they're coming down to get me!" And they did. They carried Grandma to the bosom of our heavenly Father.

What a beautiful and blessed way to enter life eternal: being carried to the arms of God by His own special agents. I imagine the angels might have appeared to Grandma the way they did to Jacob in his dream—descending and ascending heaven's ladder. They descended to earth to take into their arms one of God's special children, and carefully ascended, carrying her safely home.

What an assurance of the reality of heaven this experience of Grandma's home-going has been to me! I will never understand all the marvelous mysteries of our omnipotent heavenly Father. But until I see Him face to face, I will be content to trust the reality of Grandma's experience of angels carrying her home.

Dear God, thank You for allowing that special home-going experience for Grandma. Thank You, too, for the assurance and comfort it leaves with us who are left here. *Amen*

Putting Away Malice

Let all bitterness and wrath and anger and clamor and slander be put away from you, with all malice, and be kind to one another, tenderhearted, forgiving one another, as God in Christ forgave you.

Ephesians 4:31,32

A young mother with baby in arms sat at my kitchen table and sobbed. She was physically and emotionally abused by her husband and had left her two older children with her neighbor. I listened, we prayed together, and I shared a couple of devotional books with her before she wearily left to return home.

I continued to pray for her in the hours that followed. The next morning I was thrilled to see her with her husband at church. Later she told me how Ephesians 4:31,32 had ministered to her. She opened the devotional book to this verse during the worship service and gave it to her husband to read. He did and was visibly moved by it.

God's Word is a comfort and guide for us always and in all ways.

Slowly but surely malice and bitterness seemed to be diminishing in this marriage. It began in God's Word. God's Word and faith in Jesus Christ—who is the ultimate example of forgiveness—will sustain a strong and sound marriage.

Jesus forgave even during His supreme sacrifice on the cross. To be kind to one another, tenderhearted, forgiving one another is to be Christ-like. When we can look at a person who spitefully uses us and see a person in need of forgiveness and help, we are seeing that person with Christ's eyes.

We are often imprisoned in some way, though not behind bars as was Paul when he wrote this verse in Ephesians. Living in a dysfunctional family can be like a prison. But with God's help, through the Holy Spirit and His Word, there is hope and help. In time and with God's help, bitterness, wrath, anger, clamor, slander, and malice can not only be diffused, but be replaced by love and forgiveness.

Heavenly Father, bless the families who struggle with relationships. Help us to have opportunities to share Your Word with them so that they may know Your love and forgiveness. Through Jesus we pray. *Amen*

What Inheritance Should We Keep?

*Train up a child in the way he should go,
and when he is old he will not depart from it.*

Proverbs 22:6

When my parents died, my brothers and sisters and I met together many times to divide up the household and personal belongings. As we sorted items into five groupings for the "drawings," we prepared a sixth group, which would be thrown away. Though we kept most of our parents' things, we all agreed that a few items were of no value to anyone.

Our future is determined by our faith more than our bloodline.

I believe that we have to do some sorting of values and attitudes we inherit also. There may be parts of our heritage that shouldn't be kept and passed on. But if our training has been in the way we should go, then we should not depart from it.

No one is perfect. I've always said that I hope our children improve on their parents. We hope they will always keep that which has been right in their training, and depart from that which was wrong. No one should be bound to his or her past. Like Paul we need to forget what lies behind and strain forward to what lies ahead (Philippians 3:13).

Our past is past. Much of it involved factors over which we had no control. God's plan for our lives is to give us "a future and a hope" (Jeremiah 29:11b). The Pharisees and scribes asked Jesus why the disciples didn't live according to the tradition of elders. Jesus warned them, "You leave the commandment of God, and hold fast the tradition of men" (Mark 7:8).

Jesus didn't want us to be prisoners of our past, but sons and daughters of God! Our adoption as heirs of God frees us from any scar from our earthly inheritance. Are we allowing our heavenly Father to shape our present and future?

Dear Father, help me to hold fast to what is good and right in Your eyes. I pray that You would rid my life of all that displeases You. In Jesus' name. *Amen*

Others

Let each of you look not only to his own interests,
but also the interests of others.
Philippians 2:4

Dietrich Bonhoeffer called Paul's advice to look to the interests of others "active helpfulness."[4] I can think of so many persons who have been actively helpful to our family over the years. They have looked to our interests through small and large deeds of kindness. For some, it was simply listening to our concerns. For others, it was putting feet and hands to our needs: offering to run an errand or baby-sit; speaking an encouraging word; praying for us; or just letting us know that they cared.

When we look to the interest of others, we please our Lord.

This verse reminds me of a dear friend, Elizabeth Keller. She was a great support, and her "active help-fulness" followed us on to Atlanta. During an especially low time while Wally was in seminary, a package arrived in the mail. It contained a dozen yellow artificial roses—the plastic ones of the fifties!—but, oh, how they warmed our hearts and encouraged us!

Another person that comes to mind is Mrs. Ethel Crump at the Park City United Methodist Church, our first appointment after seminary. Periodically, Mrs. Crump would take my hand and slip a twenty dollar bill into it. With a smile she would whisper, "Now, this is for you—no one else." She made me feel so loved and appreciated.

It's not always easy to get beyond ourselves. But Paul exhorts us to look not only to our own needs, but also to the needs of others. Jesus was the supreme example of self-sacrifice and kindness. I pray that each day I will faithfully follow His example.

Dear Lord, help me to follow Your example of caring for others. In Your name. *Amen*

No Coincidences

We know that in everything God works for good with those who love him, who are called according to his purpose.

Romans 8:28

A large statue of Christ emerges from the landscape of the Ozark Mountains near Eureka Springs, Arkansas. The outstretched arms of this immense work of art seem to enfold all of God's creation for miles around.

A wonderful story is told about this statue. A person named Elna Smith provided the financial means to build it, but it was left up to the local townspeople to locate a sculptor who would be willing to undertake such a mammoth task.

God is ever at work for good in our world, even though we may not be aware of it.

It is said that only two such sculptors existed in the entire world at that time. One lived in Rio de Janeiro. The other, a man named Emmett Sullivan, was said to be residing somewhere in the United States.

A search was conducted to find Mr. Sullivan. Finally, the Eureka Springs townspeople were told that he was staying in "a small resort town in Arkansas." That small town turned out to be none other than Eureka Springs! The person who had the ability to make the "Christ of the Ozarks" become a reality was, in fact, one of the townspeople himself.

So often God goes before us and works for our good, and we aren't even aware of it. Today, the outstretched arms of the "Christ of the Ozarks" touch thousands of people each year. I know I was moved by the sight of the statue when I visited Eureka Springs. I'm grateful to God for working everything for good, bringing about experiences that are "God-incidences," not coincidences.

Loving God, thank You for working in everything for our good when we love You and seek Your will. Help us to be Your outstretched arms to those in need. *Amen*

"Lady, Speak to Me!"

For everything there is a season, and a time for every matter under heaven…a time to keep silence, and a time to speak

Ecclesiastes 3:1,7b

The street was crowded with noonday shoppers. I found myself carefully weaving in and out of the mob of people. A feeling of aloneness swept over me. I was lonely in the midst of a huge crowd of humanity.

I became "hotel weary" and stepped outside the Cincinnati hotel for a breath of air. Inside, I had been among some three hundred strangers from all over the country. The bus ride from Louisville had been very unpleasant and, in that moment on the street, I wished to be home.

Lonely people cross our paths every day. Do we see them?

Suddenly I realized that I was looking directly into the face of an elderly man. I watched him look at my name tag and listened as he slowly read out loud: "Mrs. Wallace… Thomas… Christian… Social… Relations." Our eyes met and he paused for my reaction. All around us people were rushing by, unaware of our confrontation. He read the name tag again, a little more rapidly the second time. "That's right," I responded, and before I could attempt an explanation, his eyes pierced mine. "Lady," he interrupted, "that means that you are supposed to speak to me!"

I snapped instantly out of my self-pity. Caught up in my own little world, I had failed to see the people all around me. The meeting I was attending was to train leaders in Christian social relations, and I had just learned the greatest lesson possible.

I looked into the eyes of the stranger and felt compassion well up in my heart.

"Yes, sir," I said, "You are exactly right, and thank you for reminding me!" A fleeting smile came over the old man's face, and he slipped back into the crowd.

Walking back to the hotel, I felt grateful that my eyes had been opened. I will never look into a crowd again without trying to see individual persons and speaking when it is time to speak.

Father, forgive me when I fail to be sensitive to persons all around me. Help me to walk my talk every day of my life. *Amen*

"You Still Have Me!"

For it is the Lord your God who goes with you;
he will not fail you or forsake you.

Deuteronomy 31:6b

T hat's okay, Daddy," Savannah Baffert said as she pulled herself closer to her daddy. "You still have me!" Bob Baffert held his four-year-old daughter securely in his arms as he realized his horse had lost the Belmont Stakes. "Real Quiet" had won the 1998 Kentucky Derby and Preakness, and now, by a nose, he had failed to win the coveted Triple Crown.

I can face life's losses and disappointments when I remember that I still have God.

What a blow to this trainer. It was so great that even his little girl sensed it. She offered him words of comfort and the best gift anyone could ever give—the gift of herself. "Daddy, you still have me!"

Disappointment and failures are a part of life. All of us experience them to one degree or another. Life can take strange turns. A potential Triple Crown winner can be comfortably ahead one moment and the next moment, lose by about two inches in a photo-finish race.

When tough times come and we don't know which way to turn, God simply pulls His children close and says, "You still have me!" We have a God who wants to carry our heavy loads, who wants our cares cast upon Him. We have a God who will never fail or forsake us.

The disciples were devastated after the crucifixion, but Jesus later appeared to them to remind them, "You still have me!" Later, when he ascended to the Father, He sent the Holy Spirit to be with us forever. Even if the closest of family members forsake us, we still have God. Psalms 27:10 says, "For my father and my mother have forsaken me, but the Lord will take me up."

Today I want to remember that absolutely nothing can separate me from the presence of God.

Dear God, thank You for never leaving or forsaking us. Help us to extend Your love to others by giving of ourselves through comfort and kindness. In Jesus' name. *Amen*

Layered Christians

So have no fear of them; for nothing is covered that will not be revealed, or hidden that will not be known.

Matthew 10:26

I remember vividly the first time I ate a dessert called baklava. Baklava is a rich Greek or Turkish dessert made of thin flaky layers of pastry with honey and chopped nuts between the layers. Cutting baklava with a fork meant going through every layer—pastry, honey, nuts, and all! It fascinated me and, for some strange reason, reminded me a bit of how people can be layered, too. Life can add layers of experiences, making it difficult at times to "cut through" them to the real person.

God's love can cut through all of our layers of cover-up.

The baklava also made me think about the old iron bed I slept on during my childhood. I happened to inherit the bed and decided to refinish it. The paint had chipped badly over the years, and layer after layer of paint was added to cover the flaws. I scraped, sanded, rubbed, and added coat after coat of paint remover.

Like Matthew put it: "Nothing is covered that will not be revealed, or hidden that won't be known" (Matthew 10:26). By the time my fork sliced the baklava, I could see every layer, top to bottom. By the time I got the iron bed sanded and stripped, I had seen every color that was ever put on it.

We may have layers, too, covering the real person God created. If so, God can cut through the layers: the "honey layers," the "nutty layers," the thin "flaky layers," and the "chipped and flawed layers." The Holy Spirit can remove all the cover-up if we release each layer of our being to God.

Lord, You know our hearts. You also know the pains that have caused us to put layers of protection over our hurting hearts. Help us to have the courage to be the real person You intended us to be. In Your name. *Amen*

Offer Them Christ

Go therefore and make disciples of all nations.
Matthew 28:19a

I will never forget standing at the shore near Bristol, England, where John Wesley sent Thomas Coke to America. Wesley's parting commission was, "Offer them Christ."

For David's college graduation gift we framed the print by Kenneth Wyatt entitled "Offer Them Christ." The picture holds a striking resemblance to the shoreline of Bristol today. And, surely, the challenge of the title is as true for us today as it was for Thomas Coke as he embarked for the New World.

When I offer God's love, I offer Christ.

Wesley's charge resounded again the call of our Lord to the disciples to take the gospel to the whole world. God offered to the whole world His only Son, Jesus. We are called to do the same today. Only Jesus can heal our sin-sick world. Only a Savior can mend the brokenness in families, the cynicism in the market place, the sin in society, and the corruption in governments.

We are called to walk in love as modeled by Christ. In a world mired in evil, only Christ has the answer. Bombings, drive-by shootings, crack cocaine, assisted suicide, pornography, shock radio, sexual abuse, abortion—sin's endless list makes us know we must offer Christ. He is the only hope for a hungry, helpless, and hopeless world.

Will I be found faithful today in following our Lord's great commission? How will I offer Christ to my family, my neighbor, and the world? The best way I know is to simply offer love, for I believe when we offer love we offer Christ. God is love (I John 4:8b), and Jesus said, "This I command you, to love one another" (John 15:17).

Loving Lord, I pray that each day You will so fill me with Your love that I can channel it to a hurting world. In Jesus' name. *Amen*

Hold to Tradition

So then, brethren, stand firm and hold to the traditions which you were taught by us, either by word of mouth or by letter.

II Thessalonians 2:15

Today's families, regardless of their makeup, daily face the complexities of our changing world. In the midst of this, it's heartening to see a fresh interest in establishing meaningful and enduring traditions in the home. Paul encouraged the Christians at Thessalonica to hold to the traditions which helped them through the misunderstandings, erroneous teachings, and persecution in the church.

What will our children hold on to after we are gone?

Traditions established in the home help build faith and a sense of "roots" and are a mainstay for the family. Family conferences, open faith discussions, and times of prayer—such as at mealtime, before trips, or at any time of special need—are doors for establishing good communication patterns. Bedtime Bible stories are remembered long after other activities are forgotten.

Holidays offer excellent opportunities for establishing family traditions. In our family we gather around the nativity set for a devotional time before opening our Christmas gifts. At Thanksgiving we always try to take the time at some point to name our blessings. New Year's Eve has provided a time for us to reflect on the past year, share dreams and goals for the coming year, then close the session with prayer. Another meaningful tradition for our family is to hold hands during the mealtime blessing. But I realize that for some of us the challenge is to be able to have one meal together each day.

As Christian families we are called to stand firm and hold to the traditions which we were taught. It's a heritage that God Himself established when He instructed Moses, "And you shall teach them to your children, talking of them when you are sitting in your house, and when you are walking by the way, and when you lie down, and when you rise" (Deuteronomy 11:19). If we hold fast to these traditions and to God's commandments, our families will hold together.

Loving God, bless the homes of our nation. Help us to establish the kinds of traditions that will be faith anchors for our loved ones. *Amen*

Serving Others

*The Son of man came not to be served but to serve,
and to give his life as a ransom for many.*
Matthew 20:28

Cal Turner, Jr., then President and C.E.O. of Dollar General Stores, spoke in a nearby church. He talked about his company's mission statement, which is, "Serving Others." "Serving Others" is a wonderful motto for a corporation, but it's also a wonderful motto for a Christian.

True service to others is sharing God's love in ways that the world never sees.

Jesus is our model for serving others. After he washed the disciples' feet, he told them they should wash one another's feet. The true test of faithfulness comes when we are called to serve in some out-of-the-way place where there's little chance of ever receiving any recognition or appreciation. We are called to serve—and to spread Christ's love—with no strings attached. No payment in return. No selfish, hidden motive.

I have to ask myself what motivates me to serve. Do I want to be in the limelight? Do I feel it's expected of me? Do I serve in order to receive praise and approval? Colossians 3:23 says, "Whatever your task, work heartily, as serving the Lord and not men." Christlike servanthood is prompted by love, carried out with gladness, and seeks no praise or reward. I want to serve others with this kind of a servant heart, don't you?

Lord Jesus, help me to always remember that I serve You best when I serve the least among us. In Jesus' name. *Amen*

Joy Is Our Strength

For the joy of the Lord is your strength.
Nehemiah 8:10b

*N*ehemiah took on a big task. He gave up a responsible position with the king of Persia in order to rebuild the wall of Jerusalem. But he latched onto a truth, and it made a difference in his life. Nehemiah knew his strength came from the joy of the Lord.

God's Word encourages us to be happy and have joy. Joy is a gift that God wants His children to experience. Jesus said, "These things I have spoken to you, that my joy may be in you, and that your joy may be full" (John 15:11). Joy is the second fruit of the spirit named by Paul in Galatians 5:22.

Will I bring joy or discouragement to someone today?

Joy is a part of God's nature. It is curative. It is restorative. It energizes. It empowers. Nehemiah knew this. We are learning about it. There are many walls—some to be torn down, some to be rebuilt. But, through it all, our attitude affects our coping ability and our relationships with people. Nehemiah said that it affects our physical strength, too.

Proverbs 17:22 reminds us "A cheerful heart is a good medicine, but a downcast spirit dries up the bones." We've all been around people whose attitude and spirit had sort of dried up their bones. Being in their presence for extended visits can sap us of our own spirit and positive outlook.

Christians today, like Nehemiah, are called to big tasks. We can't face them in our own strength. We need the strength of the Lord. So we must set our minds on the great gift our Lord came to bring us: joy, full joy. If we do this, our spirits will never become weak and weary in well doing, regardless of the task we are called to do.

Dear God, thank You for the strength that Your joy brings to our lives. Help me to share Your joy with others each day. I pray in Jesus' name. *Amen*

Standing Appraised

Judge not, and you will not be judged.
Luke 6:37a

I stand appraised in the presence of Jesus the Nazarene," sang the child heartily. He changed one word—"amazed" to "appraised"—in the hymn "My Savior's Love."[5] This one word made a world of difference in the hymn's meaning. Instead of standing amazed and in awe of Jesus, the child sang about being appraised or judged.

Are the faults we find in others ones that might also be in our own lives?

Changing the wording of the hymn doesn't affect the flow or tune, but greatly changes the theology. We don't stand in God's presence appraised or judged as to our worth. All of His creation is precious and important to God. God sends rain on the just and the unjust (Matthew 5:45). He loves the one who brings joy to His heart, but He also loves the one who brings grief to His heart.

The Scripture tells us, however, that there will be a day of judgment. Hebrews 9:27 says, "Just as it is appointed for men to die once, and after that comes judgement." Judging and appraising others are not our jobs. To judge another person is to take upon ourselves a right that belongs to God alone. Instead of appraising others, it might be well for us to take a long, honest look at our own lives.

Dear God, help me to see the areas of my own life that I need to improve and leave the judging to You. Through Christ. *Amen*

For His Name's Sake

Yet he saved them for his name's sake, that he might make known his mighty power.

Psalms 106:8

What's in a name? Can the name that parents give their children influence their future? Many people believe that names and nicknames can influence both positively and negatively. Nicknames that deride and taunt attack a person's self-esteem and self-image.

Perhaps this is one reason there is so much interest today in the meaning of names. Books have been written on the subject. Cards with names and their meaning are printed in billfold size and in larger sizes for framing.

Is my daily lifestyle bringing honor to the Christ whose name I bear?

In Psalm 23:3, David talks about the importance of the Good Shepherd's name when he says, "He leads me in paths of righteousness for his name's sake." In Psalms 106:8, the psalmist was talking about the trustworthiness of God as He saved the Israelites in crossing the Red Sea: "Yet he saved them for his name's sake, that he might make known his mighty power."

What about the name "Christian" that I bear as Christ's follower? Is there evidence of its influence in my lifestyle? Do I "make known His mighty power" in my day to day living?

The "being" and "doing" of our Christian walk must come together if His mighty power is going to be seen in our lives. Jesus taught, but He also demonstrated. Love, kindness, humility, patience, goodness, self-control, faithfulness, joy, peace, and all the other qualities of a Christ-centered life should be visible if we profess to be Christians. Otherwise, we negate our name "Christian."

Father, forgive me when I fail to represent who You are. Help me to influence others to want to bear Your name. For Christ's sake. *Amen*

Gentle Nudges

In all your ways acknowledge him, and he will make straight your paths.
Proverbs 3:6

Many times I have experienced what I call a "gentle nudge"—that internal nagging that won't go away until I do a certain task. The test that I use to see if this nudge is of God is three-fold: (1) It reoccurs persistently; (2) it is for the ultimate good of a person; and (3) it is often a task I do not desire to do.

The Holy Spirit always leads us—and sometimes into unexpected places.

One such gentle nudge came at the end of a hot, hectic day in July of 1976. I had attended summer school classes and was on my way home when I got caught in rush hour traffic. Adding to the frustration of the day, I had been postponed in getting my driver's license renewed. As I tried to think of what to prepare for supper, I was caught off guard by a thought: *Go visit Dorothy Kuchenbrod.*

I was sure I had misunderstood. *Not today.* I dismissed the nudge soundly and quickly. Yet the closer I got to her street, the stronger the nudge felt. *Not Dorothy, Lord. And, please, not today. Besides, she wouldn't want to see me. She might not ask me in even if I did stop.*

I came to Dorothy's street and the nudge wouldn't go away. I decided to pull off the highway. Finally, like a child obeying a parent against her will, I begrudgingly drove down Kurz Road. Still I convinced myself that I probably wouldn't recognize the house, and she probably wouldn't come to the door.

Wrong on both counts. Dorothy welcomed me as though she were expecting me. We engaged in small talk at the kitchen table for a few minutes. Her face looked tired. Her breathing sounded labored. I knew I needed to cut through the pretense and get to the real reason I had come.

"Dorothy," I stammered, "I was on my way home, but something nudged me to come by here first." Her eyes softened and she listened intently. "What I really want to say to you is that I love you, and I want to meet you in heaven one day." A big smile came over her face, and, looking me in the eye, she promised, "I will get ready." And I have the assurance that she did.

Thank You, Father, for the gentle nudges You give us. Help us to have the courage to obey them. In Jesus' name. *Amen*

Jesus Never Changes

Jesus Christ is the same yesterday and today and for ever.
Hebrews 13:8

Sometimes I don't like to admit that I'm aging. This truth came home to me recently. I keep ideas for writing in folders and place them in two different stacks. One stack is labeled "To be developed soon"; and the other is labeled "To be developed later." One day I noticed two folders adjacent to each other. One was entitled "Aging," and the other was entitled "Eternal Life/Heaven." Both folders were in the "To be developed later" stack.

> *Today I will put my trust in the One who is eternal.*

Days pass. Seasons come and go. Years take a toll on our bodies. We change. There's a bit of uneasiness attached to aging. But as I think about the concerns facing us in old age, I'm reminded that Jesus never changes. Our Scripture for today says He remains the same. His love for me that I claimed early in life has not diminished a drop. His faithfulness is constant. Psalms 100:5 says, "For the Lord is good; his steadfast love endures for ever, and his faithfulness to all generations."

The unchanging character of our Lord comforts me. It challenges me. It calls me to keep growing spiritually. II Peter 3:18 says, "But grow in the grace and knowledge of our Lord and Savior Jesus Christ." Our soul never changes. It's eternal. It's the part of us that is of God, placed in us by Him to one day return to Him. It's the "constant" part of us in a changing body, created for eternal life. Our bodies are finite. Our souls, when surrendered to our Savior, are infinite. As my physical body changes, I want my spiritual life to bring me closer to the One who is the same yesterday and today and forever.

Dear Jesus, I am so thankful that You never change. Help me to grow into Your likeness until the day I'm in heaven with You. *Amen*

Our True Self

Teacher, we know that you are true, and teach the way of God truthfully.

Matthew 22:16a

A young minister's wife said to me, "Sometimes I don't know who I am." I remember replying, "I just know I'm important to God, and that's enough for me."

One of the most important questions we will deal with in life is, "Who am I?" Not only do we search for who we are, we also wonder, at times, how others perceive us. Even Jesus wanted to know who the disciples said that he was (Matthew 16:15). It was Simon Peter who identified Jesus as His true self—the "Son of the living God." (Matthew 16:16).

When we come to know our true self, we will want to tell others about the source of truth, Jesus.

Sometimes our "true self" is not the person that others see. I believe that our true self is the person fully known to God. Jesus said, "I am the good shepherd; I know my own and my own know me" (John 10:14). The more I come to know Christ, the more I will come to know the real me. When I really believe I am made in the image of God and that I am His child, I can know that He knows all about me. Isaiah 43:4 says, "Because you are precious in my eyes, and honored, and I love you."

When we realize that our Creator loved us enough to give His only Son to die for us, we surely can believe that we are precious and honored and loved by our Father. We are His children when we accept His Son as our Savior. That makes us joint heirs with Christ.

Knowing who we are should cause us to want to reach our full potential. A person may struggle with his or her self-image, but when we come to understand our relationship with God we know who we are and whose we are. This is good news, and we need to share it with a hurting world.

Our Father, thank You that You have received us as Your children. Help us to remember that this is both a privilege and a responsibility. Through Christ our Lord. *Amen*

Enjoy the Precious Present

Therefore do not be anxious about tomorrow,
for tomorrow will be anxious for itself.

Matthew 6:34a

After the 1996 Midwest Regional NCAA victory, Rick Pitino, coach of the University of Kentucky Wildcats at that time, gave his players some profound advice: "Enjoy the precious present!" That's a bit of wisdom that each of us can apply to our lives each day. Jesus offered similar advice on living the Christian life in the Sermon on the Mount when he said, "Do not be anxious for tomorrow."

> *I want to enjoy the present moment to the fullest, for it is all I have.*

I heard someone say the other day that life is like a grammar lesson—the past is perfect and the future is tense. It's doubtful that the past seems totally perfect to many of us. It's only natural to experience some regrets, but it's useless to dwell on them. What's done is done. We are to enjoy the precious present, which is really all we have anyway. Stewing over the tomorrows ahead only serves to make us anxious and tense.

In Philippians 3:13, Paul talks about "forgetting what lies behind." We need to keep the past in the past. God can redeem our mistakes. The future is unknown, and the unknown is difficult to deal with. But God is merciful to protect us from knowing what lies ahead. It's today that matters anyway. Our precious present may not feel as perfect as winning a national basketball championship, but just being alive is a precious blessing. Today, I want to make the most of every single moment!

Lord, help me to enjoy and appreciate life in the now, forgetting what is past and taking no thought for tomorrow. In Jesus' name. *Amen*

The Lamb Is Our Shepherd

For the Lamb in the midst of the throne will be their shepherd,
and he will guide them to springs of living water.
Revelation 7:17

*W*e're familiar with the image of Jesus as both the Good Shepherd and the Lamb of God. The beloved Psalms 23 begins, "The Lord is my shepherd." Psalm 80 opens with, "Give ear, O Shepherd of Israel." Isaiah speaks of God feeding His flock like a shepherd, holding His lambs in His arms and carrying them in His bosom (Isaiah 40:11). Jesus gave Himself the title of Shepherd when He said, "I am the good shepherd" (John 10:11).

With Jesus as our Shepherd our souls can be satisfied.

I love the works of art that portray Jesus as the Good Shepherd. They always serve as a reminder to me of how Jesus, the Lamb of God, shepherds us. They show us how He protects, nurtures, feeds, leads, and even gives His very life for us. The Lamb of God, our Shepherd, leads us to living water, our very source of life.

I'm reminded of our son, David, attending a presidential prayer breakfast at which Jacob Javits spoke. Mr. Javits, suffering from Lou Gehrig's Disease, could barely speak above a whisper. Sitting in his wheelchair and assisted by a tank of oxygen, he quoted the entire twenty-third psalm. And in those moments, Mr. Javits led that audience to the very source of living water.

I have to ask myself: Does my life point people to the Lamb of God—the Good Shepherd? Am I an instrument for introducing the thirsty to the source of living water? I pray that this will be so each day of my life.

Thank You, Lord, for being our Good Shepherd. Enable us to be good shepherds for Your hungry and thirsty lambs among us. *Amen*

Altered Attitudes

This is my commandment, that you love one another
as I have loved you.
John 15:12

Showing people that we care can change attitudes. This truth came home to me a few years ago when I attended a legislative training event in Washington, D.C. One assignment was to visit a community center in the high-crime area of the inner city and talk to welfare recipients about the present welfare system.

Our cab driver warned us, "I hope you know where you're going. When you get there, go inside quickly. It may be a long time before another cabbie comes by."

Cold stares greeted us as we entered the community center. These women saw us as representing "the system," and a barrage of angry words were hurled at us.

I felt afraid. Why had I come to this place anyway? I kept reminding myself that it was because I believed that Christians can make a difference in this world. But, in that moment, I wondered if any good could come from our being there.

Empowered by the Holy Spirit, our soft answers can turn away wrath.

In my heart I knew I had to attempt to reconcile, and I prayed for the Holy Spirit to intervene.

Standing up, I began to express my heart. The group had to lower their own voices to hear me. My heart pounded fiercely as I tried to explain why we were there. "I know you all have reason to be angry, bitter, and disillusioned. We just want you to know that we care. The church cares." The room was stone silent. I continued, "We really do want to hear your hearts, and we want you to hear ours. Maybe when we go back to our communities we can make a difference."

I believe these ladies heard my heart that day. Good discussion followed. As we stood to leave, one African American woman said, "Oh, you must not go out to the street alone. We'll stand with you." They did stand with us—for the entire thirty minutes we had to wait for our cab. The power of the Holy Spirit had altered the attitudes of a group of women that day. It was an experience I will never forget.

Dear God, help Your body on earth—the church—to be a part of reconciling the world to Yourself. In Jesus' name and through the Holy Spirit. *Amen*

Focus on the Promise

For all the promises of God find their Yes in him.
II Corinthians 1:20a

For several weeks a small note was posted on Wally's bathroom mirror which read, "Glance at the problem—focus on the promise." I'm sure there were many mornings when he read the note and was encouraged for the day ahead. At other times he hardly noticed the little yellow piece of paper, let alone the meaning of the words printed on it.

In this world we will have problems, but we don't have to focus on them.

The same holds true with my life. On some days I feel keenly aware of God's power, presence, and promises. But too often, days come and go with my focus directed at my problems. If I remember God's precious promises at all, they may just get a quick glance.

How much better my days would be if I, too, practiced the "focus on the promise" admonition. Then I would be recalling such promises as—

- The promise of His presence. "I will never fail you nor forsake you" (Hebrews 13:5b).
- The promise of His help. "The Lord is my helper, I will not be afraid; what can man do to me?" (Hebrews 13:6).
- The promise of His forgiveness. "If we confess our sins, he…will forgive our sins and cleanse us from all unrighteousness" (I John 1:9).
- The promise of His peace. "Peace I leave with you; my peace I give to you; not as the world gives do I give to you. Let not your hearts be troubled, neither let them be afraid" (John 14:27).
- The promise of comfort. "Even though I walk through the valley of the shadow of death, I fear no evil; for thou art with me; thy rod and thy staff, they comfort me" (Psalm 23:4).
- The promise of eternal life. "For God so loved the world that he gave his only Son, that whoever believes in him should not perish but have eternal life" (John 3:16).

Faithful God, thank You for fulfilling Your promises through the life, death, and resurrection of Your Son, Jesus. *Amen*

The Family of God

*Above all these, put on love, which binds
everything together in perfect harmony.*
Colossians 3:14

We had no clue as to what to expect with our host Kenyan family during our visit to the Meru Province. Questions plagued us: Could we be gracious guests and eat the food prepared for us? Could we bridge the deep chasms of our cultural differences? What if an emergency occurred in our family and we could not be reached?

Night fell before we reached the Muthee home. Eunice, the hostess, peered through the darkened door as we, with her husband Justus, approached the house. Smiling broadly, she welcomed us.

The Muthee home was warm and inviting. Crocheted doilies hung gracefully on each piece of living room furniture. A container of hot coals had been placed in the grate to break the chill of the Kenyan winter evening. Shadows from the flickering flame of the lantern danced playfully all around the room.

God's love transcends nations, cultures, and colors—binding us together in harmony.

All too soon the hour grew late. We had enjoyed warm tea and coffee, and a three course meal. Calling their four children to the living room, Justus explained, "We always close out our day with family devotions." He read Isaiah 40:28-31, then asked Eunice to lead in prayer. Her remembering the joys and concerns we had shared earlier touched our hearts. Then, handing each of us a paperback hymnal, Justus led us as we joined hearts and voices in singing a hymn familiar to all of us.

We felt so blessed by this dear family. No experience in our lives has made us realize so keenly that we are all a part of the family of God. We were eight thousand miles from our home, and, yet, we felt "at home" because of the ties of God's love that bound us together.

Heavenly Father, I'm so glad to be a part of Your family. Thank You for sending Jesus so that Your love could encircle the globe. *Amen*

Angels Guard and Deliver

For he will give his angels charge of you to guard you in all your ways.
Psalms 91:11

As Wally prayed one day for his elderly parents, in his mind's eye he saw angels hovering over them. I believe this was a profound truth. There are many instances in the Bible when angels protected and delivered God's people. Psalms 34:7 says, "The angel of the Lord encamps around those who fear him, and delivers them."

I want to remember today God's activity through His angels.

I believe angels take on special bodies only when God appoints them to special tasks. Deuteronomy 33:2 says that ten thousands of angels —"holy ones"—were with Moses on Sinai. In Psalms 68:17 David records twenty thousand chariots coming from Sinai into the holy places. When King Nebuchadnezzer ordered Shadrack, Meshach, and Abednego into the fiery furnace, he saw four men instead of three. The king said, "But I see four men loose, walking in the midst of the fire, and they are not hurt; and the appearance of the fourth is like a son of the gods" (Daniel 3:25). An angel of God was present to guard and deliver these three men of God.

When Herod decreed the slaughter of innocent babies, an angel directed Joseph to flee Egypt and told him when it was safe to return (Matthew 2:3-21).

Years later when Peter was imprisoned because of his faith, four squads of soldiers guarded him. Herod failed to figure two things into this picture—the power of prayer and God's angels. The church began to pray earnestly for Peter's release, and when Herod was about to bring Peter out to meet his doom, an interesting thing occurred. An angel awakened Peter, led him out by the guards and through the gates to freedom. Then the angel was no longer present, and Peter said, "Now I am sure that the Lord has sent an angel and rescued me from the hand of Herod and from all that the Jewish people were expecting" (Acts 12:11).

There are many other accounts in the Bible of angels guarding and delivering God's people. How thankful we can be for God's marvelous provisions for us.

Dear God, thank You for sending angels to guard and deliver those dear to us. Continue to encamp around us with this loving provision. Through Christ. *Amen*

Makers of Peace

Blessed are the peacemakers, for they shall be called the sons of God.
Matthew 5:9

I'm glad this beatitude uses the word "peacemakers" instead of "peace lovers" or "peace helpers" or "peace eulogizers." Jesus didn't just love peace, He made it. I believe we're called to do the same.

Scholars of the early church suggested the meaning of this beatitude to be the man who makes peace in his own heart is blessed. I believe this is true. We do have to first be reconciled with God in our own hearts before we can be agents of reconciliation. But I believe Jesus was saying for us to do more than make peace within our own hearts.

Do I make sacrifices in order to make peace? Do my actions prove what my heart confesses?

The word "peace" in Hebrew is *shalom*, which means everything that makes for man's highest good. Surely man's highest good involves a right relationship with God and a right relationship with our neighbor. I believe we are to live out, through authentic action, all that has happened in our heart.

India's Mohandas K. Gandhi (the mahatma) was a person of authentic action. He had to solve the problem of communication in a land of, at that time, some 350 million illiterate people. These people could not be reached by radio. He knew that he had to touch the lives of his beloved people by example. So Gandhi completely identified with the masses. He took off his European garb and wore the simple peasant dress. He traveled the railways by third class. He ate nuts and curd, which was the food for those without money. He gave up the privileges of a high-caste Hindu in order to be a maker of peace.

God of peace, please forgive me for failing to walk my talk. Give me the strength, wisdom, and the courage to serve You authentically—always. *Amen*

Cracks in the Concrete

You are a chosen race, a royal priesthood, a holy nation, God's own people, that you may declare the wonderful deeds of him who called you out of darkness into his marvelous light.

I Peter 2:9

I've always been amazed at the sight of a flower or a weed that has made its way through a crack in concrete or pavement. It reminds me how perseverance pays off when we face obstacles in life.

Sunlight beckons a plant from its place of darkness under the concrete. That same sunlight will enable it to grow, blossom, and reach its full potential. So it is with us. God has called us out of darkness into His marvelous light. Jesus said, "I am the light of the world" (John 8:12a). The world would have remained in darkness had not Jesus allowed the cross to break down the partition of sin.

To whom can I offer a ray of light today?

Jesus broke the barrier that separated us from God. He allowed His light to draw us to Him. We've been set free to grow, to blossom, and to reach our full potential. When we come into this marvelous light, we are no longer restrained by the heavy weight of sin, lost under the load, or groping for a crack in life's concrete.

Because of Calvary, we are a chosen people—a people chosen to serve God. We are a royal priesthood with total access to God. We are a holy nation, different in that we are to be dedicated to do God's will. We are God's own people, with dignity and worth. We are all of this for a purpose, and that purpose is simply to share God's wonderful deeds with others.

Jesus is the Light of the world, but He also said that *we* are to be light (Matthew 5:14). There are multitudes that still struggle under heavy burdens in their lives, searching and longing for a way out of their despair. Let us always seek for opportunities to offer hope and freedom to those around us.

Loving Father, please help me to so love that Your light can shine through my life today. *Amen*

Loving God More

Jesus said to Simon Peter, "Simon, son of John, do you love me more than these?"
John 21:15

The conversation at the birthday party turned to the latest lottery jackpot. The going question was: "It's 150 million now. Do you want your name in the pot?" It seemed that the entire group, except for two ministers and their spouses, joined in the ticket buying.

I felt sick: sick at heart because our society has become so greedy and materialistic; sick inside because it feels like we have placed Jesus in a concealed cubicle of our lives to call on if we "need" Him, but out of sight of our shadowy living.

Would I be embarrassed with where my heart is if I met Christ today?

Put your name in place of Simon, and ask yourself the question, "_____, do you love me more than these?" The test for finding where we place the Lord in our lives is simply to locate our priorities. What occupies our minds? Our time? Our hearts? Jesus said, "For where your treasure is, there will your heart be also" (Matthew 6:21). The only things we will be able to take with us to heaven are the souls we've led to Christ. So the bottom line is: Do we love the things of this world more than souls?

A newscaster said recently that surveys show lottery winners are less happy after they win than before. We can spend a lifetime accumulating material wealth and make no provision for treasures in heaven. The only way to real happiness and peace is loving God more each day.

Father God, forgive me when I fail to love You as I should. Help me to put You first in my life. In Jesus' name. *Amen*

Relational Write-Offs

If you do not forgive men their trespasses, neither will your Father forgive your trespasses.
Matthew 6:15

*H*ave you ever heard someone say—or maybe have said yourself—"I don't want anything to do with him/her anymore"? Lloyd Ogilvie called this a "relational write-off," and he sounds a stern warning about this attitude in his book *The Greatest Counselor in the World.* Ogilvie says, "He [the Holy Spirit] wants us to understand that writing off another person, without even coming to the place of seeking forgiveness, puts us in the perilous position of being written off by God."[1]

We can't control all that happens to us, but we can control how we respond to it.

Forgiveness doesn't come easily, but every one of us needs to forgive and be forgiven. In order for forgiveness to take place, grace is needed. Only grace can restore "written-off" relationships. It was through grace that Corrie Ten Boom was able to look into the face of a guard at the concentration camp where her sister had died and forgive him. It was through grace that Jesus looked down from the cross and asked the Father to forgive the very ones who had participated in His crucifixion. John says in the prologue to his gospel that this grace is for all: "And from his fullness have we all received, grace upon grace" (John 1:16).

Jesus said that if we want to be forgiven by God, we must forgive. There is no sin so great for which we cannot forgive or be forgiven.

Relational write-offs caused by hurts and hatreds need to go! Bitterness and grudges cannot stay in our hearts if we expect to enter heaven. Paul said, "Let all bitterness and wrath and anger and clamor and slander be put away from you, with all malice, and be kind to one another, tenderhearted, forgiving one another, as God in Christ forgave you" (Ephesians 4:31,32).

Forgiveness doesn't mean that we wipe from our memory the word or deed that hurt us. But it does mean that we are no longer chained to that hurtful experience. Jesus would never have us write-off a soul for whom He died. Is there a relationship that you and I need to try to restore today?

Dear Father, by Your grace, help us to be able to forgive others as You have forgiven us. In Jesus' name. *Amen*

A Place to Serve

Serve the Lord with gladness!
Psalms 100:2

A doctor in our town can often be seen tending the rose garden in the city park. This is his place to serve. We all need a place to serve. In God's eyes, the small, mundane task done in His name can make a lasting difference.

Serving the Lord with gladness can be done in many ways. Speaking a word of encouragement is serving Him. Comforting a broken heart is serving Him. Sharing God's love is serving Him. Serving may happen in lonely places, like dusting and pruning alone in a city park. God has gifted each of us according to His varied grace. We just have to seize the opportunities to serve that come our way. Opportunities, such as tending to roses, may present themselves only for a season.

Today, I want to serve the Lord with gladness regardless of where He sends me.

Sometimes serving may take the form of waiting: waiting on the faltering steps of a family member or friend; waiting on a weary heart to tell of its trouble; waiting on the direction and empowerment of the Holy Spirit in our serving.

As we search for our place to serve we can be sure that what God calls us to do He has been willing to do Himself. He didn't come into this world to occupy a throne but a cross. People looked for a mighty conqueror—they found a humble servant.

Where would God have me serve Him today? Am I willing for it to be in a lonely and insignificant place? Am I willing to wait until the Holy Spirit directs me to my place to serve? And when I know where this is, will I be willing to go?

Dear Father, show me where You would have me serve You today. Give me Your Spirit so that my service will please You and bless others. In Jesus' Name. *Amen*

A Silent Night in June

Thou dost keep him in perfect peace, whose mind is stayed on thee, because he trusts in thee.

Isaiah 26:3

*P*erspiration streamed from my face as I tried to make a path through boxes in the kitchen of our new home. The jolt to one box triggered an unexpected sound from within. Slow, clippy music began to flow. "All is calm, All is bright."[2] It was the music box, shaped like a little white plastic church, packed securely for moving. *Who could possibly feel calm and bright?* I wondered.

The precious peace of the Christ child will be with us wherever we go.

Moving from one parish to another is always difficult for me. I love the people deeply wherever we go, and I always find it heart-wrenching to leave.

As I sat in the middle of the floor, I pictured that little plastic church-shaped music box playing "Silent Night." I jiggled the cardboard box a little more, hoping for a few more notes, a few more seconds of respite from unpacking still another box. But there was no more music. Perhaps the little church, too, had run out of energy.

I sat alone in the kitchen of a strange parsonage in a large and scary city and tried to sort out my thoughts. I began to feel calm inside. I once more began to see the future as bright. I knew in my heart that we would adjust to another move. The sweet notes about a Savior being born—in another strange setting and another time—began to penetrate my weary soul. And I knew we would learn to love again. We'd locate a new doctor, dentist, pharmacist, barber, and grocer, and we would find all the needed services for the health and security of our family. This has been our experience again and again with each new appointment.

And, yes, we would feel loved again by God's special people. Of this we could be sure. We had adjusted to moves to new churches before. Peace came that night, and peace will remain as long as I keep my mind stayed on the Prince of Peace.

Thank You, dear Father, for coming to earth to show us Your love and peace through Your Son Jesus. Because You are with us, we can face the unknowns of our future. *Amen*

After the Rain–the Rainbow

*I set my bow in the cloud, and it shall be a sign of the
covenant between me and the earth.*

Genesis 9:13

I love rainbows. I love their sheer beauty and the sign of hope they bring. For Noah, the rainbow in the cloud was a sign of God's covenant that a flood would never destroy the earth again.

Rainbows are a part of God's plan to give us a "future and a hope" (Jeremiah 29:11b). To have a rainbow we need rain! Without the droplets of water remaining in the air after the rain, the rainbow would not appear; sunlight would have no color. For Noah, the rainbow followed the rain.

I remember seeing a special rainbow one day. I had driven several miles in a rainstorm after visiting my mother-in-law in the hospital. Suddenly there was a break in the storm, and, right before my eyes, was a beautiful double rainbow. Two perfect arches of color—something I had never seen before.

What doubts do I hold in my heart that should be erased through God's power, presence, and promises?

I pulled off the highway to thank God for His providential care and covenant of hope. Sitting there savoring that special moment, I vowed to remember always that *after the rain comes the rainbow.* Regardless of how stormy or dark our days may be, there is hope—through Christ and His presence with us.

Wonder fills our hearts when we see a rainbow in the sky. How much more should our hearts rejoice over the assurance that God's covenant is true and can be trusted as in the days of Noah.

Loving Father, thank You that You came to give us a future and a hope through Jesus. Help us to remember Your faithfulness all the days of our lives. In Jesus' Name. *Amen*

When the Answer Is "Wait"

Wait for the Lord; be strong, and let your heart take courage; yea, wait for the Lord!

Psalms 27:14

Sometimes I feel like I'm put on hold in my prayer requests. Those are the times when the answer is simply to wait—to wait for God's perfect timing and will. Waiting is not easy, but it's inevitable.

Every day we have to stand in line, pick a number, or wait our turn. There are unexpected delays, obstacles, slowdowns. We're told that we'll be called when our table is ready, our tests come back, our papers are processed, or our order comes in. Or we are told, "I'm sorry, that line is busy. Would you like to wait?"

God is at work even as we wait.

Many of the Psalms deal with the struggle of waiting. Before the psalmist David wrote these words from our text today, he had affirmed his faith afresh. He said, "I believe that I shall see the goodness of the Lord" (Psalms 27:13a). Waiting brings us to that point of faith in the goodness of God.

Earlier in this book I wrote about our daughter's deep desire to meet the right mate and, later, her deep longing to become a mother. God has graciously granted these two desires. Now we wait for another answer to another concern: Their little daughter, Katie, an angel from God, is not talking fluently yet. We believe that she is a bright child, but we pray and wait for the joy of a conversation with Katie.

I know that God is good and that He desires good for His children. I remember the promise of Jesus in the gospel of John, "My Father is working still, and I am working" (John 5:7). And I believe that before this book of devotionals is completed, Katie will be talking much more. My heart takes courage.

Dear God, it's hard when Your answer is to wait. But You have already proven Yourself to be faithful and trustworthy. I will wait patiently for Your perfect will and perfect timing. In Jesus' name. *Amen*

Love Surpasses Knowledge

If I have prophetic powers, and understand all mysteries and all knowledge, and if I have all faith, so as to remove mountains, but have not love, I am nothing.

I Corinthians 13:2

*S*omeone has said, "I don't care how much you know until I know how much you care." Paul seemed to be saying the same thing in the "love chapter" of I Corinthians. He was advising the Christian community at Corinth that they may have an abundance of the gifts of knowledge and prophecy and even a deep faith, but all of these put together were useless without love.

So often within the church we become hung up on trivialities—where to hang a picture, who's in charge of this or that, or who will receive the credit for a completed task. We forget that we are called to the "more excellent way" as Paul describes the life of love in I Corinthians 12:31b.

It's more important to fill my heart with love than to fill my head with knowledge.

I believe any word or action by a Christian can be negated if it's not prompted and tempered by love. Love surpasses everything. Of all the gifts that Paul mentions, only one is called the greatest of all: love. Many good Sunday school lessons, sermons, and conversations have fallen on deaf ears because of the absence of love. Many good deeds are only hollow acts of the human will because they are not motivated by God's love.

I have a deep respect for the gift of a great mind, but the far greater gift is love. In fact, the kind of love that Paul was talking about is God Himself. As I John 4:8b says, "God is love."

Loving God, You are the source of every good and perfect gift. Help me to seek daily to live the more excellent way by being a channel of Your love. *Amen*

The Sign of a Dove

This is my beloved Son, with whom I am well pleased.
Matthew 3:17

Our friend Eugene Dunn loved the many songbirds that visited his back yard. He carefully placed the bird feeders so he could enjoy the birds from the back windows of his new retirement home. All kinds of birds came—robins, wrens, cardinals, bluebirds, yellow finches, and orioles. From dawn to dusk they came, and ate, and sang.

God sends signs of His presence when we need them most.

During the last days of Eugene's brave battle with cancer, his hospital bed was placed near a window. It seemed that each singing bird had its own special song for Eugene, and on the day of his death a strange thing happened. Shortly after his body had been taken from the home, the songbirds were silent. Not a sound came from the backyard. The birds were not only silent, they were gone! In their place a group of beautiful doves had quietly settled around the feeders.

Louise, Eugene's wife, noticed this phenomenal happening and called her daughters, Lynn and Kathy, to the bedroom window. "Look, you all," she spoke softly, "The doves have come! They're saying to us that your daddy is at peace, and we must be at peace, too!"

Doves are symbols of peace. They are a sign of God's pleasure, too. At the baptism of Jesus, the Spirit of God descended from heaven like a dove and lighted on Jesus. Matthew, Mark, and Luke record that, at this appearance of the dove, a voice from heaven acknowledged Jesus as Son of God in whom He was well pleased (Matthew 3:17; Mark 1:11; Luke 3:22). And I believe God was also pleased the day another son, Eugene, came into His very presence.

Signs of God's peace and pleasure are precious to us—especially at the home-going of a loved one. I can imagine that Eugene now enjoys the sweet music of celestial songbirds—nonstop! Nothing stops their singing in heaven—no darkness, no pain, no death, no grief. There won't even be any need for signs of God's peace and pleasure in heaven, for we'll be in the very midst of both, forever.

Loving Father, the timing of Your presence is perfect. Thank You for the many ways You show us that You care. *Amen*

Clipped Wings Renewed

Be renewed in the spirit of your minds.
Ephesians 4:23

I used to watch my mother gently clip the wings of young chickens in order to keep them in a fenced area. It seemed a little cruel to me for her to do that at the time, but she would patiently explain, "Their little wings will soon grow out again, when they are older and stronger." I came to understand that if the chickens flew over the fence they could be run over by farm equipment or maybe be killed by an animal. They weren't ready to fend for themselves. Their wings would soon grow out again—completely renewed and possibly stronger than before.

Since God wants the best for His children, we can trust our entire lives to Him.

Clipped wings *can* be renewed; they will grow out again. So it is with our "clipped wings"—our wounded spirits, our weary bodies and minds, our burdened souls, and our ears numbed by noise. God promises to "make all things new" (Revelation 21:5). That's good to know—and remember.

Burned out energy *can* be restored. Tired, weary bodies and minds *can* know rest and refreshment. Wounded spirits *can* experience healing. Heavy hearts *can* be lifted. It takes time. It may require some intentional waiting on the Lord. It may mean that we have to stay planted where we are for awhile longer while we mature some more. And it may require us, like the little baby chicks, to be nourished awhile longer. We need to be fed by God's Word if we are to be equipped for the next phase in our life.

Mother knew what was best for the little chickens. She never clipped their wings enough to do any permanent damage. Rather, she tried to protect them from pain. She would never have wanted them to remain fenced in forever. Growth and strength and renewal came to their clipped wings as they waited.

God, in His infinite wisdom and love, allows growth times for us—times for us to be renewed in our spirits. I want to be sensitive to ways I can help this happen.

Loving God, thank You for healing our clipped wings. You always bring renewal at the times and in the ways You know are the best for us. I can rest today in this assurance. *Amen*

Mother's "Checkedy" Apron

Fathers, do not provoke your children to anger,
but bring them up in the discipline and instruction of the Lord.
Ephesians 6:4

*M*y mother had a gentle way of letting us know of her disapproval. She would say, "I guess I'll just have to turn you across my checkedy apron." I don't remember her ever following through with that particular warning, but we knew what she meant. At times with our own children I've said something like, "Where's my checkedy apron?" They understood what I meant.

We can either provoke our families to anger or provide encouragement for them.

Parents have a heavy responsibility to balance discipline with encouragement. Paul says in Colossians 3:21, "Fathers, do not provoke your children, lest they become discouraged."

I like the story of Benjamin West, one of England's most celebrated artists under King George III. Young Benjamin was babysitting his little sister, Sally, while his mother was out. He found some bottles of ink and, being the budding artist that he was, attempted to paint a portrait of Sally. When his mother returned she found ink stains everywhere—on the floor, table, and chairs. She surveyed the mess, and then, seeing the picture, said, "Why, it's Sally!" With that she bent down and kissed her young son. Later Benjamin West said, "My mother's kiss made me a painter."

My mother's checkedy apron warning remains in my memory as her gentle way of bringing us up "in the discipline and instructions of the Lord," (Ephesians 6:4). And I'm grateful.

Heavenly Father, help us as parents to be slow to anger, lest we cause someone to stumble. In Jesus' name. *Amen*

What's the Elevation?

The wise man's path leads upward to life.

Proverbs 15:24a

One of the highlights of my parents' later years was our trip together to Washington, D.C. Mother was particularly interested in the elevation signs along the way. She kept a running record of our vertical distance above sea level, and really didn't mind our chuckles when she'd whip out the little notebook from her purse at the sight of a new elevation sign. If we traveled several miles without seeing a sign, mother quietly asked, "Wonder what the elevation is here?"

What is my elevation point today? Have I let life bog me down, or am I pressing toward the goal of the "upward call of God in Christ Jesus?" (Philippians 3:14).

I've reflected many times on my mother's attention to our upward climb, and I have realized that all of her life was an upward climb. Before our family owned a vehicle, Mother faithfully walked the steep hill to church each Sunday. Every trip to see her aging mother involved climbing many hills, often by horseback. She sang about going up Redbud Hill as she neared Grandma's house. Trying to keep a home running smoothly with five children was often a steep climb. Fighting lung cancer was an upward struggle, too.

But through it all Mother's path led her upward, ultimately to eternal life. Her vantage point today is perfect. No more need for signs and notebooks. No more struggles to reach the next elevation point. She's reached the pinnacle: at home with God!

Loving Lord, strengthen me in my climb today. I want to be faithful to You all along the way. In Jesus' name. *Amen*

Mother's Tithe Account

*Each one must do as he had made up his mind,
not reluctantly or under compulsion.*
II Corinthians 9:7a

After my mother's death, I found a record of her income from sewing for people. Representing what was probably a week's work, her note read, "Dress…$5.00, Cut off pants…$1.50, Hem skirt…$1.00." For me this yellowed piece of paper was a reminder of my mother's faithfulness. She wanted to be very sure that she tithed every cent that she earned. I always knew she tithed her income, whether it was a payment for hemming a garment or interest from a small CD account. And here was tangible evidence for me once again of her example of the good life.

It's not the amount given but the spirit of the giver that's most important.

Paul says that each of us must do as we have made up our mind. Mother made up her mind to provide a service for her friends, and because of her warm, friendly spirit, she was offered more work than she could do. People often not only took home a garment that she had created or repaired, but also experienced renewal of spirit for having been with her.

Mother made up her mind to be faithful to God and return to Him at least 10 percent of her earnings. She carefully placed her tithe money in a small black leather change purse. She never gave reluctantly nor under any sort of compulsion to do so. Rather, she gave with joy and gladness, and I know she experienced God's love in a special way because of her cheerful giving. I'm so thankful for this rich legacy.

Heavenly Father, help me to faithfully follow the example of my mother in both my giving and my serving, for You were her example. In Jesus' name. *Amen*

Come Home, It's Suppertime

I am the bread of life, he who comes to me shall not hunger,
and he who believes in me shall never thirst.
John 6:35

Suppertime was a special time for me on the farm. Mother would call to us in her own special way, "You all come on. Supper's ready!" It meant the chores were done, and all seven of us would gather around the kitchen table. I can almost still smell the aromas coming from the kitchen. Much of what we ate was the result of her labor in the garden and canning. There was always enough for all of us and a special spot at the table where each of us sat.

I need to go to the Lord's table and remember what He has provided for me.

I miss sitting around my parents' table. But I'm so thankful that there's another table provided for me— the Lord's Table—and He continues to call us to it. This table was made possible by sacrifice also—the supreme sacrifice of our Savior on Calvary. There's food at God's table for all His children. We're all welcome. There's a special spot provided for each of us.

We truly come home when we come to the Lord's Table to partake of Holy Communion. We need this time at His table often, because it is there that we remember who we are and whose we are.

I can no longer gather at my parents' table, but I am comforted to know that I can go to my heavenly Father's table. There I can partake of the symbols of His body and blood that will sustain me eternally. There is no more hunger and no more thirst for those who come to Jesus and believe in Him.

Thank You, dear Father, for giving us the bread of life. Help me to bring others to Your table. In Jesus' name. *Amen*

The Power of a Look

And the Lord turned and looked at Peter.
Luke 22:61a

*H*ave you ever wilted from the power of a look? I have. I well remember the power of my mother's look. She was a person who didn't correct unless there was a real reason for it. She didn't often raise her voice to reprimand her five children. But more than once, from the choir area of our little country church, I felt her look at me. I knew I shouldn't talk during the service but temptation sometimes overcame me. I wanted to look away when her eyes met mine, but I knew I couldn't. I would just nod to her to say I had gotten her message.

I want my life to be pleasing in God's eyes.

What's in a look? There can be anger, gentleness, love, hate, understanding, discipline, compassion, and forgiveness. What did Peter see in the Lord's look? The Scripture doesn't tell us. But it does say that Peter remembered how the Lord had said Peter would deny Him before the cock crowed three times. Along with this remembrance, there was probably regret, repentance, and fear in Peter's eyes. And there was probably hurt and disappointment in the eyes of Jesus. But whatever look was exchanged between them that night, we know that later Jesus called Peter the rock (Matthew 16:18).

My mother's look called me to attention. The Lord's look caused Peter's memory to be so clear that he went out and wept bitterly. We need looks that call us to attention and commitment. We need the eyes of our heavenly Father upon us always. I'm glad this is promised in His Word: "For the eyes of the Lord are upon the righteous" (I Peter 3:12a)

Dear God, thank You for watching over us. Call us by the power of Your look to walk faithfully with You. *Amen*

Whose Hand Directs Us?

My times are in thy hand.
Psalms 31:15

Strolling by a new Ripley's "Believe It or Not" museum, I noticed a large round ball out front. Water quietly trickled over it causing it to move easily in its concrete socket. The ball was so large a long-armed man could not reach around it.

Hands of all kinds were upon the ball—big hands, little hands, black hands, white hands, male hands, female hands—all guiding it. After a few minutes of watching the huge hunk of marble roll around in its watery, hollow socket, I walked on.

How does my life reflect the One who holds it?

As I walked I began to think about my own life and whose hand directs it. What sways me this way or that? Which outside force influences me most? Some of the time, like the marble ball in its socket, I feel pushed and pulled in a dozen directions. Oftentimes I feel that I accomplish little and that I am just moving around in circles. There are also times when I feel that the world is passing me by like the people passing Ripley's.

But, if I'm really honest with myself, I remember that there are many helpful hands upon my life. These are the hands of my family, friends, and, most importantly, the hands of my heavenly Father.

Family hands can guide us to a point. Hands of friends can offer encouragement and love. I thank God for these human hands. But I want my times, my experiences, and my life to be in His hands. I want the Holy Spirit to flow over me like water over the marble ball, helping me stay centered in His will.

Human hands could move the Ripley marble ball *in* the socket, but no human could move it *out* of the socket. Human hands can affect my life, but no person or circumstance can move me from the palm of God's hand.

Dear Jesus, keep me centered in the palm of Your hand, for this is where I belong. *Amen*

Gold Vault Next Right

My God will supply every need of yours according to his riches in glory in Christ Jesus.
Philippians 4:19

While driving near Fort Knox, Kentucky, I noticed a road sign that read, "Gold Vault Next Right." Here was the beginning of a set of directions that would lead tourists to the place where most of our nation's gold bullion has been stored since 1937. It was a simple marker, but one that would lead to the storage place for this country's standard of value.

God's wealth in Christ Jesus is available for all who seek it.

As I drove along and looked at the gold vault on my left, I began to think about this source of much of America's riches. I thought of another Source of riches—a never-ending supply of them.

Paul said that God would supply every need according to His riches in Christ Jesus. These are riches that are not stored in a vault but in a person. There are no impurities in these riches. No alloys. Just pure love and all the gifts of the Spirit.

We can follow roadside signs that eventually take us near the Gold Vault at Fort Knox, but that's all. No stopping. No tours. No entry. Guards are there to see to that.

But receiving the riches of Christ Jesus is free. The price has been paid. There's no entry charge, no guard to turn you away. In fact, our Lord invites us to share in the abundance of His blessings.

If the gold supply were to be drawn upon at Fort Knox, it would eventually run out. Not so with our God. His supply is enough for our every need always. It's up to us to draw upon it whenever the need arises.

Dear God, You have blessed us so abundantly through the gift of Your Son. As we receive in abundance, help us to give generously in return. In Jesus' name. *Amen*

A Season for Everything

For everything there is a season,
and a time for every matter under heaven.
Ecclesiastes 3:1

I learned something about orange trees this week. Driving through some orange groves in central Florida and enjoying the sweet aroma of the blossoms, I was surprised to see the trees were producing both oranges *and* blossoms. I never knew before that any fruit tree could bear both ripe fruit and blossoms at the same time. I have observed apple, pear, peach, and plum trees many times while growing up on a farm. In every instance, the blossoms came first and then the fruit.

In what season should my life be today?

Two weeks earlier I helped lead a retreat during which we discovered our need for disengaging ourselves for a while. We need to rest now and then. To emphasize the point I said to the group, "Even fruit trees must have a time of dormancy to rest." Now I know the orange tree, at least in the warm climate of Florida, continuously bears fruit or blossoms or both.

As I've reflected on this new insight, I've recalled how our Lord directed the disciples to "come away by yourselves to a lonely place, and rest awhile" (Mark 6:31). But going apart and resting doesn't mean that all activity shuts down. Rather, resting is preparation for productivity. In fact, resting is productive. It's a time when fresh, creative ideas bud and blossom. It's a time when the Holy Spirit prepares us for fruit-bearing days ahead.

The writer of Ecclesiastes talked about a season for everything. We all need a season for rest and renewal, for new ideas to bud and blossom, for bearing fruit. I want to live wisely each day of each season of my life.

Dear God, You have blessed us with so much. In every season of my life, help me to be in Your perfect will, living each moment for You. In Jesus' name. *Amen*

A Faith Stand-In

He said to them, "Where is your faith?"
Luke 8:25a

I remember our son David coming to the place in his life when he said, "I just don't believe I will ever meet the right girl to marry." Wally and I could usually encourage him by saying, "Oh, you will meet her, David. God has her picked out already. Just have faith!"

When God's plan becomes our plan we have a future filled with hope.

Over the years we prayed for the persons our two children would one day marry. Both of them were in their early thirties before meeting their mates, and at times both wondered where and when, if ever, that right person would come along.

Finally one day David said, "I just give up on finding the one that's right for me. Maybe God expects me to stay single all my life." I saw he meant it this time, and I searched for one more word of encouragement. I wanted to say, "David, where is your faith?" Instead I said, "David, I still have faith that God will bring the right person into your life. Would you let me be faith for you until your faith returns?" "If you want to," he answered quietly.

I had never offered to be faith for someone before. In fact, I don't believe that was my own thought. It came from God. He knew He was saving Karen Muselman to be our son's wife! God *does* have a plan for us. He promised in Jeremiah 29:11, "For I know the plans I have for you…plans for welfare and not for evil, to give you a future and a hope." God's plan for David and Karen unfolded before too many months passed, and I'm so grateful for being allowed to be a "faith stand-in."

Dear God, thank You for supplying all our needs. Strengthen our faith each day, I pray. In Jesus' name. *Amen*

Cheerful Generosity

God loves a cheerful giver.
II Corinthians 9:7b

*O*ur daughter-in-law Karen recently hosted a cookware party in her home. To her surprise over seventy people came. She made up her mind before the party began that she would give one-half of the "reward" for hosting the party to a nearby mission. The sales representative caught the spirit and said she would donate half of her profit that evening to the mission also.

A few days later the Louisville Courier Journal carried a story about Cal Turner, Sr.'s death. Mr. Turner founded the chain of Dollar General Stores in 1955, and over the years his charitable foundation gave millions to worthy causes. Most recently, Mr.

Cheerful giving develops Christ-like living.

Turner gave, on two separate occasions, a thousand dollars to each of the ninety churches in his home county in Kentucky. His philosophy was that part of the fun of having money was giving it away.

Cheerful giving. Karen cheerfully gave a portion of her cookware to a mission in Lexington. Mr. Turner cheerfully helped untold numbers of persons from his abundance. Both gave without reluctance or compulsion, but from a loving, generous heart.

Have we found a way to channel to others a part of our financial blessings? Or are we like the Dead Sea—dead because it receives water yet never releases it? The sea has no outlet, therefore it is stagnant and lifeless. Our lives will become stagnant and lifeless, too, if we don't share some of what God has entrusted to us.

Is our generosity cheerful? It really is more blessed to give than to receive (Acts 20:35). John 1:16 says, "From his fullness have we all received." We all have something to share. It's not the amount of our gift or the circumstances in which we give that matters the most. Rather, it is the cheerful heart that is important to God.

Dear God, You are the giver of all that we have and are. Help us to give cheerfully of our abundance for we know this pleases You. In Jesus' name. *Amen*

Feeling Like an Orphan

For my father and my mother have forsaken me,
but the Lord will take me up.
Psalms 27:10

*M*ost of us at one time or another have struggled with our identity. It might have been that first day in a new school when we felt so alone and unknown by anyone. Maybe it was that first day on a new job or a time of deep grief over the loss of someone dear to us.

Each of us can share God's love with someone today. Johnny felt lost and alone and, at times, worthless. His situation was unlike any of the above—his problems stemmed from a broken home and being rejected by both of his parents. Neither parent wanted Johnny to live with them, and he was sharp enough to recognize it. He spent most of his time moving about, staying with a grandparent, or a friend or at the spouse abuse center.

Johnny soon became involved with the wrong crowd. His once bright mind became dull and corroded; his once sensitive spirit became callused. For awhile, we were able to keep in touch with him, and then contacts became more and more difficult.

One day while having my devotional time, I read Psalms 27:10, "For my father and my mother have forsaken me, but the Lord will take me up." I wanted so much to share these words with Johnny, but could not reach him by telephone. So I put these and other comforting verses on a cassette tape and mailed them to his last address. I later found out that he received them and was blessed by them.

There are so many people like Johnny in this world that feel lost and lonely, insignificant and discouraged. People feel rejected by family and even by God. Somehow those of us who know God's love must find a way to share it with the Johnny's all around us. When they feel forsaken, they need to hear that God is with them.

Dear God, thank You for never forsaking one of Your precious children. *Amen*

Pray Before You Plan

Commit your work to the Lord, and your plans will be established.
Proverbs 16:3

*P*rayer was a vital force in organizing Kentucky's first Korean United Methodist congregation. When Wally began serving as district superintendent of the Louisville South District of the United Methodist Church, he found a manila folder marked "Koreans." Inside was a stack of letters from Korean people in the Radcliff-Fort Knox area requesting help in organizing a new church.

Months of meetings soon began, often fraught with frustration and discouragement. Finally, the Korean dream became a reality, and the new church was officially organized. The pastor wept and said, "We tried and tried to get our church started, and when all else failed, we committed it to prayer."

I'm sure the prayers of those faithful Korean Christians did help their dream come true. But like most of us, they planned before they prayed. If we could only remember to pray first and commit our work to the Lord, our plans would be established.

God knows what is best for us, therefore we need to seek first His wisdom and will.

It would be well if all of us committed ourselves to prayer, as do the Korean Methodists at Kwang Lim Methodist Church in Seoul, Korea. I am told that on any given Sunday, one can see thousands of people streaming in and out of this church. When asked the secret of their rapid growth, prayer is always given as part of the answer.

The Kwang Lim Church has built their World Prayer Center for additional emphasis on prayer and spiritual formation. This center has overnight accommodations for over 800 persons and over 100 private prayer rooms. Outside these prayer rooms are kneeling benches for people to meditate and pray as they wait to go inside.

We may not have access to a World Prayer Center, but we *can* remember to pray before we plan.

Dear Lord, I commit myself and my work to You today so that Your plans for my life can be established. *Amen*

Letter of Recommendation

*You yourselves are our letter of recommendation, written on your hearts,
to be known and read by all men.*
II Corinthians 3:2

*Y*ou've heard the old adage that you are the only Bible someone may ever read. The truth of this statement took on new meaning recently as I reflected on this verse from II Corinthians. It caused me to deal with some questions: Does my life recommend Christ? Would a nonbeliever want to follow Jesus from the evidence written on my heart? Can the difference He makes in my life be seen clearly? I hope so. I want it to be so. But if it is so, what criteria will be present in my life?

My life is a human letter: what or whom will it recommend today?

I believe that my life, if it is to recommend Christ to a skeptical world, must be:

1. *Credible.* The love of Christ must be written so indelibly on my heart that it's believable.
2. *Clear.* My life must be readable as an open book and open to scrutiny and study by others.
3. *Consistent.* Christ-like qualities must be seen in my life each time it's observed.
4. *Convincing.* The truth of Christ should be observable in my life through His power and presence at work in me.

Letters of recommendation on paper are valuable when we want to be believed. But a person's life—imprinted indelibly by the ink of the Holy Spirit—is even more convincing. The message of who Christ really is and what He can mean in a life is believable when observed in a person's day to day living. A letter on paper can be misinterpreted, even if it's read over and over. But when Christ is seen in a life over and over, that life will be a valid witness—credible, clear, consistent, and convincing. I want my life to always recommend my Savior and Lord. Don't you?

Loving God, You sent the ultimate love letter when You gave us Your Son. I want Him to be known and read by all who see my life today. I ask for Your help that it might be so. *Amen*

Careless Words

Be not rash with your mouth...therefore let your words be few.
Ecclesiastes 5:2

*H*ave you ever been around someone who just plain talked too much, never allowing the listener to get a word in edgewise? Or have you been in the company of someone who was spreading idle gossip?

Careless words. Jesus had something to say about them in Matthew 12:36,37: "I tell you, on the day of judgement men will render account for every careless word they utter; for by your words you will be justified, and by your words you will be condemned." Earlier in Matthew—in the Sermon on the Mount—Jesus admonished the people not to swear, but to "let what you say be simply 'yes' or 'no'; anything more than this comes from evil" (Matthew 5:37). If a person has character and is trustworthy, there is no need for extra, careless words. The truth found in our talk should be such that requires no oath.

Will my words justify or condemn me today?

Some of the most significant eternal truths in God's Word are brief. Think of the message in I John 4:19: "We love because he first loved us." Or consider the message on the nature of Jesus in the two words, "Jesus wept," following the death of Lazarus (John 11:35).

Careless words cannot be retracted. Like feathers from a pillow that have been scattered by the wind, they are gone forever. I want my talk to be simple, clear, and kind. I want my words to always be few enough to allow time to hear another's heart.

Lord, help me to speak in such a manner that will not only bring You honor, but will build up Your body on earth. *Amen*

Heaven Can Wait

Every one turns to his own course,
like a horse plunging headlong into battle.

Jeremiah 8:6b

I was driving recently on a two-lane highway and fell behind two trucks hauling caskets. On the back of each truck was the company's slogan, "Drive carefully—heaven can wait." On my return trip home during the same day I found myself following still another one of these casket trucks with the same slogan on the back. By this time the message began to sink in.

Am I living every minute of my life carefully each day?

What is my rush today? I asked myself. I couldn't pass the trucks on the curvy road even if I tried. I watched while other travelers drove as Jeremiah described: going their own course like horses rushing headlong into battle. It just wasn't worth the rush, and besides, the slogan was right: heaven *can* wait.

There is a story about a revival preacher who asked for a show of hands from all those who planned to go to heaven when they died. The response was unanimous, except for one old gentleman. He didn't budge, so the preacher thought the man didn't understand the question. A little more loudly this time, the preacher repeated his question. Same response: unanimous except one. Not being able to stand it any longer, the preacher walked down and stood in front of the silent and somber man. "Brother John," the preacher began, "You *do* want to go to heaven when you die, don't you?" The old man replied quickly, "Oh, yes, Reverend, but I thought you might be getting up a load tonight!"

Someone has said that if we combined every wonderful experience of an entire lifetime we would only know a fleeting second of what heaven is like. I do want to go there! But in the meantime, I want to *live carefully*. I want to make the most of every day while heaven is waiting.

Dear Lord, You set the example for living life carefully. Help me to make the most of every minute I have on earth, looking forward to being with You for eternity. Through Christ. *Amen*

Clay in the Potter's Hand

Like the clay in the potter's hand, so are you in my hand.
Jeremiah 18:6b

*A*s a child I loved to make mud pies. I soon learned that the mix of dirt and water had to be just right or the clay would not be moldable. My cousin and I spent many hours rolling out clay to represent various breads and food items. Even today I enjoy kneading bread dough.

Jeremiah learned an important lesson at the potter's shop. When something went wrong with a pot, the potter didn't throw it away; he turned the messed up object into a new creation. The two things required for this were patience and perseverance. The potter had no choice but to stay involved in the remolding process. Otherwise the clay would harden and no longer be pliant.

There is no better place for clay than in the hands of a loving Potter.

God stays involved in our messed-up lives if we allow Him. The Master Potter can transform our flaws and failures. He never leaves us or forsakes us. II Corinthians 5:17 talks about new creations by the touch of God's hand, "If anyone is in Christ, he is a new creation; the old has passed away, behold, the new has come."

God saw how much we needed help in our sinfulness and sent us a Savior. Paul reminds us of how much God loves us and wants to touch our lives. In Romans 5:18 Paul says, "God shows his love for us in that while we were yet sinners Christ died for us." Love can do no more than this: Love can provide a way for our formation and re-formation.

Dear God, thank You for the supreme sacrifice of Your Son in order that we can become new creations. I pray that You will continue to mold and shape me into Your image. Through Christ I pray. *Amen*

Safety Through the Storm

Behold, there arose a great storm on the sea, so that the boat was being swamped by the waves; but he was asleep.

Matthew 8:24

While crossing the English Channel by boat from Amsterdam to London, our family encountered a violent storm. Knowing that our boat was old and headed for dry dock to be repaired added to our alarm. Huge waves slapped against us. The ride became a roller coaster—continuous nosedives followed by abrupt tilting backwards. The old hull cracked and moaned as it struggled to stay intact.

Will my faith free me from fear today?

Most of the five hundred passengers became seasick. The infirmary ran out of medicine for motion sickness. Hardly anyone was sitting upright. Over and over I prayed for safety and remembered John 14:27b: "Let not your hearts be troubled; neither let them be afraid."

I also remembered another storm in another place and another boat being "swamped by the waves." Fear was a part of that scene as well, but there was one striking difference. One passenger in that boat was not afraid. Jesus was sleeping so soundly through the storm that He had to be awakened by the disciples. Matthew 8:26 tells us that Jesus simply asked them, "Why are you afraid, O men of little faith?" He then rebuked the winds and sea, and a great calm followed.

Storms of adversity may come to all of us, but Jesus is very near to us in our need. He shares the difficult and scary times with us. He is the same Lord today as He was on the stormy Sea of Galilee.

When we feel swamped by the waves of sickness, financial stress, misunderstanding, depression, or whatever comes our way, Jesus will be there to see us safely through these stormy times. Lamentations 3:22 says, "The steadfast love of the Lord never ceases, his mercies never come to an end." Truly God's faithfulness is new every morning!

Loving God, thank You that when the storms of life are raging, You stand by us. In Jesus' name. *Amen*

Tunnel Time

I have come as light into the world,
that whoever believes in me may not remain in darkness.
John 12:46

O ne way of getting to the other side of a mountain or a body of water is to go through a tunnel. Our children loved tunnels. They always asked their daddy to blow the car horn when we drove through a tunnel. They loved the echo from the horn and the cacophony of other horns joining in. Knowing others were in the tunnel with us added to the excitement, and, too soon, we would see light at the other end.

Roads and bodies of water have tunnels, and life has some tunnels, too. All of us have had these dark, tunnel times. Christians have slumps. There are times when we wonder if our prayers go anywhere, and maybe even sometimes feel forsaken by God. We know what dark days of the soul feel like. The psalmist expressed his tunnel time when he said, "How long, O Lord? Wilt thou forget me for ever?" (Psalms 13:1a).

We can't remain in darkness when we know the Light of the world.

I don't believe God sends our tunnel times, but He allows them. It is during these times that His image is produced in us. Like a photo being developed, the image is sharpened in the darkroom. It's during the dark time—when we can't see our way clearly—that we are most likely to rely on God.

There is a host of hurting people in the tunnels of life who don't know the source of light. Jesus said that He is the light of the world (John 8:12); We are to be light, too (Matthew 5:14). We are to be light to the discouraged and to those who have lost their way.

We know that morning follows night. Springtime follows winter. We know that the resurrection followed the dark tomb. We know that there is light at the end of the tunnel, even before we see it. We know we don't travel alone. We know that even when we face the tunnel of death, God will be with us. So we will fear no evil, and the light on the other side of this tunnel will never dim. Thanks be to God!

Lord, help me to remember that tunnel times are temporary, but Your love is eternal. In Jesus' name. *Amen*

Thank You

We give thanks to thee, O God; we give thanks;
we call on thy name and recount thy wondrous deeds.

Psalms 75:1

A sincere "thank you" doesn't require an elaborate array of words. Actually, these two words are sufficient if they are spoken from the heart. This truth was brought home to our family through an orthodox Jewish friend who was our family doctor for five years. Dr. Maher Speevak was a loving and kind man—a person whose gentle ways drew our children to him.

Are my prayers authentic and sincere, or are they a jumble of high-sounding words?

Though we insisted, Dr. Speevak never allowed us to pay him for his services. So, as often as possible, we had him in our home for meals. Though it was a meager attempt at repayment, and the food was never as kosher as it should have been, he always seemed to enjoy these times with us around the dinner table.

Often we asked Dr. Speevak to pray our blessing for the food. He would bow his head and say a heartfelt "thank you." That was it. No more words. Sometimes our children would giggle a bit in amusement at his brief blessing. Then he would look us in the eye and say, "Well, isn't that sufficient?" It was. In Dr. Speevak's grateful heart he had called on God and recounted His wondrous deeds in two brief words. He had said all that was necessary and had expressed himself in the way that was appropriate for his personality.

An orthodox bachelor Jew can sit at the table of a Christian minister and his family and, through his sincere "thank you" to our common God, lift us all in a moment of deep gratitude. I won't remember many eloquent table graces I've heard over the years, but Dr. Speevak's genuine "thank you" will be remembered always.

Heavenly Father, You've taught us that the "prayer of a righteous man has great power in its effects" (James 5:16). Help me to pray with power. *Amen*

Queen Anne's Lace and Georgia Vines

For she has done a beautiful thing.
Matthew 26:10b

Growing in many fence rows and along Kentucky's highways are two wild-flowers: Queen Anne's Lace and Georgia Vine. Queen Anne's Lace is a cluster of tiny white flowers shaped like a small, flattened umbrella. Georgia Vine is a bright orange flower shaped like a trumpet. Both are often looked upon as a nuisance by farmers and the state highway department.

I gained a new appreciation of these two lowly plants one summer when I attended a family reunion in my home church in rural Cumberland County. Walking down the aisle of the little white church, I spotted a beautiful bouquet of Georgia Vines and Queen Anne's Lace centered on the communion table. Though it was skillfully arranged, I knew that the person who was responsible for the bouquet had probably never taken a class in floral design. I recalled the many Sundays of my childhood when I had seen similar flower arrangements placed lovingly on the same table by the same woman: "Miss Willie," as we referred to her.

Today I want the Master Designer to put His touch on my life.

Beauty is truly in the eye of the beholder. For the farmer or highway maintenance crew, the plants are a hindrance and need to be destroyed. But to this dear lady, these flowers are works of art waiting to adorn "God's house."

Our lives, I believe, are like Georgia Vines and Queen Anne's Lace. They hold possibilities to display beauty or they hold possibilities to produce irritation. It is only as we let the Master Designer form and transform us that we will provide joy to those around us.

Dear Father, Creator of all we are and ever hope to be, mold us into Your likeness so that we may bless others along life's way. In Jesus' name. Amen

Tumbleweeds and Trees

He is like a shrub in the desert…He is like a tree planted by the water.
Jeremiah 17:6a,8a

I remember the first time I ever saw tumbleweed. Our family was driving across the Western prairie en route to California. For miles the only moving things we saw were those dead looking balls of stubble. What once was a thriving green plant had lost its grip from the earth and withered. And, without anchor, the tumbleweeds rolled aimlessly, guided only by the wind, until they landed against a fence or into a ditch.

In whom I put my trust will determine whether my life is like tumbleweed or a tree.

Jeremiah uses the simile of the non-Christian life being like a shrub in the desert, and the life of a Christian being like a tree planted by water. Contrasted to the small, dead, rootless shrub, that person who puts his or her trust in God is like a tree, the largest of all living plants. This person's faith is rooted deeply, staying in touch with its very source of life. The "tree person" doesn't "fear when heat comes, for its leaves remain green, and is not anxious in the year of drought, for it does not cease to bear fruit" (Jeremiah 17:8).

I believe God calls us to be trees, not tumbleweeds. Trees never stop growing as long as they live. They may suffer from storms, fires, insects, disease, and even people, but when their roots stay anchored firmly to their source of life their life can be restored. Our lives and our homes can be like trees if we put forth the effort to make them so and stay anchored to *our* source of life. God wants us to bear fruit and flowers, to put down deep roots in Him, and be a source of comfort and strength during life's struggles and storms. I believe the day in which we live demands no less.

Loving Lord, forgive me for the times I fail to be anchored to You. Thank you, Lord, for loving us unconditionally, whether we are tumbleweeds or trees, and help me each day to grow into Your likeness. In Jesus' name. *Amen*

"God's on Earth, Too!"

For God is the king of all the earth….
Psalms 47:7a

*I*t was difficult to walk away from the breathtaking beauty of the Grand Canyon. I lingered a little longer than the others in my family as crimson streaks of sunset settled across the western sky. Tourists soaked in the sheer majesty of the scene and a hushed silence fell over all of us. I was awestruck as I looked out over that vast sepulchre carved out over the years by the constant erosion of the mighty Colorado River. I sensed a special presence all around us.

I want to always have a childlike faith.

Too soon the sun was no longer in sight and tourists moved toward the parking lot. Falling along behind two small boys, I could not help but overhear their conversations. They were in a deep discussion on how the Grand Canyon was formed. One boy said, "God didn't help make this big canyon, because He is in heaven." The other little boy stopped deal still and blurted out, "But don't you know that God's on earth, too?"

As I walked toward our car, the profound truth of that statement sank into my mind. Oh, what a difference that would make in our world and in our lives if we never lost sight of that fact. He *is* on earth—in the person of the Holy Spirit. It's no wonder that the prophet Isaiah said a long time ago, "A little child shall lead them" (Isaiah 11:6b).

Father, let me never lose sight of Your powerful presence all about us. Thank You for the blessing of the faith and wisdom of little children. *Amen*

The Responsible Life

Look carefully then how you walk, not as unwise men but as wise, making the most of the time.

Ephesians 5:15,16

While touring one year in Salt Lake City, Utah, our family visited Temple Square and the Mormon Tabernacle. Our guide was a bright, young man who was giving himself as a missionary of the Church of Jesus Christ of Latter-Day Saints. His real drawing power was his sincere belief in and dedication to his church.

How does my life reflect meaning and purpose today?

As we sat waiting for the Mormon Tabernacle Choir to sing, hundreds of young men who were in training to be missionaries sat directly in front of us. I remember thinking that these young people have already looked carefully at how they should walk. In fact, they must be so convinced of this that they are willing to give two of the prime years of their lives to it.

Regardless of their doctrine of faith, these Mormon young adults challenged me by the example of their dedication. I felt compelled to examine my own life. Am I living out my days as though I know the meaning and purpose of life? Am I living responsibly? Do I make each day, each hour, each minute count for eternity? What about the times I fail to show Christ's love to the "least of these"? Do I always try to stop, or at least discourage, gossip? Is my forgiveness genuine toward that person who may have despitefully used me? Do I speak words of kindness and encouragement at every opportunity?

These questions of self-examination are endless and could be asked daily. But more importantly, God's love, mercy, and enabling power are boundless. This gives me hope for living the responsible life and making the most of the time.

Loving God, forgive me for the times I fail to walk carefully and wisely. Show me Your way each day. In Jesus' name. *Amen*

We Need a Light

Again Jesus spoke to them, saying, I am the light of the world;
he who follows me will not walk in darkness, but will have the light of life.
John 8:12

Atop a hill overlooking beautiful Lake Junaluska in North Carolina is a large lighted cross. It is said that during the Depression years funds were not available to keep the cross lighted the year round. So the lights on the cross were turned off during the winter season.

The Southern Railway winds its way through the mountains in this area. The story goes that the train employees who made the daily run by Lake Junaluska missed the lighted cross greatly during those dreary winter months. They missed it so much that they decided to take up a collection among themselves to help with the power bill. The cross became lighted once more and continues to inspire all that view it to this day.

> *How willing am I to sacrifice so that the Light of the world can be lifted up?*

These railway workers *needed* the light of the cross. They said that it reminded them of home, of their families, of their faith in God and each other. The lighted cross became their beacon of hope—a daily reminder that they need not "walk in darkness." The Junaluska cross became a "light of life" for them to the extent that they willingly sacrificed a part of their meager salaries to keep the lights burning.

Just as the railway employees needed the light of the cross during the dark days of the Depression, so do we today. Our roads in life lead us over steep mountains, through deep, dark valleys, and around dangerous bends. But a beacon is available always to us through Jesus, the Light of the world.

Dear Father, forgive me when I fail to walk in Your light. Help me to be able to disperse a little darkness in someone's life today. *Amen*

Passing Through the Waters

When you pass through the waters, I will be with you;
and through the rivers, they shall not overwhelm you.
Isaiah 43:2a

While attending the World Methodist Conference in Hawaii in 1981, our daughter Debbie came close to drowning. Without realizing it was happening, the ocean's undercurrent moved her farther and farther from the shoreline. Suddenly a bystander's urgent cry shocked us to reality: "That girl has drifted too far!" He raced toward the water, and seconds later he swam back, holding Debbie safely in tow.

The Lord comes to us at our point of deepest need.

One moment we were a family enjoying a few minutes of the majestic beauty of the white-capped blue Pacific. The next moment we were experiencing a near tragedy. The waters almost overwhelmed Debbie, but, thank God, someone saw her in time.

Often life's circumstances can feel just as overwhelming. We pass through deep "waters" that hold potential danger and suffering, but God has promised to be with us through it all.

Sorrow can be deep waters. Most of us know what it feels like to be overcome with grief. Whether this grief stems from loss through death, divorce, financial crisis, or some other trial, we can claim God's promise: "Lo, I am with you always" (Matthew 28:20b).

Sin can lull us into deep waters because its undercurrent is subtle and insidious. When we're drifting we may not see dangers ahead. But I Corinthians 10:13 tells us that with each temptation God is faithful to provide a way of escape.

Coping with sickness can be a time of deep waters, too. Those dark nights of the soul seem to stalk every family at some point in life. During these times our Lord hovers ever nearer. When we can no longer walk alone, He carries us. Paul said in II Corinthians 12:9 that God's power is made perfect in weakness.

I am so thankful that our rescuer is with us through the deep waters of life. But, like Debbie in her time of danger, we must trust the One who knows the way to safety.

Merciful Lord, thank You for Your watchful care over us, not only in the deep waters but also all along the shore. *Amen*

Our Good Samaritans

A Samaritan, as he journeyed, came to where he was;
and when he saw him, he had compassion.

Luke 10:33

A gloomy cloud hung low that muggy July day in 1973 as we prepared to leave. Unable to shake my unusual feelings of apprehension, I shared them with Wally. He reasoned, "We need to get on the road. Mom and Dad have already started by now."

There seemed to be no *real* reason not to take our two children to meet their grandparents at a halfway spot on I-65. They had looked forward to this annual visit. We started our journey south, and about thirty minutes later we were hit head-on by a tractor trailer truck pulling a mobile home. God in His wonderful mercy spared all four of us from death.

To whom can I show mercy and compassion as I journey through this day?

I recall my simple prayer as I realized what had happened. "Lord, please help us." And He did. Good Samaritans—all total strangers—began to minister to our needs. A woman shared her clean beach towel for my bleeding face. A policeman took our shivering children out of the drenching rain and put them in his car. A trucker used a log chain to pull the wreckage off Wally's crushed leg. Someone covered him with a tarpaulin to keep him dry as he lay on the pavement. Another truck driver agreed to search until he located Wally's parents at a nearby rest stop.

All the other good Samaritans who came our way made the difficult days and months that followed easier. They truly were our ministering angels. We can never thank all these people or attempt to repay them—except to be good Samaritans ourselves.

Thank You, Lord, for sparing our lives. Help us to be faithful in sharing Your love with the broken in our world. In Jesus' name. *Amen*

Our Bad Side

Do ye look on things after the outward appearance?
II Corinthians 10:7a (KJV)

*O*h, you have your *bad side* turned toward Wally!" our friend said to me in dismay as she entered the hospital room. I can still feel the sting from that remark. In my heart I knew what she meant; she was concerned that no added stress be put upon Wally since his injury in the accident was much more serious than mine. But my heart was also telling me that I was doing well just to sit by his bedside, bad side or no bad side! The stares at my facial cuts and bruises as I came to the room were enough. Once inside, I didn't care to be reminded again of how I looked.

Today I will try to see the real person behind the scars and bruises.

Since that time I've pretty well covered my facial scars with makeup. I seldom think about them once they are covered, but I've often thought about the "bad side"—the scars and wounds each of us has on the inside. My friend saw my outward appearance; she didn't know what was in my heart that day in the hospital room.

Do we do the same? Do we tend to see only outward appearances? Most of us have some bruises and scars that we've sustained in life. Sometimes these manifest themselves through negative attitudes, fear, worry, intolerance, envy, jealously, lust, greed, low self-image and numerous other ways.

When these are called to our attention we feel the sting. We feel misunderstood. We try to cover the scars that cause the hurt. But, like me with my makeup, the cover-up is only temporary. Eventually the makeup either comes off or is removed.

Only God's love can cover the scarred, bad sides of us. Only His love and healing grace as revealed on Calvary can cover the scars of sin in our lives—both hidden and revealed. I Peter 4:8 says, "Above all hold unfailing your love for one another, since love covers a multitude of sins." I'm so glad that God looks through eyes of love—not at the outward appearance, but at our heart.

Lord, thank You for accepting us as we are—bad side, scars, warts and all! May Your love continue to make us whole. *Amen*

His Grace Is Sufficient

He said to me, "My grace is sufficient for you."
II Corinthians 12:9a

*A*fter our family was involved in the automobile accident, I felt a deep desire to share a verse of Scripture with our congregation. Doubts about attempting to stand before a crowd of people began to plague me. Could I keep my composure? Would the people be repulsed by the bruises and stitches on my face? Would my word mean anything to anyone?

That first Sunday morning back at church found me walking to the pulpit. I looked into the eyes of a loving congregation and simply said, "What I want to tell you today is that God's grace is sufficient." I said very little more except to offer my sincere thanks for their arms of compassion that had been extended in countless ways to our family.

God's wonderful free grace will sustain us, both in life and in death.

Years later I received a call from a member of that church who had just undergone heart surgery. He said, "Do you remember the verse you shared at church after your accident?" It seemed like ages ago, but I remembered. "Yes," I answered. "Well," he said, "I'm calling to tell you that the same Scripture has just brought me through heart surgery!"

God's grace is truly sufficient for injuries, for surgery, for thorns in the flesh, and even for the thorns on the brow of our Lord. Grace is a gift from God unearned. It's a gift worth receiving; in fact, it's priceless!

Merciful Father, we are so grateful for Your grace made possible through our Lord. Help us to experience it each day of our lives. Through Christ our Lord. *Amen*

A Gift of Love

For the wages of sin is death, but the free gift of God is eternal life in Christ Jesus our Lord.
Romans 6:23

*D*avid got to know six-year-old Johnny during a summer YMCA camp. They stayed in touch the following fall, and one of David's roommates in college became interested in helping the little boy. Johnny had longed for a new bike for his birthday, so the roommate offered to buy one. David immediately called Johnny's mother to see if giving him a new bike would present any problem. Her initial response was silence, then quiet sobs. David's first thoughts were, *I've blown it. I've made her feel inadequate as a mother.*

How can I share God's free gift of love with someone today?

Shortly, Johnny's mother regained her composure and explained to David that the gift was an answer to prayer. She was a single parent, struggling financially, and unable to buy her son the gift he wanted most.

So David made the three-hour round trip to Madisonville and delivered the new bike in time for Johnny's birthday. The little boy was ecstatic! He repeatedly hugged the bike and David. David asked, "Johnny, do you know *why* this bike was given to you?" "Because you knew I wanted one!" he answered with a tinge of arrogance. David pursued the question, "But for what other reason, Johnny?"

Seconds passed. Then looking soberly at David, Johnny replied, "Because you love me."

David smiled, knowing Johnny had learned the deeper meaning behind the gift. He said, "That's right. It *is* because I love you. Now, listen carefully. Someone gave me a gift of money that bought the gift for you. I didn't earn or deserve the money. Neither did you earn or deserve it. It is purely a free gift of love."

Johnny listened intently as David continued. "This is like God's free gift of love through his Son, Jesus. We really don't deserve it. We didn't earn it. But He gave us Jesus simply because He loves us so much. Now, Johnny, every time you look at this bike, remember God's gift of love to you." Johnny's expression showed that he understood, and his life since then has proven it.

Father, thank You so much for the gift of eternal life through the greatest gift of all—Your only Son. In His name. *Amen*

From Hardship to Happiness

I consider that the sufferings of this present time are not worth comparing with the glory that is to be revealed to us.
Romans 8:18

Standing for one's convictions isn't always easy. Our children experienced many struggles during high school and college days because of their commitment to the Lord. Some of those experiences were very painful. During one of David's struggles in college, I remember sharing the analogy of how the butterfly suffers to break its way out of the ugly, binding cocoon. It's a difficult process that requires time and energy and perseverance. But the joy of freedom at last, when the shackles of the cocoon are gone, makes it worth it all.

Our Savior and Lord was also a suffering servant.

Struggles can be redemptive. Hardship can lead to happiness. I'm told that if someone were to try to help the butterfly break out and set it free prematurely, it would never be able to fly! The struggle and suffering required to sever the bondage of the cocoon are necessary to produce strength enough to soar later. The end result of the hardship for the butterfly produces happiness.

Sometimes we feel weighed down and totally depleted of energy and motivation due to suffering. We may feel that God has hidden His face from us. Hebrews 12:11 says, "For the moment all discipline seems painful rather than pleasant; later it yields the peaceful fruit of righteousness to those who have been trained by it."

David endured the taunts and threats at Vanderbilt. The struggles David experienced on campus didn't feel redemptive when they occurred. But later he was elected student body president and established a multi-million dollar minority scholarship fund for forthcoming generations. Had David not been faithful to God during the times of struggle, I doubt that either of those accomplishments would have happened.

Like the butterfly breaking out of the bondage of its cocoon, our struggles will all be worth it. Let us stand firm in our faith!

Dear God, thank You for life's experiences that train and strengthen us. You are faithful, and we know that You will not allow our experiences to be wasted. Through Christ our Redeemer. Amen

Direction for Our Steps

A man's mind plans his way, but the Lord's directs his steps.

Proverbs 16:9

*D*uring his early twenties, David spent a summer in Washington D.C. working as an intern for Senator Howard Baker. The area of the city in which he lived was not the safest place to be. More than once David experienced some frightening moments, but each time he felt God directing his steps.

What a comfort it is to know that even in our times of fear and loneliness, we are never alone.

One of these times occurred as David returned to his boarding house after picking up a "care package" from home. He noticed two men parked in a car by the curb whose eyes seemed glued to the package. Picking up his pace, David whispered a prayer for protection. Suddenly the car doors opened and one of the men demanded, "Whatcha got in the box, boy?"

Wanting to pitch the box and run, David recalled his grandma's towels inside. Then he blurted out the truth, "All that's in this box is towels and sheets that belonged to Grandma. Please don't take them!" The two strangers stomped angrily back toward their car. David walked on in the safety God provided.

On another occasion David found himself lost. That can happen easily in Washington with its "spider web" layout of streets. Dusk was falling and no one was in sight to offer direction. Fear and loneliness felt overwhelming to him as he searched for street signs.

Suddenly a beautiful butterfly appeared. Even with the shadows of night all about, the butterfly was bright and colorful. He said he felt as if God were reminding him of His presence with him, even in the heart of our crime-ridden nation's capital.

Shortly, David saw a familiar street sign. God had once again ordered his steps. He was not far from his boarding house after all. But, more importantly, he was very close to his heavenly Father who directed him all the way.

Loving God, I am so grateful that, through Your Holy Spirit, You always direct our steps. Help us to stay sensitive to Your direction. In Jesus' name. *Amen*

In God's Image

God created humankind in his image.
Genesis 1:27a (NRSV)

*H*ave you ever walked by mirrors that distort your image? You suddenly find yourself staring at a person with toothpick legs, a squatty, broad body, and a head that hardly looks human. This experience can make you want to find a mirror that will give you a more accurate picture—quickly.

Mirrors can reflect images we don't like. It's interesting to observe people as they pass a mirror. Some straighten their hair or clothing. Some pull their shoulders back for better posture. Some appear pleased with the picture of themselves. I usually think or say something about my need to lose weight. Stepping into a bathroom recently, I noticed a painful grimace on a person's face. As she looked into the mirror, I spoke to her reflection. "Is anything wrong?" I asked. "No," she answered softly, "I'm just giving myself a good talkin' to about my weight!"

The only reflection of ourselves that really matter is the image we see in God's eyes.

We need to remember that God's image of us is not the image we see in a mirror. It is not the image we hold of ourselves or the image others may hold of us. If we could see ourselves as God sees us, we would see ourselves as precious and honored and loved (Isaiah 43:4). God's image of us comes from his heart. We are precious—so important to Him that He would allow His Son to die for our salvation. We are honored—even to the point of calling us His children and joint-heirs with Christ. We are loved—He said it through His Word, through His Son, through His actions.

When we are convinced of how God sees us, it makes a difference in how we see ourselves. How do you see yourself today? Is there a part of you or of your past that makes it difficult to feel loved and accepted? Then trust God's Word that reflects how He sees us: precious and honored and loved.

Loving Father, help us to see others and ourselves through Your eyes. In Jesus' name. *Amen*

Nurseries for Christians

*Train up a child in the way he should go,
and when he is old he will not depart from it.*

Proverbs 22:6

*I*n a back alley of Gloucester, England, the Sunday school was born. In the early 1780s Robert Raikes began gathering a group of poor and uneducated children from the streets to hold the first sessions of school on Sunday. No public schools existed at that time. Raikes, a newspaper editor, used his newspaper to promote the school on Sunday, and it made a great difference. The children grew up to be godly parents and raised godly children. These areas where the Sunday school began became the most orderly and peaceful in the city.

We are never too young—or too old—to be trained as Christians.

It's no wonder that during our visit to this area a few years ago, we could sense the awe and gratitude toward this man from the townspeople. We were told that preachers of that day frowned on this new type of school, but a man called John Wesley stepped in. He was one of the few churchmen who saw the potential this new idea held. Wesley suggested that these schools on Sunday could become nurseries for Christians.

Nurseries for Christians! Isn't that the very heart of the Sunday school program? It's what we need today—all of us, children, youth, and adults. We all need a place where we can be loved, nurtured, and cared for. We need a place where we can be trained in the way we should go; we never outgrow this need.

Robert Raikes had a great idea, but he also put muscle to it. The Sunday school didn't just happen. He went to the poor districts in Gloucester and brought the pupils to class. If they needed clothing, he saw to it that they had some. Then Wesley added his support and encouragement, all of which was needed for the Sunday school to be successful. How grateful I am for those persons who helped birth and nurture this vital part of the church—nurseries for Christians—down through the years.

Loving Father, thank You for those who have gone before us and made the way easier for us. Help us to be nurtured so that we in turn may nurture others. *Amen*

Cleansing the Soil

If we confess our sins, he is faithful and just, and will forgive our sins and cleanse us from all unrighteousness.

I John 1:9

How could a common potato remove salt from soil? I pondered that thought as Wally, Debbie, and I traveled the beautiful countryside of the Netherlands. A land that once was covered by the North Sea had become productive. Through a feat of modern engineering, dikes were built and salty seawater was drained from much of the area.

What area of my life needs God's cleansing and healing touch today?

But it was the Irish potato that became the answer to cleansing that soil of the excess salt. The Dutch farmers discovered that if potatoes were planted for several years in succession they absorbed enough salt to make the soil usable. These potatoes could not be eaten; they were laden with salt. Tons of potatoes were sacrificed during this cleansing of the soil.

As I listened to our tour guide, I began to think of what Jesus did for us. Our lives were full of sin. They were unproductive. There was no way that we, in our own strength, could rid our lives of sin's residue. We could have the appearance of being cleaned up—drained of the most obvious sins and hidden from sight. But sin, without Jesus entering the depths of our souls for cleansing, is still on the inside.

It is through the sacrifice of Christ that the soil of our soul is cleansed. It is only through the entry of God's Son into this world that we can ever be salvaged from sin's destructive power. Through Christ our lives can be freed from sin and become productive and beautiful!

Loving Father, we praise You for giving us Jesus—Your sacrificial Lamb—in order that we may be cleansed and made whole. In Jesus' name. *Amen*

Hope for the Future

There is hope for your future, says the Lord.
Jeremiah 31:17a

*N*orman Cousins said, "The medical profession would cease to exist were it not for the hopes of patients."[1] Hope is certain. It is alive. It is real. We can hold onto hope when we go through life's difficult times.

None of us escape suffering and disappointment. We know what it means to have a dream die and face the challenge of dreaming a new dream. With hope in our hearts we can look beyond the temporary trials to a better day. Hope lifts our eyes and hearts to the One who can and will make things happen. Things may not happen in the way we want, but we can trust the end result to ultimately work for our good.

Christian hope opens the door to the future.

We live in a cynical world. The world doesn't encourage or nourish hope. Only God can instill hope in our hearts. Only a resurrected Christ can assure us that hope conquers. Only the Holy Spirit can empower us to live through the dark days and believe better days are ahead.

We can believe God's Word that says there is hope for the future. Even if we never realize our dreams here on earth, we who are in Christ can know that one day in heaven things will be better. Sin, suffering, and sorrow are temporary. I Peter 1:3 says, "Blessed be the God and Father of our Lord Jesus Christ! By his great mercy we have been born anew to a living hope through the resurrection of Jesus Christ from the dead."

We can have hope for the future *and today* when we put trust in the living Lord.

Dear Lord, thank You for the assurance of that which we cannot see. We place our trust in You because You are the source of hope. *Amen*

God Watches His Children

For the eyes of the Lord are upon the righteous,
and his ears are open to their prayer.
I Peter 3:12a

*I*t was reported recently on television that a man in Staten Island, New York, built a hedge maze on his property. The maze, built in memory of his wife, was to be a place for their children to play.

Realizing the children might sometimes become frightened and lost in the hedge maze, the owner built a castle overlooking the play area. From a lookout tower in the castle, someone could keep a watchful eye on the children. If one child became frightened the watchman would be sent immediately to comfort and help the child.

Will I see the needs and hear the hearts of the lost today?

This seems to be a modern day parable of the way our heavenly Father watches His children. Peter was talking about this in our passage for today. It is comforting to know that God watches over us through the mazes of life. His eyes are always upon us. His ears are always open to us. When we are lost and become frightened, He sends His Counselor to guide us and His angels to guard us. God is so good!

Heavenly Father, thank You for Your watchful eye and listening ear. Help us to not only receive Your care, but share it with Your children. In Jesus' name. *Amen*

We Need a Bethany

Jesus came to Bethany where Lazarus was, whom Jesus had raised
from the dead. There they made him a supper.

John 12:1b,2a

*J*esus must have stopped often at the home of Mary, Martha, and Lazarus. They were close friends, and enjoyed meals together. The Scripture says, "Now Jesus loved Martha and her sister and Lazarus" (John 11:5).

Jesus needed a place to go like this home at Bethany. He needed a haven where He could leave the dusty road awhile and be nurtured and loved. We all need a Bethany. Pastors and Christian workers especially need a Bethany. A pastor is expected to be an administrator, counselor, financial expert, preacher, friend, and, in many cases, a spouse and parent as well.

Those who help others need to recognize the need for help as well.

When does the pastor have a Sabbath? When does he or she have an opportunity to receive spiritual nourishment? Too often the answer is never, resulting in burnout, depression, anger, and bitterness.

Jesus knew the need for replenishing the soul. He practiced going apart with both His Father and friends. He encouraged His disciples to do the same. After one of their missions, the disciples reported to Jesus all they had done and taught. He knew they needed rest. "Come away by yourselves to a lonely place, and rest awhile," He advised (Mark 6:31). William Barclay calls this the "rhythm of the Christian life": serving people and returning for renewal.[2]

We can face life more successfully if we find a time and place for our Bethany. When God touches our deepest longings and needs, nurtures us, and empowers us, then we, like Jesus, can move back out on the dusty roads of life.

Dear God, help us to find our Bethany where we can be restored. And, as our spirits are renewed, help us to return to serving others. In Jesus' name. *Amen*

Promises Proven True

This God—His way is perfect; the promise of the Lord proves true.
II Samuel 22:31a

One of the first four-word sentences spoken by our little granddaughter Katie was, "I will stay still." These words made all of us happy, not only because of her beginning awareness of the need to follow instructions, but also because she was simply talking!

I doubt that Katie kept that promise of staying still very long, but God's promises are kept. They can be trusted. After hearing of Katie's "I will" promise I began to think of the many "I will" promises of our Lord. Here are only a portion of them:

Today and everyday I want to say what I mean and mean what I say.

- I will make you fishers of men (Mark 1:17).
- I will give you the keys of the kingdom (Matthew 16:19a).
- I will give you rest (Matthew 11:28).
- I will pray the Father, and He will give you another Counselor, to be with you for ever (John 14:16).
- I will come again and take you to myself (John 14:3).
- I will not leave you desolate; I will come to you (John 14:18).
- I will draw all men to myself (John 12:32).
- I will love him and manifest myself to him (John 14:21b).
- I will raise him up at the last day (John 6:40b).

All the promises of Jesus are proven true. Our willingness to believe them can make all the difference in our lives. Family and friends may make promises that cannot or will not be kept, but not so with our Lord. His Word and His deed are one and the same. Wouldn't it be wonderful if this could be said of us who bear His name?

Dear Lord, we believe and take comfort in the promises in Your Word. Help our lives to reflect this trust. In Your name we pray. *Amen*

Our Seal of Heritage

He has put his seal upon us and given us his Spirit
in our hearts as a guarantee
II Corinthians 1:22

Family heritage is important. Our son makes sure that the "R" for his middle name of Radford is always in his name. He's even had an ordination certificate and church marquee redone because the "R" was left out of his name. Our daughter used the longer version of both grandmothers' first names when naming our granddaughter Katherine Elizabeth.

With God's seal on my soul, I want my life to reflect His Son.

Family names and crests are important. A set of crests hangs in our den. But far more important is the seal of Christ on our lives. He not only has put His seal on us, but also confirms it in our hearts through the Holy Spirit—as a guarantee! II Timothy 2:19 says, "But God's firm foundation stands, bearing his seal: 'The Lord knows those who are his.'"

The Greek word for seal means genuineness of ownership. When God's seal is on us and His Spirit has been given to us, we are no longer our own. Only God can claim genuine ownership. He, through the sacrifice of His Son Jesus, paid the price for us. Paul reminded the church at Corinth, "You were bought with a price. So glorify God in your body" (I Corinthians 6:20). In other words, we need to live in such a way that others will know God's seal is on us.

Our earthly heritage is important, but the seal on us as a child of God is much more important. With this blessing comes responsibility. Ephesians 4:30 says, "Do not grieve the Holy Spirit of God, in whom you were sealed for the day of redemption." I'm thankful for the seal of my heritage, but more thankful for God's seal on my soul.

Holy Spirit, thank You for sealing my inheritance as a child of God. Help me never to forget that I belong to Jesus. In His name. *Amen*

The Spirit Makes the Master

*Create in me a clean heart, O God, and put a
new and right spirit within me.*
Psalms 51:10

A sign at one of the entrances to the campus at Western Kentucky University in Bowling Green, Kentucky, reads, "The Spirit Makes the Master." I don't know the origin of this quote, but I believe it's a statement of truth. *Webster's New World Dictionary* defines a person's spirit as the "thinking, motivating, feeling part of man."[3] Without spirit we would be lacking in courage and vigor. Without spirit we would merely exist rather than seek the higher purpose for living.

Will my contact with people today leave them discouraged, unaffected, or lifted up?

Along with a clean heart, the psalmist David was praying for a new and right spirit. This could well be a model daily prayer for each of us. I know that my heart needs cleansing and my spirit needs to be renewed and made right—every day of my life.

Our spirits can be either energized or depleted by another person's spirit. We've all been around those persons who drain us, leaving us feeling exhausted. There are those persons who have little effect on us; we soon forget the time spent with them. But there are those with the right spirit who strengthen us, encourage us, and lift our spirit. We remember our time with those persons long after we leave them. They help us reach our full, God-given potential. They enable us to master our goals. They inspire us to live out our days feeling that life is worthwhile. It's the person with the contagious, positive spirit that will likely master the challenges and struggles in day-to-day living. I want to be this kind of person every day.

Loving God, create in me a clean heart and put a new and right spirit within me each day. Help me to be a help instead of a hindrance. In Jesus' name I pray. *Amen*

Feeding the Soul

Jesus said to them, "I am the bread of life; he who comes to me shall not hunger, and he who believes in me shall never thirst."

John 6:35

The soil must have certain nutrients. When these nutrients become depleted, they need to be added to the soil. Farmers test the soil to see exactly what nutrient is missing. If the soil that grows our food is depleted of these nutrients, then people have to take vitamins and mineral supplements to make up for the soil's deficit.

Christ offers us life now and in eternity. It's up to us to receive it.

Our bodies need certain nutrients in order to function properly. And just as the soil and human body require nourishment, so does the soul. When Jesus called Himself the "bread of life," He was saying that just as bread sustains life, our faith is sustained by our relationship with God. Jesus is the essential nutrient for the feeding of the soul. The hungry heart can never be satisfied without Christ. No searching of the human mind or longing of the human heart can be fully satisfied without Jesus. He said, "I am the way, and the truth, and the life; no on comes to the Father, but by me" (John 14:6).

Nothing nor anyone except Jesus can satisfy the emptiness experienced when we neglect the bread of life. Sports can't fill this void. Material things can't fill it. People can't fill it. Jeremiah 31:25 says, "I will satisfy the weary soul, and every languishing soul I will replenish."

We're told that when a person is starving for food, he will feel the pangs of hunger only for a time. When he becomes weak and dulled he loses the desire to eat. Spiritual starvation works much the same way. At first we really miss reading God's Word and our devotional materials. We feel the void when we fail to pray and wait upon the Lord. We miss worshiping in God's house. Then we begin to become weakened and dulled. We lose our desire to feed our souls. Spiritual starvation takes hold, and the door for Satan to enter has been flung open.

I trust that your reading these words today has reminded you to return to your soul's only way to survive: Jesus.

Father, help us realize the subtle danger in neglecting to nourish our souls. Woo us back to the bread of life every day. *Amen*

An Inner "Have-To"

He said to them, "How is it that you sought me?
Did you not know that I must be in my Father's house?"
Luke 2:49

Have you ever experienced a feeling of "I must"? I call such an experience an "inner have-to." Jesus was twelve years old when an inner compulsion caused Him to remain in the temple long after His parents had left. Mary thought He was with Joseph and Joseph thought He was with Mary. But Jesus was with neither of His earthly parents because He felt He must be with His heavenly Father.

The Holy Spirit empowers us to carry out each and every inner "have-to."

There is a story of a Mexican family in southern California. The mother died leaving a family of eight children. The oldest girl, at age sixteen, was very small and frail, and she felt the load of caring for the whole family upon her shoulders. Tenderly, she kept the children clean, fed, and in school. One of the neighbors complimented her for doing this, but also said, "You don't have to. You could get out of it." The young girl reflected for a moment on the idea of being free from her labor, then replied, "Yes, that's true. But what about the 'have to' that's inside me?" She knew about an inner compulsion that went beyond the outward call of duty.

Another example took place one evening at David and Karen's home. Just as Debbie and Steve were leaving, they saw a furniture truck pull up in front of the house. Steve said immediately, "We can't leave now. They will need our help placing the furniture." He knew that furniture would take some time to unload, and that David had an early appointment at the church. At the risk of being late arriving home, an "inner have-to" turned them around to go back and help.

Jesus embodied that quality of love that goes beyond the expected. He began modeling it at the early age of twelve, and it compelled Him ultimately to go to Calvary. Throughout His life, He acted out of His conviction. In John 9:4a He said, "We must work the works of him who sent me, while it is day." That challenge is ours as well.

Father, because of Your love shown to us through Jesus, we have experienced love. Help us to do what Your love is calling us to do. In Jesus' name. Amen

Jesus at Our Fingertips

In thy presence there is fullness of joy,
in thy right hand are pleasures for evermore.
Psalms 16:11b

Parents can learn a lot from children. I know I've learned a lot from mine. In times of trial and trouble David has often touched his thumb and four fingertips to spell J-E-S-U-S. This quick and simple activity can be done anytime and anywhere, but it is a powerful reminder that Jesus is as close as our fingertips.

Jesus said, "I am with you always, to the close of the age" (Matthew 28:20b).

The disciple Thomas was distressed at Jesus telling about His plans to go to the Father. Thomas told Jesus he didn't know the way to where He was going. Jesus reminded him that the answer was close to him—at his fingertips—when He said to Thomas, "I am the way…" (John 14:6a). Later on, Thomas actually had to place his fingertips in the scars in Jesus' hands in order to believe that He was Christ resurrected. As close as our fingertips—that's where Jesus is!

In our times of darkness and doubt, we can remember just how close Jesus is to us by spelling His name on our fingertips. He's all we need; He is the way to the Father. Touching the fingertips doesn't summon Jesus to us—He's already there—it just serves as a reminder of His closeness.

So, today when I feel alone—separated from family, friends, or maybe even distanced from my heavenly Father—I want to remember that I am not alone. I may try touching my fingertips spelling J-E-S-U-S to once again experience that joyful sense of nearness to my Lord.

Dear Jesus, I am so thankful that You never leave us or forsake us. Help me to always remember just how near You are to me and my family. *Amen*

Altar in the Hayloft

There he built an altar to the Lord, and called on the name of the Lord
Genesis 12:8b

*A*bram built an altar under "the oak of Morah" at Schechem (Genesis 12:6). Wally's dad made an altar out of a bale of hay in the hayloft of his dairy barn. There, like Abram, he called on the name of the Lord. After the morning chores were completed, Mr. Thomas would make his way up to the hayloft. And before he began his day, he lifted each member of the family to God in prayer.

Where and when will I make my altar today?

For a long time none of us knew about this sacred spot in the barn loft. Then one day Mr. Thomas told Wally he had something to show him at the barn. The dairy cows, the milking machines, and the cooler—all the equipment was sold many years ago. Wondering what there could yet be to see in the old, empty barn, Wally obediently followed his aging dad. They slowly climbed the stairs to the hayloft and made their way over to the northeast corner. His dad stopped, looking wistfully down at the bale of hay. Finally he said, "Son, that's where I kneel every morning and pray for my family."

Today, Mr. Thomas is no longer with us. Yet, a special presence seems to linger there in the hayloft, especially over in that northeast corner. One can almost hear the echo of a low, gentle voice lifting the names of his family to a loving heavenly Father.

Family altars—will they become completely extinct? I pray not, because I believe that today more then ever they are needed. Those prayers prayed by Mr. Thomas were simple, sincere words, not long, high-sounding phrases. But they came from a heart filled with love. I believe they've made a difference in each of our lives. I believe, too, that God will meet each of us at our special altar, be it under an oak tree, in the hayloft, or in a closet. The important thing is that we find a place—our place—to call on the name of the Lord.

Loving Father, help me to find a time and a place to call on Your name every day of my life. *Amen*

A Love Cover

He brought me to the banqueting house,
and his banner over me was love.

Song of Solomon 2:4

When my mother was buried in the city cemetery in Burkesville, Kentucky, my brother Allen added a special touch to the gravesite. He brought fresh, green sod from the yard of our home and carefully placed the "love cover" over our mother's grave. He said, "I thought Mother would need a blanket."

Whether our needs be great or small, God's love can cover them all!

This verse of Scripture from the Song of Solomon is an expression of human love. But it is also expressive of the deepest love of all: God's love for His children. His love for the world was so great that He was willing to give up His only Son to cover the world with love. The world desperately needed a blanket of love, so God brought love from His home—heaven—and covered us all through the sacrifice of Jesus.

God's banner of love covers all our needs—our sickness and our sin, our doubts and our discouragement. It covers our heartache and sorrow when we place our loved ones beneath the sod. And, in life, His banner of love is our shelter from the storms that lash out at us.

What in your life needs a covering of love today? Your finances? God's Word says, "My God will supply every need of yours according to his riches in glory in Christ Jesus" (Philippians 4:19). Are you discouraged or depressed? Psalms 55:22 says, "Cast your burden on the Lord, and he will sustain you." Do you feel lonely and forsaken? Jesus promises, "I will not leave you desolate; I will come to you" (John 14:18). Are you afraid? Jesus said, "Let not your hearts be troubled, neither let them be afraid" (John 14:27b). Do you feel condemned? Romans 8:1 promises, "There is therefore now no condemnation for those who are in Christ Jesus."

I don't know the area of your life that needs a cover of love today. But I do know that there is *no* need beyond God's reach, whether it is a gravesite or a grave sin.

Heavenly Father, thank You for covering this world with Your wonderful love through Your Son, Jesus, our Savior. *Amen*

The Whole Armor

*Put on the whole armor of God, that you may be able
to stand against the wiles of the devil.*
Ephesians 6:11

The sign on David's shower stall simply said, "armor." It was a daily reminder for him to put on the whole armor of God before facing the day ahead. Even though the devil is a defeated power, he is alive and well. It's up to us to arm ourselves and take authority in Jesus' name in order for the devil to flee. I Peter 5:8 says, "Be sober, be watchful. Your adversary the devil prowls around like a roaring lion, seeking some one to devour."

Paul knew what a Roman soldier's armor looked like; he had been chained to one. Part by part Paul translates the Roman armor into Christian terms:

Paul knew the importance of each part of the armor, but he reminds us to put on the whole armor.

1. *The belt of truth.* In the Roman soldier's tunic, the belt gave him freedom of movement. Because we know truth, we can move quickly and confidently against the evil one.
2. *The breastplate of righteousness.* The Roman soldier wore the breastplate in front and back. When we know who we are in Christ, our self-esteem is covered; it cannot be damaged by Satan on any side.
3. *The sandals of peace.* The type of sandal worn by the Roman soldier was thick-soled and stubbed with nails to give him stability and protection in battle. We can have this protection and peace.
4. *The shield of faith.* The Roman shield was heavy enough to protect the warriors from the fiery darts of the enemy. Faith protects us from Satan's fiery darts of doubt, discouragement, temptation, and mistrust.
5. *The helmet of salvation.* The helmet protects our minds from being muddled and making us vulnerable to the devil's lies.
6. *The sword of the Word of God.* Hebrews 4:12a says, "The word of God is living and active, sharper than any two edged sword." The Holy Spirit can enable us to know the exact verse to use in combat with Satan.

Lord God, thank You for providing a protective armor for us. Help us to always wear it well and faithfully. *Amen*

God Is Good

*For the Lord is good; his steadfast love endures for ever,
and his faithfulness to all generations.*
Psalms 100:5

*J*ust as I began my devotional time, the telephone rang. Debbie's worried voice began, "Mom, Katie is lifeless. She won't eat. She won't speak. She just lies on the couch." I asked if they planned to take her to a doctor, remembering that Katie's pediatrician never works on Saturday. In fact, it was sometimes difficult to see any doctor on Saturday. In the background I heard Steve say, "We'll try," and Debbie hung up.

As your days, so shall your strength be (Deuteronomy 33:25b).

This was the third time for Katie to be sick during the few weeks that school had been in session. Heavy weariness hung over me as I glanced down at my daily prayer list inside the cover of one of the devotional books. Tears overflowed, and I opened my heart to God. "Lord," I prayed, "I can't name all of those people this morning. You know who they are anyway. I'll just bring Katie to You. Lord, please intervene." I sat there staring at the prayer list, wondering how God would work good out of this one.

Exactly ten minutes from the first call, Debbie called back. The tone of her voice was different now. "You won't believe this, Mom! Dr. Salisbury is not only in her office today, but she can take Katie as soon as we can get there."

The God of fresh starts had intervened. Tomorrow will bring more challenges, but our God will be there!

What do you face today? Whatever it is, rest in the assurance that our good God is faithful. His love is steadfast. His mercies are new every morning—customized for each day!

Thank You, dear Lord, that You know our needs and meet them according to Your will. Help me to walk by faith each day and know that You are working all things together for our good. *Amen*

Same on the Inside

Man looks on the outward appearance, but the Lord looks on the heart.
1 Samuel 16:7b

Though we don't like to admit it, most of us have a prejudice of one kind or another. Many of us form opinions before all the facts are known. Often we have biased attitudes which are influenced by our background, temperament, and experience.

Bishop Lawi Imathiu of Kenya shared the story of his prejudice at the Family Life Conference in Nairobi in 1986. His wife Florence experienced a miscarriage and was very ill. He sought desperately among his people for the O+ blood she needed, but found none. Struggling with where to turn for help, Bishop Imathiu met with some white missionary friends. He

If we are in Christ, we are the same on the inside.

shared with them his wife's dire need for a blood transfusion. The missionary friends quickly responded with an offer to give the needed blood.

In relating this story, Bishop Imathiu flashed that big, broad smile of his and with complete honesty confessed, "I really didn't want my wife to have white blood." But, being gravely concerned about her health, he sought the advice of her doctor. The bishop said he wasn't quite ready for the reply, "Oh, of course we can use the blood. Blood is blood!"

So, reluctantly, Bishop Imathiu agreed for the "white blood" transfusion. He said he watched carefully as the first drops of it entered his wife's bloodstream, asking her often if she felt all right. Then he looked straight at some sixty of us from around the world and said, "You know, that white blood really worked!" Mrs. Imathiu improved rapidly, and later she was able to become pregnant again. She gave birth to a healthy child.

Bishop Imathiu concluded his story with his own special kind of candor, "You know, that child was as black as any of the others!" Then in deep sincerity, he added, "Underneath our skins, we are all the same."

Father of us all, thank You for reminders that we are one in You, through Christ our Lord. *Amen*

Redeeming the Times

Thou hast led in thy steadfast love the people whom thou hast redeemed.

Exodus 15:13a

We all have situations in our lives that seem scary, even impossible to get through. A friend called recently to share her deep concern about a potentially divisive situation in a local church. Her heart was already heavy with the needs in her own family, and her voice reflected the weight of her burdens.

Jesus saves our souls and our situations as we place our trust in Him.

As I listened to her talk, I prayed that God would give me wisdom to communicate some word that would be helpful. These thoughts began to flood my mind, and I shared them with my friend: 1) Fight fear; 2) place the church's problems in God's hands; 3) claim Romans 8:28; 4) expectantly watch for the way God will work this for good; 5) seek truth in everything; and 6) take a stand for the truth. I suggested that she say, "Jesus saves _____," and fill in the blank with a name or a concern.

I certainly have no unique wisdom of my own—only that which is available to all from God. I *do* believe that the Holy Spirit helps us in our weakness (Romans 8:26) and teaches us all things (John 14:26).

A week passed and another telephone call came from my friend. This time I could hear in her voice the peace and victory that was in her heart. She said, "There is already evidence of good coming out of this church situation. Truth is being sought *and* discovered." She paused a few seconds and then said, "God is working this for good! I'm trying your suggestion of saying, 'Jesus saves _____,' placing my need in the blank. You know what? It's working, too!"

As with Moses, God's faithfulness is new every morning. Thanks be to God!

Dear God, our times are in Your hands. Thank You for being our Redeemer. In Jesus' name. *Amen*

The Mold Squeeze

Don't let the world around you squeeze you into its own mold.

Romans 12:2 (PHILIPS)

A young pastor had great dreams for making a difference in the world. He found a wonderful wife, graduated from seminary, and was assigned a two-point circuit. He began to share some fresh ideas with his people. Imagine his disappointment when he began to hear the following words adamantly proclaimed from his members: "We've never done things *that* way." The mold squeeze was on! These words can stifle creative leadership and even hinder the work of the Holy Spirit.

Are my convictions and actions tempered by the ways of tradition or by the will of God?

Changes come slowly in the church. New ideas in programming, modes of worship, and outreach ministries are often accepted slowly, if at all. Jesus knew about the squeezing mold of traditionalism. He broke tradition when He ate with sinners and when He healed on the Sabbath.

Jesus always stayed true to His convictions for what was best for the people. His disciples were hungry one day, and Jesus broke with tradition and allowed them to pluck ears of corn on the Sabbath. Love was more important to Jesus than the Law.

Are our lives love-focused? Are we avoiding the world's mold squeeze? Fitting into someone else's mold may be the easy route to take, but it isn't likely to be the way that pleases the Lord. God never changes, but His ways of blessing the lives of His people are forever fresh!

Dear Father, give us courage and boldness to follow Your leading in all things wherever we are. In Jesus' name. *Amen*

Drifting With the Flow

Blessed is the man who endures trial, for when he has stood the test he will receive the crown of life.

James 1:12a

As a small child I wondered why the ferryboat on the Cumberland River had to go *up* the river in order to go directly *across* to the other side. The ferryman patiently explained that in crossing the river, the boat drifts slowly downstream. In order for him to reach his destination on the opposite riverbank, he had to travel against the current several yards upstream.

God is our refuge and strength, a very present help in trouble (Psalms 46:1).

Maneuvering a boat upstream against the natural flow of the water is not an easy task. Neither is it easy for Christians to resist the pressures of the secular world. Business leaders know the temptation to follow the line of least resistance when facing ethical decisions. Politicians know about the pressures of following their deep convictions when they differ from their constituents. Youth experience the power of painful peer pressure. It's not easy to endure trial, but it *is* possible.

Like rowing a boat upstream, protecting one's integrity requires determination and deep commitment. It requires an intentional decision to refuse the route of easy drifting. Easy drifting results in falling short of one's goal. Easy drifting causes us to land in undesirable harbors.

Life will always be an upstream challenge. Yet nothing can overwhelm us as we acknowledge that God is with us. His strong arm can protect us from drifting and carry us safely to the other side.

Dear God, give us the courage to stand for our convictions and the strength needed to refuse drifting with the flow. In Jesus' name. *Amen*

Enthusiasm

Never flag in zeal, be aglow with the Spirit, serve the Lord.
Romans 12:11

"Why is that man making so much noise?" whispered the little boy sitting on the bench in front of me. Bending close to his ear, his mother replied, "He's our camp meeting preacher." In a voice no longer a whisper, the little boy asked, "BUT WHY IS HE SO LOUD?" Laying her paper fan aside and sighing deeply, the young mother attempted still another explanation, "Because he's excited. Now please be quiet!"

My mind began to wander from the preacher's message as I began to think about my own enthusiasm. It was obvious that the evangelist felt enthusiasm. The congregation seemed to be caught up in it. Even a small child was curious about it. Suddenly, the evangelist bellowed out the clincher, "Friends, enthusiasm is a fault for which we all should be accused!"

Psalm 68:3 says, "Let the righteous be joyful; let them exult before God; let them be jubilant with joy!"

At that point I began to deal with the question: *Does my enthusiasm rise or fall according to the circumstances around me?* It's easy to be excited at a ball game or a birthday party. But what about when a negative remark has been made or a "cold shoulder" has been felt? What about the dull, rainy days or the spiritually dry times? Would there be enough evidence to accuse me of having enthusiasm?

Charles Wesley wished for a thousand tongues to sing his Redeemer's praise. If I had only *one* more way to express praise, would I? Paul says that our zeal—our enthusiasm—should never grow weak. Rather, we are to be aglow with the Spirit.

I believe it is only through the aid of the Holy Spirit that joy and enthusiasm can be an abiding part of our day-to-day living.

Dear God, help me to rejoice and be glad because of Your presence with me. Thank You for the honesty of little children who teach us great truths. In Jesus' name. *Amen*

We Never Walk Alone

If we live by the Spirit, let us also walk by the Spirit.
Galatians 5:25

"Your splintered hip may not hold together on its own," came the somber prediction from the bone surgeon. We knew the dim prognosis was realistic. Wally's hip that was crushed in an automobile accident was rejecting the metal pin. There was no choice but to remove the pin.

In what part of my walk today do I need God's help the most?

It was difficult news to hear. Wally had spent four months in a wheel chair and on crutches. He enjoyed the short time of moving toward normalcy, and now he had to do it all over again. Only this time, the hip would have to function without the metal reinforcement. "It's in a thousand pieces," the doctor had described the crushed bone before the initial surgery. He was truthful when he said the splintered bone might not hold together on its own. But we knew that Wally was not alone, for God, our wonderful "I Am," was with us.

Luke 24 tells us about two pilgrims walking the dusty Emmaus Road and how they realized the risen Christ was walking with them. This same Christ who walks with us promised that He would "never fail you nor forsake you" (Hebrews 13:5b). And our Lord is trustworthy.

The metal pin was removed. It was a scary time when Wally put his full weight on his legs, this time without the metal reinforcement. But he was not on his own. The Holy Spirit was present, enabling and empowering each step that he made. Today, the injured leg is stronger than ever!

Do you sometimes feel that you are walking alone in your own strength, fearful of what lies ahead? You can find comfort and courage as Jesus did. Knowing He was facing the cross, He said, "He who sent me is with me; He has not left me alone" (John 8:29a). Wally and I have found this promise to be true—we never have to walk alone.

Loving God, we are grateful for the assurance that we don't have to walk alone. Help us to never lose sight of Your presence through Your Holy Spirit. *Amen*

Mother Duck's Path

Make me to know thy ways, O Lord; teach me thy paths.
Psalms 25:4

I watched the mother duck and her twelve ducklings move from their nest to the lake behind our parsonage. During this journey, the mother duck nudged her babies across more than one busy street, over a four-foot rock wall, and down fifteen steps to the lake. She communicated with her babies constantly, and it was obvious that they understood clearly.

Once the mother duck was at the water's edge, she *really* talked! Ever so slowly she ventured a little further into the water. She dropped her bill into the water and out again, as if she were saying, "Come on, my children! Now you know the way! I've taught you my path."

I've reflected on the example this mother duck set for her little brood. She showed them the path of:

> *If we knew that people were following our path and example, would we make any changes?*

1. Love—by caring for her babies during the weeks of incubation, hatching and during the preparation for leaving the nest.
2. Patience—by carefully and slowly leading the baby ducks from the nest to the real world for which they were created.
3. Courage—by going before the baby ducks, ever guarding them through dangerous traffic and over rough terrain.
4. Freedom—by coaxing and encouraging her babies into the water and showing them the way out into the deep.

Mother duck taught by example. She went ahead of her babies so they would have the courage to follow. We've all had examples to follow; all of us are called upon to be an example. I Timothy 4:12 says, "Set the believers an example in speech and conduct, in love, in faith, in purity." We can be this kind of an example if we follow the model of our Lord who is the Way.

Dear Lord, help us to follow Your path. Help us to trust You. Protect us over the rocky places, and give us the courage to step out in faith when You call us to a task. Through Christ. *Amen*

Transforming the Ordinary

What mighty works are wrought by his hands!
Mark 6:2b

*A*s I folded the clean dish towels, I recalled the many times I had used them at Wally's parents' home. They were a part of the boxes of memories included in our part of the "divide-up." There was the terry cloth towel, the outdated linen "calendar" towel, and there were the towels made from feed sacks.

When God places His hand upon us, we are never the same again.

The feed sack towels, especially, were reminders of my own childhood. Some were faded, floral towels. Others were solid white ones that had become a bit dingy over the years. The floral ones reminded me of the excitement I felt when we were able to get feed for the animals in several floral sacks that matched. Then my two sisters and I knew that one of us would soon have a new dress!

But in this stack of dish towels was one feed sack towel that stood out above all the others. It was a pure white one, and on each end a bright red, hand-crocheted lace had been added. As I held it I thought of the transformation that had occurred with this towel. My mother-in-law brightened its dinginess with commercial bleach, then her hands added the crowning touch of lace. Through her talent of crocheting, an ordinary feed sack was transformed, and the difference her touch made was noticeable and beautiful.

That's how it is when God touches our lives. Through Christ, ordinary persons become brand new creations (II Corinthians 5:17). His hand upon us cleanses us and crowns our lives with His glory. He changes the common and makes it special. He turns darkness into light. He transforms despair into hope. He turns failure into success, sickness into health, death into life!

I need God's transforming touch on my life today.

Dear God, thank You for the power of Your transforming love through Christ Jesus. Help me to not only treasure this rich inheritance, but also share it with others. In Jesus' name. *Amen*

A Time of Silence

For everything there is a season, and a time for every matter under heaven: a time to keep silence, and a time to speak.
Ecclesiastes 3:1,7b

*D*o you ever wish for a time of total silence? Do you need those times when the television is off, the telephone stops ringing, sirens stop sounding, and even the voices of those you hold dear pause for a few minutes? In the book of Ecclesiastes, Solomon tells us there is a time to keep silent.

Sometimes we accomplish more, inflict less pain, create less conflict, and damage less when we keep silent. Our silent times can be our most productive times.

Am I willing to wait in silence in order to better know God?

My niece Judy Branham recently taped five hours of oral history as she listened to her father, my brother Windell, recount his life. This required a good bit of silence on Judy's part, but the results were well worth it. Those tapes are a priceless treasure. Every family member now knows something more about themselves, because we have listened in silence to this description of Windell's life.

When we are willing to wait upon the Lord and listen to Him, the results are worth it. The blessing gained will be a treasure. Time spent in waiting upon the Lord and listening to His still small voice is never wasted. As we come to know more about Him, we come to know more about ourselves.

There are many precious promises about waiting upon the Lord:

- They who wait for the Lord shall renew their strength, they shall mount up with wings like eagles, they shall run and not be weary, they shall walk and not faint (Isaiah 40:31).
- For God alone my soul waits in silence; from Him comes my salvation (Psalms 62:1).
- For the creation waits with eager longing for the revealing of the sons of God (Romans 8:19).

Father, forgive me for failing to listen to You. Help me to remember that time spent with You is the most precious and productive time I'll spend each day. In Jesus' name. *Amen*

Bring to Remembrance

The Counselor, the Holy Spirit, whom the Father will send in my name, he will teach you all things, and bring to your remembrance all that I have said to you.

John 14:26

We lost a dear friend recently. For many days before the death, both Wally and I felt we should call this person. Neither of us acted on our thoughts, and both of us confessed our regret when the word of his death came. God brought this person to our remembrance, but we pushed the thought aside. We became so consumed with what we thought was urgent and important.

The Holy Spirit brings thoughts to my remembrance, but it is up to me to respond.

This experience is not an isolated event; far too often I fail to act on the Spirit's gentle reminders. But from now on, I am committed to trying harder to be sensitive to His leading. I find that often during my morning devotions names of persons are impressed upon my mind. I may not have thought of these persons for weeks or even months. I try to follow up with a card, telephone call, or visit. Sometimes the response confirms God's perfect timing in bringing them to my remembrance.

I'm grateful when God teaches me lessons on remembering. Paul expressed it so well in his letter to his friends at Philippi: "I thank my God in all my remembrance of you" (Philippians 1:3).

Whom would God have me remember today? If I will be still and listen, the Holy Spirit will let me know.

Dear Lord, help me to be still and know that You are God. And as You speak to my heart, help me to respond in the way that pleases You. *Amen*

God's Keys Are Different

I will give you the keys of the kingdom of heaven.
Matthew 16:19a

Lord, help me reach a telephone, I prayed as my truck engine slowly began to die. Creeping along the shoulders of the road with the caution lights blinking, fear welled up within me. Daylight was fading quickly. The noise under the hood worsened. Finally a food mart came into view. I held my breath as the truck crept across the busy highway. Once in the security of the parking lot, the truck motor completely died.

Two hours and a replaced alternator later, the station attendant asked for my keys. I reminded him that he had taken them when he hitched the wrecker to the truck. His face fell; my keys were lost.

> *I will not put my trust in the keys crafted by man but in the keys created by God Himself.*

A locksmith came and replaced the truck key, and the station attendant confidently said, "You can feel safe to drive your truck home now." For the first time during the entire ordeal, tears began to fill my eyes. "I can't go home because I can't get in my home! *I have no keys!*" I said, wanting to add, "*REMEMBER?*"

My watch said 9:00 P.M. as I slumped down on the hard, cold metal bench to wait. I felt homeless and helpless. Wally was in California attending a church meeting. I had been sick for three days and only ventured out long enough to make a brief funeral home visit. *Why had I not stayed home where I belonged?*

After five phone calls I finally located someone with a key to the parsonage. The next morning my keys were found, bent and broken, on the pavement where the truck was hitched to the wrecker. I held the pieces of the keys in my hands. Just seeing them again brought some comfort, but they were useless now. Not one key would work. I recalled the words of Jesus to Peter, "I will give you the keys of the kingdom of heaven." Jesus was speaking of keys that are different. They are lasting. They can be trusted. They open the door to eternal life. These are the keys I want.

Dear Father, thank You for giving us Your Son to open the door to eternal life. Thank You, too, for Your protection and help. In Jesus' name. *Amen*

Beyond Creation

I will lift up my eyes to the hills. From whence does my help come?
My help comes from the Lord, who made heaven and earth.

Psalms 121:1,2

I love being outside. I love digging in God's good earth and planting bulbs and seeds. I have had meaningful worship experiences outside, under a quiet canopy of stars at a retreat. Some of the most memorable times of my life have been when I've experienced nature in all its splendor: seeing the awesome beauty of the Grand Canyon; flying over the amber waves of grain of the Midwest; and feeling the cool spray of mist from Niagara Falls while gazing at the rainbow arched over us. These and many more experiences have centered my thoughts on our Creator God.

This is my Father's world, but I will look to Him for my help.

Nature reminds us of our Creator, but I believe there's more to worship than just being in the outdoors. We must look beyond all the splendor of God's world to God Himself. And God not only wants us to have solitude in the midst of nature, but He also calls us to fellowship with other Christians. He calls us to be challenged by the spoken Word. He calls us to Holy Communion—to remember our Lord's sacrifice for us and experience His grace anew. We might experience an understanding of God's call upon our lives while out in nature, but I believe it would more likely happen in a house of worship.

God reminds the sun to rise and set each day. He directs the fowl of the air to migrate to warmer climates in the winter. God dresses the flowers in all their splendor in the springtime. It is God who planned for the caterpillar to burst from the cocoon into a beautiful butterfly. But of much more importance—of ultimate importance—is God's Son, Jesus, who burst forth from the grave and assures us of life eternal if we believe in Him.

The psalmist looked up to the hills, needing help. He found his answer beyond nature. He found it in the very Creator Himself. You may be searching for help today. If you are, look to the first-born of all Creation as the psalmist did; look to our Savior and Lord!

Dear God, it is beyond my comprehension that You created all the universes. Yet You are at home in my heart, and I am so thankful. Through Christ my Lord. *Amen*

Shared Burdens

Bear one another's burdens, and so fulfill the law of Christ.
Galatians 6:2

At the close of a meeting of pastor's wives, we began to share prayer requests. It seemed that grandmothers in particular were sharing needs of their grandchildren. It occurred to us that we should begin a grandmother's prayer group, and a few months later we met for the first time.

En route to the first prayer meeting, one of the grandmothers who was in my car expressed her reluctance to share her granddaughter's needs. Most of us could identify with those feelings. But once we were together, the Holy Spirit seemed to remove our apprehensions. One by one we shared our concerns. I began by telling of Katie's struggle with autism, then other needs unfolded: Attention Deficit Disorder, Osteogenesis Imperfecta, Diabetes, Treacher Collins Syndrome, Obsessive Compulsive Disorder, profound deafness, and unexplained weight loss and weakness.

A good way to love our family is to pray for them.

We were amazed at the range and severity of our grandchildren's problems, but we felt in our hearts that we had found the key to facing them. We would simply bear one another's burdens, and bring all of them to God in prayer.

Our shared burdens have become lighter burdens. We're seeing improvement in our grandchildren. There is power in prayer. This fact has been documented over and over. Scientific studies at Princeton University and other places are opening doors for increased consultation and cooperation between doctors and clergy. James 5:16 says, "The prayer of a righteous man [or grandmother] has great power in its effects."

Sharing burdens with one another and with God has been a beautiful blessing for this group of grandmothers. Christ has promised that "where two or three are gathered in my name, there am I in the midst of them" (Matthew 18:20). The grandmothers in our prayer group have seen the truth of this promise.

Loving Father, thank You for the blessing of grandchildren. We ask for Your continued healing touch on them and all our loved ones. Through Christ our Lord. *Amen*

A Clear Call

He who calls you is faithful, and he will do it.

I Thessalonians 5:24

*D*inner bells were an important part of my childhood. The dinner bell was used to send out a clear call at mealtime: It was rung to call the family home to eat. But at hours other than mealtime, hearing the dinner bell ring meant there was an emergency of some sort in the community. It could be a serious illness, a death, a fire, or any number of situations. But the reason for ringing the dinner bell had to be clear and honored.

Are we listening to God's clear call?

We can depend on the One who calls us to serve. His clear call may be to return to Him for sustenance and replenishment—so our strength can be renewed and we can return to our fields of labor. His call may be to respond to the emergencies in the lives of His children. His call may be to help the hurting and minister to the needy.

Whenever God calls us, we need to respond. His summons is certain. It can be depended upon because He is faithful. May we always be listening to His clear call upon our lives.

Heavenly Father, thank You for calling us to Your table and to Your service to others. Help us to keep our ears attuned to You and readily respond. In Jesus' name. *Amen*

The Limit of the Possible

Can you find out the limit of the Almighty?
Job 11:7b

A young missionary in China wrote these words to me in 1994: "God can do nothing for me until I get to the limit of the possible." I can attest to the truth in this statement. It's at the point of full surrender that God can step in and do for us what we thought impossible. When I exhaust my own wisdom and strength—and fully trust God to work in my life—He never fails to do so. "All things are possible to him who believes" (Mark 9:23b).

We limit the possible, I believe, by our spirit of hopelessness and lack of faith. I know that my faith is neither what it should be nor what I want it to be. But, like the father asking for his son's healing in Mark 9, I can ask for help by saying, "I believe; help my unbelief!" (Mark 9:24b). Feeling that God's power is limited can inhibit or prohibit God's work in our lives. But to approach anything in a spirit of faith is to make it a possibility.

Will I remember God's limitless power when I feel I've come to the limit of the possible?

The moment that I exhaust my own strength is the precise moment that God can move upon the scene. Job, in the midst of all of his suffering, asked the question, "Can you find out the limit of the Almighty?" (Job 11:7b). He answered himself by saying, "It is higher than heaven…deeper than Sheol…longer than the earth, and broader than the sea" (Job 11:8,9).

God's power and love are limitless! When we realize we have come to the limit of the possible in our own human strength, then all things become possible if we only believe.

Lord, I do believe. Please help me when my faith weakens to always remember that with You all things are possible. *Amen*

Light for the Journey

Thy word is a lamp to my feet and a light to my path.

Psalms 119:105

The headlights of my car pierced the early morning darkness. I felt hopeful that the two-hour trip ahead to attend an autism workshop would be worthwhile. *Just concentrate on driving safely along this dark, lonely road*, I reminded myself.

"The people who walked in darkness have seen a great light" (Isaiah 9:2a).

After about an hour on the road I began to notice long shadows cast across the newly mown pasture fields. A heavy dew hung like shimmering diamonds on the grass reflecting the rays of the sun.

What a beautiful sight to behold! Yet this scene didn't prepare me for the experience that was to follow. In what seemed like an instant, a dazzling bright light penetrated the car's rear window.

I slowed down. Reflected in the rear view mirror was the most beautiful sunrise I have ever seen. White, billowy clouds hovered over the visible half of the sun's bright orange circle. *This is just too beautiful to miss,* I said to myself and pulled off the road to enjoy it.

I felt very close to Christ in that moment, and remembered that Jesus called Himself the Light of the world. The psalmist promised that God's Word would be a lamp to our feet and a light to our path. Sunrises last only for a short time, but God's Word can be light to our path forever. That is, it can be if we read, study, and store it in our hearts. It can guide our paths always, at any hour of the day or night and at any age or stage.

When our way becomes dark with illness, disappointment, discouragement, or problems of any kind, we can know that we have access to the Light of the world. And the best part is that this Light for my path will be bright and new every morning!

Dear God, thank You for sending Your Son into our world of darkness. Help us to be a light to others along the way. Through Christ our Lord. *Amen*

Luke, Bearer of Light

Walk as children of light.
Ephesians 5:8b

I am so thankful that before I completed this book of devotionals, our grandson Luke Christian Thomas was born. Our son David and wife Karen waited until his birth to reveal the baby's name.

Standing outside the delivery room, David proudly held their first-born son. Moving the blanket a bit for the family to get a better look, he said, "This is Luke Christian Thomas, and he's perfect!" David then explained the meaning of the name. He said, "Luke means 'bearer of light.' Christian is Karen's Grandpa Muselman's first name which means 'follower of Christ.'"

How will my life be a light to others today?

As family and friends lingered at the nursery window, I thought about this beautiful name. A follower of the Light carries the light to a dark and needy world. What a blessed thought! I felt in my heart that this little baby—a gift from God—would one day help dispel the world's darkness. Luke Christian will, on the grayest of days, be a beam of brightness.

That's our call, too, isn't it? Paul told the Christians at Philippi that they were to shine as lights in the world (Philippians 2:15). Our countenance should reflect our Lord. Psalms 4:6 says, "Lift up the light of thy countenance upon us, O Lord!"

Luke Christian, before we really get to know you, we love you. In time you will come to know and love Jesus, the Light of the world. Jesus said in John 12:36, "Believe in the light, that you may become sons of light." Go forward unafraid, Luke Christian Thomas. Follow Christ and bear the Light!

Loving Father, help us to be faithful followers of Your Son, Jesus. May the light of Your love be seen in our lives for Your glory. In Jesus' name. *Amen*

Echoes of the Heart

The Lord called me from the womb, from the body of my mother he named my name.

Isaiah 49:1

Much is being written today about a baby's ability to hear and even recognize certain voices from the mother's womb. All of this seems much more believable since I've seen Katie respond to songs which were sung to her before birth. Her Uncle David wrote a special song for Katie, and this tune was one of the first she hummed as a toddler. Even today she can be totally frustrated, and when she hears this melody, she attends instantly. Music echoes in the heart of Katie.

Our Creator God can speak to our heart, regardless of our age or circumstances.

Now David and Karen have a child of their own, and I'm sure Luke will love music, too. Many tunes were placed in the hearts of these children while in their mothers' wombs. In the same way, I believe the echoes of God's heart reach ours even before we are born. Isaiah said that God called him from his mother's womb. God spoke to Jeremiah and said, "Before I formed you in the womb I knew you, and before you were born I consecrated you" (Jeremiah 1:5a). God knows us by name.

Surely if God is mindful of us even before we are born, we are precious and important to Him. We are, in fact, too precious to be viewed as just a mass to be destroyed at will. Life in the womb can receive the sound of a voice and the sound of music. The Gospel of Luke says that an angel spoke to Zechariah about the son that Elizabeth would bear for him. He said the son, John, would be "filled with the Holy Spirit even from his mother's womb" (Luke 1:15b).

If God is so mindful of the unborn, surely, then, we must love and respect His creation. For the heartbeat of the unborn child truly echoes in the heart of God.

Dear God, when we remember how You loved us even before we were born, we are amazed. Thank You for holding us always in Your heart. Through Christ our Lord. *Amen*

The Upward Call

*I press on toward the goal for the prize of the
upward call of God in Christ Jesus.*
Philippians 3:14

*I*n one particular parsonage in which we lived, I enjoyed devotional times in front of the bedroom window. The yard on that side of the house was terraced into three gently sloping levels. When our daughter Debbie first saw the yard at this parsonage, her reaction to the sloping terrain was, "What fun the grandchildren will have someday, running up and down those little hills." But from the vantage point behind my desk, the levels of the yard seem to remind me more and more of life itself. Hills, mountains, smooth places, more struggles, but always moving onward and upward.

Are we preparing for the place God has prepared for all who heed His call?

In the Scripture above, the apostle Paul was talking about enduring. In our Christian walk, we climb, we press on, we persevere. We also experience those brief times of "leveling off" when we catch our breath. We can never relax our efforts nor lower our standards in order for the climb to be made easier. And we can't look back. In Philippians 3:13 Paul says we are to forget what is past and strain forward for what is ahead.

There *is* a prize that awaits us on higher ground. At the top level of our yard is an overgrown thicket. I know there is a house on the other side of the thicket beside our yard, even though it's concealed. I know what's beyond this upward journey in life, too. I know there's a heavenly home for me—a "house not made with hands" (II Corinthians 5:1b). I know it's there because my Lord promised it when He said, "I go and prepare a place for you" (John 14:3a).

So we press on toward the goal for the prize of the upward call. What's the prize? The *place* is the prize? Oh, yes, His presence during the climb seems prize enough, but there's *more* when we reach the higher ground!

Dear God, Your call is ever before us. Help us to be strong in our upward climb. In Jesus' name. *Amen*

Show Me Their Heart

Search me, O God, and know my heart! Try me and know my thoughts!
Psalms 139:23

We were busy preparing a meal for the Habitat for Humanity work crew when someone walked up beside me. Speaking in an intense, angry whisper, she said, "I don't think I can bear to work with that woman another minute!" I asked whom she was talking about, and she carefully nodded in the direction of another kitchen helper.

We need to sense the pain in people's hearts more than we need to see their actions.

I understood how she felt. This person had also irritated me. Our "thorn in the flesh" had been sharp-tongued and bossy all week. I let my frustrated friend empty herself of her pent-up feelings. Then I asked, "Have you ever looked into her eyes?" "No," she replied, "I can hardly bear to be around her that long." "Well, try to see the pain in her eyes which probably reflects the pain in her heart," I said, and went about my work.

A few weeks earlier I probably would not have given this advice. But I heard Jan Johnson speak at a recent meeting for spouses of ministers. Jan suggested that we pray for the people who irritate us and ask God to show us their hearts.

The psalmist David knew what it was to be seen in the heart. In fact, he asked God to do just that. "Search me," he said, "And know my heart. Try me and know my thoughts!"

It is comforting that God looks upon our hearts and not our glaring eyes. Psalms 44:21 says, "Would not God discover this? For he knows the secrets of the heart." We would do well to pray with David, "Create in me a clean heart, O God, and put a new and right spirit within me" (Psalms 51:10).

Today, when we are tempted to be critical of someone, let us remember to look at his or her heart. If we will do this, our own hearts will more likely remain pure.

Heavenly Father, search me and know my heart. Help me to be more sensitive to others. In Jesus' name. *Amen*

Compassion Communicates

But a Samaritan, as he journeyed, came to where he was;
and when he saw him, he had compassion.
Luke 10:33

I was struck by the words of a mourner in front of Buckingham Palace following the tragic death of Diana, Princess of Wales. Speaking to a reporter about the royal family, this person said, "They're not normal—they don't show feelings." I cannot judge the accuracy of this statement. I'm sure the royal family experienced deep grief but did so in private. People express grief in different ways

The statement by the mourner caused me to wonder just how much compassion he was feeling for the royal family. It has caused me to think of how much compassion I show to those who are hurting from day to day. Paul advised the faithful at Colosae to "put on...compassion" (Colossians 3:12). He speaks of kindness, lowliness, meekness, and patience, too, but he lists compassion first of all.

Every time we share God's love with someone in need, we communicate compassion.

God's compassion for a lost and dying world moved Him to give His only Son for our salvation. Jesus was often moved with compassion for the people in need around Him. He grieved with those in sorrow. When Lazarus died, He wept. He was so moved with compassion that He healed the sick, made the lame to walk again, restored sight to the blind, and even brought life back to Lazarus. Jesus was moved with compassion for the woman caught in adultery and offered forgiveness and acceptance.

What is our response to someone in grief or in need of forgiveness, healing, and acceptance? Would a stranger observe our compassion as "normal," or do we conceal our feelings? Jesus set the example of compassion by loving us enough to go to the cross for us. Are we willing to show our gratitude by sharing His love with a hurting world?

Loving God, help me to be faithful in showing Your love and mercy with my neighbors in need today. In Jesus' name. *Amen*

Shelter from the Storm

*O Jerusalem, Jerusalem...How often would I have
gathered your children together as a hen gathers her brood
under her wings, and you would not!*
Matthew 23:37

A vivid childhood memory of growing up on the farm is that of a sudden fierce thunderstorm. Crops were beaten to the ground. Rich top soil washed away to the river. Worse than anything that happened was the number of baby chickens that drowned. Normally, the mother hens gathered the little chickens under their protective wings, but not this time. Perhaps the storm came too suddenly.

How often do we reject God's extended arms of love and mercy?

Dozens of bright yellow, fluffy baby chicks lay strewn around the chicken coops. I remember my deep feelings of disappointment in the mother hens. Their shiny, slick feathers would easily have deflected the water. Instead, the down of the baby chicks soaked it up, and many drowned. My mother tried desperately to coax the hens into the coops where they could call their chicks to safety, but to no avail.

Picking up one of the little chickens, I cradled its lifeless form in the palm of my hand. *Maybe it could be revived*, I thought, and I began to stroke its head every so gently. I found myself completely caught up in loving this small part of God's creation. The yellow fuzz began to dry. It actually began to feel warmer! *Could I be imagining a faint sound? There it was again.* Clear, but weak, little chirps came from the limp form.

Suddenly, little black eyelids fluttered as the once unconscious chick came back to life. My mother could hardly believe what happened. She looked at me and spoke a profound truth that day. "You know, if you could have loved all the other little chickens like that, they might have lived, too!"

Recalling that incident over the years, I realized anew the deep longing of Jesus to gather the people of Jerusalem from the storms of their life into the safety of His sheltering arms. Today, as then, the choice is ours to receive His gift of life and life eternal.

God of compassion, thank You for restoring us to life when we place ourselves in Your hands. Through Christ. *Amen*

The Enduring Marigold

For you have need of endurance, so that you may do the
will of God and receive what is promised.
Hebrews 10:36

"I cut down those old ragweeds!" my nephew proudly announced. "Those things were taking over your flower bed!" I didn't have the heart to tell him that he had just destroyed my bed of marigolds.

After a day or two passed, I noticed that three marigold plants were still standing bravely among the wilted ones. These marigolds grew to be some of the prettiest ones I have ever seen. It was as though, having come through a time of trial, they were now basking in their full beauty.

With God's help, we will be able to endure the dry times and storms of life.

One of the qualities I admire most about the marigold is its ability to withstand hardship and dry times. When the moisture is scarce in the soil, the roots seem to grow down deeper and deeper. One would be hard-pressed to find a wilted marigold from lack of water. Its leaves may become brown, but the blossom will continue to radiate bright yellow and orange colors.

I'm glad I gained a new appreciation for the common marigold that day my nephew cut down the "ragweeds." Its odor is still unpleasant, but with time scientists will probably be successful in developing an odorless variety. I believe the marigold can be an example for us. We, too, can rise from our disappointments and even our disasters. We, too, can reach down into our deeper resources during life's dry times. Wherever we are planted, we can be a source of hope and encouragement to those around us.

Gracious God, help me to stay rooted and grounded in my faith and be an encourager to others who may be struggling with life. In Jesus' name. *Amen*

No Fruit

You will know them by their fruits.
Matthew 7:20

I faithfully nurtured the tomato plant in our backyard throughout the summer. The plant itself became strong and bloomed profusely, but never once did I spot a small green tomato on its branches.

July and August came and went with no evidence of tomatoes except for the blossoms. I longed to experience the fulfillment of watching even one tomato form, grow, and ripen to be enjoyed by our family at the dinner table. But it never happened.

Before I am critical of another's life, I need to take a look at my own.

Near the end of that summer, my patience with the barren vine wore thin. *I might as well cut it down,* I thought. It would never benefit us, and, besides, I could use that spot in the yard for fall mums. At least *their* blossoms would open into the full beauty for which they were intended.

As I went for the garden hoe, I was taken aback by a sobering question from my Creator God: *What if I cut you down each time you fail to bear fruit for me?* How often my life has failed to produce that fruit for which it was intended. Yet, God has continued to nourish my soul, given me opportunities to produce fruit, and even provided me with living water.

I am so thankful that His patience with me endures forever and that He is a God of second chances. But I know that Jesus expects my life to bear fruit. He said in John 15:16, "You did not choose me, but I chose you and appointed you that you should go and bear fruit and that your fruit should abide; so that whatever you ask the Father in my name, he may give it to you." He wants me to not only bear fruit, but to bear fruit that will abide—that will stand the test of time. The fruit I bear must be more than a blossom; it needs to reach maturity. I pray that this will be so.

Merciful Father, thank You for being patient with us even when our lives aren't producing fruit as they should. *Amen*

Blossoms in the Dessert

The wilderness and dry land shall be glad,
the desert shall rejoice and blossom.

Isaiah 35:1

The drought in Kentucky during the early summer of 1988 was devastating. Crops began to die in the fields. Parched grass along the median of the state's highways was vulnerable to cigarettes thrown carelessly by passing motorists. Charred patches were a continuous reminder of man's thoughtlessness.

Driving through this area a few weeks later we saw a different picture. Life-giving rain had fallen in abundance since we last passed that way. Now in the place of burned grass there were green areas; in the place of charred earth, new life was bursting forth.

Today, will I encourage or discourage those with whom I come in contact?

This experience was something of a parable of life for me. Circumstances can mar—even destroy—the growth and beauty that God intended for us. We sometimes become discouraged and wonder if our lives will ever feel whole and normal again. But the goodness and providence of God comes to us in time—in *His* time—restoring, refreshing, renewing, and redeeming.

Just as the good rain renews and restores parched grass, so does our heavenly Father bless and restore our lives. He is good. He is sovereign. His mercy endures to all generations, not only in the trials but in the triumphs as well. And I believe that God wants each of us to help restore people in the droughts and deserts of their life.

Dear God, in the dry times of our soul, renew us with Your living water. *Amen*

The Gospel Makes a Difference

For freedom Christ has set us free; stand fast therefore,
and do not submit again to a yoke of slavery.

Galatians 5:1

During our visit to the Meru province of Kenya, our hostess, Eunice Muthee, made a statement I will never forget. She said, "The gospel of Christ has made such a difference for the women of our country."

Eunice was a devoted mother and wife. She was a college graduate, trained as a teacher. Her husband and extended family respected her. Because of the change the gospel made in her life, she realized a freedom that many of her African sisters did not know. Through the power of the gospel, she had experienced freedom as a whole person. As a child of God she knew her worth in His eyes.

Once we are free in Christ we are free indeed!

Because of the difference the gospel had made in her area, a hospital was built. Schools were established. A training school for pastors flourished. Eunice's home was Christian, and life was good.

The gospel of Christ transformed Eunice's life as it does all of our lives. Christ sets us free! II Corinthians 3:17 says, "Where the Spirit of the Lord is, there is freedom." We don't have to remain in *any* kind of bondage. The yokes that would enslave us in America may be different than the yokes of slavery in another part of the world. But it is the same God who brings freedom through Christ to the world. Thanks be to God!

Loving Father, we are so grateful for the freedom we can know through Your Son, Jesus. Help us to share the good news of the gospel so that others can experience the difference Christ makes. *Amen*

First Things First

*Seek first his kingdom and his righteousness,
and all these things shall be yours as well.*
Matthew 6:33

The African lunch was finished and we asked to see the "mother church." Our host, Justus Muthee, several times had referred to his own congregation as a "mother church"—a church that sponsored the birthing of new churches.

We walked across a large grassy field where Wally had preached, through an interpreter, to twelve congregations assembled for morning worship. The scene of that service will be forever etched in our memory.

Is seeking first God's kingdom the priority in my life?

Five hundred hungry hearts came searching for spiritual food that day. Some had walked barefoot on the dusty dirt roads since daybreak to attend. They knew what seeking His kingdom was all about. The women who took the offering were stooped from the weight of the coins.

Nearing the site of our host's church, a cool, gentle breeze reminded us of the presence of the Holy Spirit. Justus pointed out beautiful Mt. Kenya in the background. "That's where our people believed that God dwelled before the Christian gospel reached us," he explained.

Rounding a thicket, Justus pointed to an incomplete structure made of hand-hewn rocks. "This is our new building!" Justus announced proudly. "Where is the big mother church?" we asked. "You mean that you helped build three mission churches, and your own building isn't finished?" Solemnly Justus replied, "That's what the gospel teaches: 'Seek first His kingdom and all these things will be added'"

The truth of that promise was totally believable in that moment. Justus went on, "Oh, we'll soon finish our building. We had a *harambe*—the other churches helped us raise 360,000 shillings. That's more then enough to finish our building!"

The people in the Meru province of Kenya showed us how to take the gospel seriously. They sought God's kingdom and reaped a great harvest of God's good gifts. How thrilling it would be if North American Christians could catch that beautiful spirit of *harambe*!

Heavenly Father, Help me to seek first Your kingdom every day of my life. *Amen*

Ministry of Encouragement

Therefore encourage one another and build one another up,
just as you are doing.
I Thessalonians 5:11

I can be an encourager today—if I'm willing to take the time.

We stopped to visit the sixth church on that Sunday in the Meru province of Kenya. Our African host, Justus Muthee, proudly showed us the five other churches. During the morning we saw scores of children assembling for Sunday school. Time was running out for our visit there, and we didn't want to miss this last church. But neither did we want to miss our bus back to Nairobi.

Assuring us that the "experience is more important than time," Justus took us to the Githonga Methodist Church. Inside, a crowd of people were singing jubilantly. I asked if this was an afternoon worship service, and our host explained that the congregation had simply come together for prayer and encouragement.

Prayer and encouragement. My mind flashed to our churches in America. These two vital elements of a healthy church aren't always present in the Western world. I wondered that day, and still do, would we be willing to give up a Sunday afternoon to meet for prayer and encouragement? Could we even admit that we need prayer and encouragement?

I heard Dr. E. Stanley Jones say that the greatest ministry of the future is the ministry of encouragement. We need encouragement. We need prayer. Paul recognized this need as he wrote of his longing to visit the Christians in Rome: "that we may be mutually encouraged by each other's faith" (Romans 1:12).

I believe that encouragement can be given—and received—through simple ways. Sometimes a smile, a hug, a telephone call, a note, or a word of sincere praise can change a person's outlook on life. We may never meet together on a Sunday afternoon as do our brothers and sisters in Africa, but we can be involved in our own ministry of encouragement where we are.

Our Father, help us to be sensitive to those about us, and find ways to offer encouragement. In Jesus' name. *Amen*

Increased Burdens, Increased Help

Cast you burdens on the Lord, and he will sustain you.
Psalms 55:22a

Forever etched in my memory is the scene of rural Kenyan women carrying heavy loads of sticks on their backs. Day in and day out, these women gather the needed wood for fires to cook the day's rations. Then they faithfully trudge back to their huts to cook and feed their hungry families.

Burdens of one kind or another are common to all of us. One person may struggle to simply supply the food for the daily needs of their family. For others, the burden may be a crippling or fatal disease, parenting a disabled child, or making ends meet financially.

As God receives our burdens, He gives us His blessings.

Dave Dravecky pitched for the San Diego Padres and the San Francisco Giants baseball teams. He developed pain and soreness in his pitching arm and tests revealed that he had cancer. He had surgery followed by months of rehabilitation. Later the cancer returned. He broke his arm and it had to be removed. Dave Dravecky was not a loser. With the loss of his arm, he received increased help from God. Today he gives his testimony about God's grace in his life.

The Kenyan women knew what it was to have help from the Lord, too. I saw hundreds of these women walk to an outdoor worship service—many barefoot—and I knew the source of their daily strength. They knew about casting their burdens on the Lord and experienced His sustaining grace.

Are you carrying a heavy load today? We may not be bent low with a roll of sticks on our backs like the Kenyan women, nor suffer from cancer as Dave Dravecky. But whatever our need may be, God's grace, strength, mercy and peace can be ours—today and forever.

Dear God, thank You for receiving our burdens and sustaining us every day—all along the way. In Jesus' name. *Amen*

Words in Season

A word in season, how good it is!
Proverbs 15:23b

You at least advanced the ball!" a friend said to Wally after he made a poor golf stroke. Wally was disgusted with his game of golf, but these words from his friend were an encouragement. They were "in season."

A kind word of encouragement is always in season. Matthew 12:34 says, "Out of the abundance of the heart the mouth speaks." Jesus was saying that if a heart is filled with goodness, good words will flow from it. On the other hand, if the heart is filled with evil, evil will flow out.

Will the words I speak today be acceptable in God's sight?

The book of James, in chapter 3, says that it is easier to control a horse, guide a ship, or tame the wild than to control the tongue. We need to do like my kindergarten student said, "When the devil says 'Be mean,' I just keep my mouth shut."

All of us can recall times when words have stung us. If we were really honest, we probably can recall times when our *own* words have stung others. I ask God each day to bridle my tongue, but I haven't arrived yet in this area. We can pray like David in Psalm 141:3: "Set a guard over my mouth, O Lord, keep watch over the door of my lips!"

One word, regardless of how innocently it is spoken, can discourage or hurt. It can do damage to a person's reputation and spirit. It can destroy close relationships.

Proverbs 15:1 says, "A soft answer turns away wrath, but a harsh word stirs up anger." Wally's friend spoke a kind word of encouragement. It helped him to move on to the next stroke in the golf game. I'm grateful for people who know when to speak a good work in season and help us move on in life.

Lord, I pray that today You will set a watch upon my lips. Help me, by Your grace, to guard each word I speak. *Amen*

Soul Drought

*Jesus stood up and proclaimed, "If anyone thirst,
let him come to me and drink."*
John 7:37b

The sun dried the grass until it became straw. Pastures became barren and herds of livestock were sold. Cracks in the earth formed. Crops and shrubs died. Spirits were low. All of this happened in Kentucky during the drought of 1999.

The good earth must have water to support life. So must we as Christians have the water of life. Jesus reminded the woman at the well that the water she was taking back to her village would not quench their thirst. He said to her, "But whoever drinks of the water that I shall give him will never thirst" (John 4:13).

As we receive the living water, we must be channels, not reservoirs.

People try one thing after another to quench the thirst deep within their souls. They experience something like the starvation described in Jeremiah 2:13, "For my people have committed two evils: they have forsaken me, the fountain of living waters, and hewn out cisterns for themselves, broken cisterns that can hold no water."

Only Jesus can provide "living water" (John 4:10) which becomes "a spring of water welling up to eternal life" (John 4:14). Life's parched, lifeless wasteland can become restored when we come to the source of the living water. Only He can change the soul's drought in a parched and thirsty world.

Dear God, thank You for providing for this thirsty world a source of life—the living water. We praise You that, through Jesus, we can have abundant life now and forevermore. *Amen*

The Unclouded Day

The Lord will not forsake his people; he will not abandon his heritage.
Psalms 94:14

Jessie suffered from dementia for several years and grew progressively worse. Most of her ability to carry on a conversation was gone, but she could still remember the words of favorite hymns. Earlier in her life she had neatly recorded songs in a notebook. Now, when she was asked if she would like to sing, she would eagerly reply, "Help me get started."

What am I storing in my heart and mind for the cloudy days of my life?

All Jessie needed was someone to sing or read the first few words of a favorite hymn—like "The Unclouded Day"[1]—and she could sing all the stanzas perfectly.

Even with her clouded mind, she could reach into the deep recesses of her memory and recall the words to hymns. She could recall the image of her home far away—where no storm clouds, nor pain, nor suffering, nor death would ever come. Jessie could still get in touch with God, and attest to the fact that "the Lord will not forsake his people."

I believe as a person's memory is slowly deteriorating, the last part to go is the part that is in touch with the presence of God. That is why hearing Scripture read aloud or hymns sung are so comforting to the critically ill. When we know our Creator and Sustainer, that knowledge will be with us to the end.

Is something clouding your life today? Maybe it's sickness, sorrow, stress, family concerns, financial burdens, discouragement? Whatever it may be, just know that God has not forsaken you. Reach into your mind and heart, and sing or say the words of a favorite hymn or passage of Scripture that is buried there. It's amazing how quickly this can help drive the clouds away!

Loving Father, I am so thankful that You never leave us nor forsake us. Strengthen our faith in the heritage that we have in You. Through Christ. *Amen*

Always Remain Teachable

My son, do not forget my teaching.
Proverbs 3:1a

Wally gave David and Karen some words of advice during their wedding ceremony, "Always remain teachable." I believe this is good advice for newlyweds or for anyone.

None of us ever "arrive"; we never learn all there is to know. We are always in need of being taught truth. Jesus is our example for seeking truth. As a twelve year old, He lingered for three days in the temple, "Sitting among the teachers, listening to them and asking them questions" (Luke 2:46). Jesus was hungry to be taught and eagerly searched for knowledge (Luke 2:49).

Are we, like Martha, distracted by useless things in our life?

As an adult, Jesus encouraged others to be willing to listen and to be taught. He saw this attitude in Mary, the sister of Martha and Lazarus. The Scripture says that Martha received Jesus into their home, but "she had a sister called Mary, who sat at the Lord's feet and listened to his teaching" (Luke 10:39). The verse that follows hits me, for it says Martha was "distracted with much serving" (Luke10:40).

The one thing that is needed in many of our lives is to always remain teachable. In order to know and accomplish God's will, we must stay open to truth. God's Word is the living truth; we can learn new insights each time we study it. The psalmist David said, "Teach me to do thy will, for thou art my God" (Psalms 143:10). Can we sincerely pray this prayer? The master teacher is ready, willing, and able to hear and answer us.

Loving Father, You have promised to teach us all things through Your Holy Spirit. Teach me Your wisdom, Lord. *Amen*

God in the Far Away Places

But thou, O Lord, be not far off!
O thou my help, hasten to my aid!
Psalms 22:19

Recently I awakened in the night with these words strongly impressed upon my mind and heart: "God in the far away places." Nothing more. I pondered these words and prayed that God would help me understand their meaning.

Far away places. *Where are the far away places in my life?* I wondered. *Could it possibly be that God is reassuring me that He cares about every concern that lies heavy on my heart?* I believe that was it. God knew my concerns: David's upcoming trip to South Korea; autism and illnesses in the family; loved ones away from God.

There is no limit to God's loving presence.

The list of needs grew, but so did my confidence that no circumstance in my life is beyond God's reach! I recalled the psalmist David's words: "Whither shall I go from thy Spirit? Or whither shall I flee from thy presence? If I take the wings of the morning and dwell in the uttermost parts of the sea, even there thy hand shall lead me, and thy right hand shall hold over me" (Psalms 139:7,9,10).

No situation can ever come to our lives that the love of God cannot touch. Paul reminds us in Ephesians 3:19 that this kind of love "surpasses knowledge." He knows *all* our needs. His love provides for us the Holy Spirit to be with us in all of our "far away places." Yet He is as close as our breath.

The psalmist pled with God to "be not far away." We can take comfort in the fact that wherever we are, whatever our concerns may be, God will "hasten to our aid." Claiming this truth can make all the difference in our lives.

Dear God, thank You so much that You go the distance with us. Strengthen our faith and trust in you. In Jesus' name. *Amen*

Mother's Rose

The grass withers, the flower fades;
but the word of God will stand forever.
Isaiah 40:8

*F*ollowing my parents' deaths, my brothers and sisters and I divided their personal items. One of the last items was in their rose garden. Normally, people don't move rosebushes from a yard, but Mother's roses were different—at least in her mind. One by one she had planted a special rose for each of her five children. She would proudly point to the bush that was planted in honor of Windell, Allen, Geneva, Jewell, and me.

Reminders of our Lord's victory over death are all about us.

None of us wanted to leave "our" rosebush to new owners or tenants. So we each dug up our roses and planted them in our own yards.

I took some of the good Cumberland County soil to Louisville, hoping to make the transition easier for my rosebush. After patting the mulch around it, I breathed a prayer that my bush would live and thrive in its new location. It did live and throughout the summer produced beautiful, velvety roses.

When the next spring arrived, I was thrilled to see the reddish sprouts bursting forth. They grew quickly and soon a hearty rosebush was well on its way. But, not for long. During one of my morning checks on the rosebush, I found nothing there. It was gone. Totally. Obviously a wild rabbit had feasted on its tender branches. Tears flowed as I sat by the "crime scene." *That dumb rabbit,* I mumbled. *If I could only put my hands on it.*

I quickly purchased enough chicken wire to encircle the spot where Mother's rose had grown, in faith that it would sprout again. Sure enough, near Easter, the rosebush that had nearly been destroyed was now alive! I was filled with joy and was reminded of the power of the resurrection in a fresh way that Easter. But I knew that even at best, Mother's rose would not flourish indefinitely. Thanks be to our Lord that He came back to life—*eternal* life! As Christians, we can live forever with Him.

Loving God, thank You for Your plan for life—and new life—on earth. But more than this, thank You for the assurance of life eternal. Through Christ our Savior. *Amen*

Upward Bound

The wise man's path leads upward to life.
Proverbs 15:24a

From my kitchen window I've enjoyed watching the daily changes in a new plant. Another beautiful pink blossom can be spotted nearly every day as the vines inch upward on the trellis. I go outside often to gently guide the tender tips of the vines around a stake.

To whom can I extend God's love today?

About a week ago I began to notice two vines dangling haphazardly from the top of the trellis. I tried to encourage them to curl around an empty stake close by and grow downward, but they have stubbornly refused. It even seems that their growth has slowed down since the vines have no way to continue upward.

Then it occurred to me—the plant was *created* to grow upward. God placed within its genetic makeup a plan for it to climb higher and higher as long as there is a support system on which it can rely. Isn't that true with us in our Christian walk, too? God created us to one day return to Him, but, like the plant, we need a support system. We need the dependable love and care of families and friends. We need the daily nourishment and guidance from God's Word. We need the gentle nudges of the Holy Spirit.

Today my sister, Geneva, who also gave me the plant, gave me two tall reeds to use as extensions of the trellis. Now, the plant can continue its upward climb for which it was created. We, too, are encouraged to keep moving upward in our journey through the many extensions of God's love to us through others. I want to keep climbing upward. I want to be sensitive to others, and offer help and love to those that are struggling and faltering along the way.

Dear God, please strengthen me in my upward climb. Guide me when I falter and lose my direction. Help me to be an extension of Your love to others. In Jesus' name. *Amen*

It's Today Now

This is the day which the Lord has made; let us rejoice and be glad in it.
Psalms 118:24

*L*ittle Danielle had questioned her grandmother all day about when we would arrive. Her grandmother, my sister Geneva, answered patiently over and over, so Danielle continued to ask the question.

Later that afternoon as we sat on the front porch, Danielle asked her grandmother a profound question: "Mama G," she said, "Is today *now*?" My sister replied, "That's right! Today *is* now, and aren't we having fun?!"

I recalled that conversation as I lay awake that night. Today *is* now. This day with which God has blessed us is here. This moment, this very second, is all we have. This small slice of eternity is ours to enjoy—now!

> *Rejoicing in each day will make our yesterdays and tomorrows better.*

We need to seize each moment of each day because each moment is precious. It will never be repeated. It will never be duplicated. Our tomorrows are yet unknown. Our yesterdays are forever gone.

So often I rush through the day, trying to accomplish all the goals I've set. I rush from one meeting to the next. I spend senseless energy regretting something that occurred yesterday. I sometimes dread tomorrow. It is all so futile when all any of us have is today.

It's today now! Let us rejoice and be glad in it!

Father, I thank You for each precious moment of each new day. Help me not to waste such a gift. *Amen*

Root Systems

As therefore you received Christ Jesus the Lord, so live in him,
rooted and built up in him and established in the faith.
Colossians 2:6,7a

*T*he root system of trees fascinates me. Trees are held in place by roots. They receive their water supply and nutrients through their roots. Roots that grow deep into the soil provide needed support during fierce storms.

Some trees grow in large clusters. Their root systems interlock and actually give to each other needed support and strength. A lone tree can be easily uprooted, but a supportive network of tree roots can share in the burden of holding each tree firmly in place.

What kind of root system am I developing today?

In this way, families have much in common with trees. Children are like tree limbs: they depend on their root system for support and nourishment. If a part of a tree is damaged or diseased, the whole tree is affected. So it is with the family. A supportive network in the family will enable it to weather difficult times. Family ties form a powerful base for strength and stability.

Trees don't spring up overnight. For a tree to grow strong and reach its full potential, time is required. Time is required to build strong family root systems, too. There will be storms to weather, dry times to endure, and injury with which to cope. Families need to stay close to each other, share needs with each other, and draw strength from our common source. When this happens, they, like trees, will be strong and stable.

Likewise, Paul admonished the Christian family at Colosae to be a support for each other. He told them to be built up and rooted in Jesus. Root systems are a part of God's providential plan for His body (the church), for families, and for the trees on His good earth.

Heavenly Father, help us to be mindful every day that stability is possible only as we remain rooted and grounded in Your life-giving love. Through Christ. *Amen*

Making Someone's Day

Be kind to one another.
Ephesians 4:32a

*A*s I walked to my car in the grocery store parking lot, I kept hearing coins hit the pavement behind me. Turning around I saw a smiling teenage boy with his left hand cupped in front of him. "I believe you've dropped some change," I said. He cheerfully replied, "Oh, I'm just making somebody's day!" and continued dropping shiny new pennies all around him.

Whose day can I make happier today?

I put my groceries in the car and returned the grocery cart. By this time all the pennies had been picked up. For several people that day, their morning had been "made" by a cheerful young lad with a handful of pennies.

Each of us has opportunities each day to spread some cheer. Acts of kindness, though as small as a copper penny, not only bring joy to the recipient, but also please God. Proverbs 14:31 says, "He who is kind to the needy honors him." Someone has said that kindness is Christianity in work clothes.

The persons who picked up the pennies were not likely to be needy of material goods, but all of us are in need of kindness. A kind deed may cost little or nothing, but can bring priceless joy to someone's dreary existence. An anonymous writer has penned these words on sharing deeds of kindness:

Have you had a kindness shown? Pass it on!
'Twas not given for you alone, pass it on!
Let it travel down the years, let it wipe away another's tears,
Till in heaven the deed appears, pass it on!

Heavenly Father, help me to find ways to show Your love and kindness wherever I go. In Jesus' name. *Amen*

What's Behind the Door?

*Now faith is the assurance of things hoped for,
the conviction of things not seen.*
Hebrews 11:1

"What's behind the door?" was an expression used by a friend from my childhood days. Often before others finished eating, this elderly gentlemen would glance at the hostess. Then, with a twinkle in his eye, he would ask the same question each time: "What's behind the door?" It was his way of asking, "What's for dessert?"

We can be sure of Christ's sweet presence each day of our life.

He hoped for a dessert after each meal, and though the dessert might not be anywhere in sight he believed that it had been prepared. On one occasion, he asked his daughter-in-law this pointed question. She turned and whispered to those near her, "Wonder what Grandpa would say if I got the broom from behind the door?"

Expectation. Faith. Belief that a dessert had been prepared. How different our lives might be if we truly believed Psalms 84:11: "No good thing does the Lord withhold from those who walk uprightly."

It took some faith for this elderly man to believe that something good had been prepared for dessert. Our lives would hold greater joy and expectancy if we could have the faith that our Lord has good things in store for us just behind the next door in our lives.

Loving Father, thank You for blessing our lives in bountiful ways. May we live each day in the expectancy of Your power and presence with us. In Jesus' name. *Amen*

Continuous Growth

Grow in the grace and knowledge of our Lord and Savior Jesus Christ.
II Peter 3:18a

*H*aving grown up in Kentucky, which has four distinct seasons in the year, I am always fascinated by the areas of the world where continuous growth occurs. During a visit to Kenya, I noticed ten-foot poinsettia plants laden with bright red blossoms. Ageratum flowers and yam plants looked like trees to me. In areas that receive adequate rainfall, gardens grow year round.

Of particular interest to me were the short stalks of corn planted along the road embankments. The stalks were stunted, and the ears were only nubbins: small and undeveloped. Sloping sides of the road were difficult to cultivate, and I wondered if the planters had access to fertilizer. I'll never know about the final outcome of those corn crops, but I did notice one thing in particular: even though circumstances stunted the plants, they *were still growing.*

Is my spiritual growth a bit stunted like the roadside corn, or thriving and blossoming like the poinsettia tree?

Am I willing to plant seeds of faith during difficult situations? Am I willing to nourish my efforts through regular Bible study, prayer, and worship? Am I determined to grow during the dry or rainy days of life? It is always growing season with Jesus, regardless of the circumstances. It's up to me to access the Source of life to make it happen.

Heavenly Father, help me to tap into Your continuous, sustaining love, so that I can be fruitful and faithful in serving You. Through Christ I pray. *Amen*

A Model for Humility

Whoever humbles himself like this child,
he is greatest in the kingdom of heaven.
Matthew 18:4

*J*esus loved the children. He used them as a model of humility for adults. Scripture says that children were brought to Jesus that He might touch them (Mark 10:13). The disciples rebuked Jesus for taking the time to be with the children, but Jesus elevated children as being the greatest in the kingdom of heaven.

As children of God, are we truly modeling the humility of a child?

Jesus even went so far as to say that if we receive a child, we receive Him (Matthew 18:5). In Matthew 18:10 Jesus spoke about children's special angels in heaven who "behold the face of my Father." Jesus said that it is not the will of God for one of these little ones to perish (Matthew 18:14).

Jesus wants us to model the humility of a child. When His disciples—His closet friends—were arguing over who would be the greatest in His kingdom, he called a child to Him. He told the disciples that unless they became like a child, they wouldn't enter the kingdom of heaven (Matthew 18:3).

This is a difficult admonishment for us in this self-sufficient age. It's not easy to be humble. But according to our Lord, having the humility of a child is a requirement, not a choice.

Loving Father, help us to depend on You as a child, to love You as a child, to be as humble as a child, and to trust You as a child. In Jesus' name. *Amen*

Bad Company

Do not be deceived: "Bad company ruins good morals."
I Corinthians 15:33

*I*t's better to be alone than in the wrong company." This was my mother's advice as I entered my teen years. The older I get the more I appreciate her words of wisdom. Peers can be either a positive or negative influence; they are a powerful force in shaping character. Paul warned the Christians at Corinth that bad company can ruin good morals.

Being alone in a group or refusing to go along with the crowd is not always easy, but it *is* possible. It's not easy to turn down one's best friend when asked the answer on an exam. It's not easy to refuse to add a tidbit to the flow of gossip. It's not easy to say "no" to smoking, drinking, or doing drugs. It's not easy to live alone and try to make ends meet when others move in with their significant others in order to "save money." It may be hard to leave the party after work and go home to the family. But it is possible.

When we feel alone, we need to remember that we are not alone; God is with us always through His Spirit.

We should not be deceived into believing that temporary acceptance is more important than lasting joy and peace. The world can't give these or take them away. These blessings come from a close, committed walk with Christ, and this walk may be in a direction different from our peers.

Dear God, thank You for providing a Counselor for all of life's journey. When our friends and peers disappoint us, we can be in good company with You. Through Christ. *Amen*

Help My Unbelief

*Immediately the father of the child cried out and said,
"I believe; help my unbelief!"*
Mark 9:24

An alcoholic man decided he'd had enough to drink. Walking along a country road one day, he said to his sister, "I'm going to quit drinking!" Rejoicing over his new commitment, the sister suggested that he begin by destroying the bottle in his coat pocket. "Just throw the stuff away," she encouraged him. "Oh, no!" the brother replied, "I *am* going to quit, but this bottle cost too much to throw away!"

Faith assures us of things not seen.

The man sincerely wanted to give up the habit of drinking, but he needed help with that part of himself that wouldn't let go. How often do we say we are going to do a certain thing only to realize a little later that we really aren't ready to pay the required price? We believe, but need help with our unbelief—like the father of the sick child in the Scripture.

Jesus reminds us in Matthew 19:26 that all things are possible with God. The alcoholic man had some degree of faith that he could give up drinking, but his desire to do so wasn't great enough. Had he surrendered totally that day, perhaps his life would have been different.

Our lives, too, can be different and set free as we surrender our unbelief. Maybe the beginning point is to admit that we do have doubts and unbelief at times. Mark 16:17a says, "And these signs will accompany those who believe." Like the father with the sick child, our prayer can be, "I believe; help my unbelief!"

Father, thank You for accepting us as we are. Enable us to have faith enough to live victoriously. In Jesus' name. *Amen*

Nibbling Away at Life's Treasures

You then who teach others, will you not teach yourself?
While you preach against stealing, do you steal?

Romans 2:21

My Moonpie was missing! I looked forward all morning to recess when I could eat it. Sitting at the double desk in my one-room school, I once again checked to see if I possibly had overlooked it. I could just taste the rich chocolate covering, and I could visualize the marshmallow creme filling as it stretched on and on when I broke the Moonpie apart. My mouth watered at the very thought of it!

The teacher proceeded with teaching the seventh graders how to spell "M-e-d-i-t-e-r-r-a-n-e-a-n" and I continued my search for the lost Moonpie. Just then I found what I was afraid I'd find—an empty wrapper. I looked at the girl who shared the double desk, and I thought I detected a twinkle in her eyes. "Do you know what happened to my Moonpie?" I whispered. "A little mouse got it," she said, looking all the while like the cat who ate the canary.

Today and always I want to do to others as I would have them do to me.

"That's not fair! You know that was mine and I was saving it until recess!" I said, almost in tears now. "But I just ate it a crumb at a time," she rationalized. "Like a little mouse!"

Some fifty years later, I can still remember the disappointment of losing that Moonpie. Nickels were pretty scarce, and it wasn't every day that I got to buy something from my Aunt Jessie's grocery store. But as the years have passed, I have reflected on this incident and wondered, in all honesty, how often I have "nibbled" away at someone's simple pleasure. What about the times I have become irritated with family or friends? What about the times when I might have found it a bit difficult to rejoice at another's accomplishments? Have I sometimes wanted to teach others when I was the one who needed teaching? The lesson for me from the Moonpie experience is to be careful that I never deny another person any of life's simple pleasures.

Father, You bless us in so many ways. Help me never take these blessings for granted nor take them from one of Your children. *Amen*

Hidden Patches

But who can discern his errors? Clear thou me from hidden faults.
Psalms 19:12

As we anticipated retirement, we began to get rid of some household items. We gave each of our children a cedar chest. One had belonged to Wally before we married. The other had belonged to his parents.

A rush of memories swept over us as we emptied the contents of each chest. There were baby clothes, toys, pictures, crocheted doilies, ruffled curtains, Wally's high school diploma, and his wedding shirt. It was the wedding shirt that caught my eye: starched, ironed, and neatly folded. It was a bit yellowed, but it looked like he had not "gotten the good" out of it.

Jesus sees our patches, but He also sees our potential.

After the clothes from both chests were washed, I ironed the wedding shirt first. Every button was still in place. Neither the collar nor the cuffs were frayed, and I was a bit puzzled. Then I saw the secret: hidden patches on the back and left arm of the shirt. I had not seen the torn places when the shirt was folded or when I tossed it into the washer. But, now, under the pressure of the hot iron, the flaws were in full view.

I finished ironing the shirt, buttoned it, and then folded it again. As I put it away, I began to remember that it was Wally's mother who had tried to salvage the torn wedding shirt. She extended its life by patching it, but the telltale flaws were still there.

How about our own lives? Do we ever *appear* prim and proper—starched and all buttoned up—while keeping our patches hidden? Underneath it all, are our lives flawed and in deep need of repair? We need washing and cleansing. We need the worn places reinforced. We need the torn places patched and healed.

God not only discerns our errors, the psalmist said, but He also clears us from our hidden faults. All we have to do is open up the cedar chest of our hearts and allow Him to make us whole again.

Thank You, dear God, for loving us—hidden patches and all! Through Christ, our wounded healer. *Amen*

The Care Bears

Cast all your anxieties on him, for he cares about you.

1 Peter 5:7

*B*illy was one of the most complicated little persons I have ever known. Daily episodes with him included his falling out of his chair intentionally, jumping up and dashing across the room, crawling under desks, hiding in the closet, hitting someone, or destroying school supplies. His school counselor imformed me that his home life contributed to the whole problem.

Still, some days were almost unbearable. The only respite I had was story time. Billy would actually listen for a few minutes. When it came time for him to choose the book, he chose not one, but three. His favorite stories were about the "Care Bears."

How can I show someone today that I care and that God cares?

As I read page after page about these special little bears that care about every problem, I noticed Billy weaving his way through the twenty-four other first-graders sitting on the floor around me. Soon he reached my knees and began tapping—gently at first, and then more insistently. I patted his hand, hoping the delay could last until I finished the book. No such luck. "Mrs. Thomas," he whispered, "Are these little bears for real? Are they *really* real?"

I looked deeply into the pleading blue eyes of a little boy who longed to believe that someone—even some *thing*—cared for him. My mind scrambled for answers that would somehow comfort Billy in his deep hunger for love. "Billy," I said, "This is a story about bears that are only toys. But these bears can be your friends. Even though they can't feel and really care, they can be your toy for real."

I knew by the look in Billy's eyes that I had not given him the answer he needed, so I stumbled on. "Only people can really care, Billy, and I care about you." He dropped his head and sadly muttered, oblivious of the children around him, "My mama and daddy don't love me."

"Billy, you *are* loved. Your heavenly Father loves you very much." The closing bell ended that conversation, but I was more convinced than ever that the world longs to know that someone cares. It's only through us that they will ever know.

Father, help me see beyond offensive behavior—regardless of age—and hear the deep longings of the heart. *Amen*

Help in Trouble

God is our refuge and strength, a very present help in trouble.

Psalms 46:1

A sudden burst of smoke came from under the hood of our car. I suggested to Debbie to pull off the road as soon as possible, wondering all the while what could be wrong.

Within two minutes a young man in a sleek, red sports car pulled off the highway and parked near us. Fear gripped my heart. "Lord, please let him be a nice person," I prayed. "Having trouble?" he asked politely, to which we answered a faint, "Yes."

How can I be a help to someone in trouble today?

Raising the hood, he soon discovered that the main radiator hose had burst. Antifreeze covered the motor, causing billows of smoke to continue to rise.

The incidents that followed were not coincidental. We needed a telephone and spotted one nearby. An auto parts store in the area was open that Sunday morning; they usually opened at 1 P.M. The young stranger very capably remedied our problem, and we were soon on our way to church.

Before we left though, I handed the man a twenty-dollar bill and thanked him sincerely. "I don't want pay for what I've done," he said. I told him he must accept the money because he had been an answer to prayer. Then I explained that since our family was involved in an auto accident in 1973, we make it a habit to pray before we start on trips. I said, "So you are the answer to our prayer this morning!"

Smiling, he looked me in the eye and said, "I believe that's right. I didn't know why I felt I should put that toolbox in my car today. And I couldn't understand why, when I signed in at the National Guard a few minutes ago, they told me I had the day off. I guess this is why." Then with a faraway look in his eyes, he added, "My mom calls me up real often and gives me Scripture verses." I told him to be sure to tell his mother that her faith was lived out through her son that day. God had truly been our very present help in our time of trouble.

Heavenly Father, my heart overflows with gratitude for the wonderful ways you protect and help us all along life's way. Help me to be ready and willing to help others in need. *Amen*

Pictures of Jesus

He said, "Abba, Father, all things are possible to thee; remove this cup from me; yet not what I will, but what thou wilt."

Mark 14:36

Seven pictures depicting the life of Jesus hung in full view from where I sat in the small rural church. There was one of Christ holding a lamb; one of Him knocking at the door; one sending forth the disciples; one in the Upper Room; and three scenes of Jesus in the Garden of Gethsemane. Each of the three Garden scenes was different.

Why, I wondered, *were there three pictures in one little church of Jesus praying in the Garden?* My next questions answered the first: I*s there a scene in the life of our Lord more vivid, more excruciating? Was there ever a time when He felt more deserted by His closest friends?*

How willing am I to follow the example of Jesus?

"Could you not watch one hour?" our Lord sadly asked of His disciples in Mark 14:37. Lonely, searching, struggling, and shedding drops of blood, Jesus submerged His will with the Father's as He prayed in the Garden, "Yet not what I will, but what thou wilt" (Mark 14:36b). After hours of deep struggle, it was in the Garden that Jesus conquered Calvary

So as I sat in the little church, I realized that we need reminders of who our precious Lord really is. We need them in our places of worship. We need them in our homes. We need the nurturing care of the Good Shepherd. We need to hear His knock at our heart's door. We need to hear His call to go into all the world. And we need to be reminded that if we are to know peace, ultimately we must surrender our wills to His.

Looking at the many scenes in Christ's life before me that day, my heart was filled with gratitude for the example of our Lord. And I felt grateful, too, for this little church which placed before her people reminders of how we are to live.

Lord, help us to stay on our knees in our "gardens of Gethsemane" until we are willing to do Your perfect will. *Amen*

Work Rewarded

*But you, take courage! Do not let your hands be weak,
for your work shall be rewarded.*

II Chronicles 15:7

You probably have never heard of "YOGOWYPI." This acrostic for "You Only Get Out What You Put In" has become the name of a youth group at Lindsey Wilson College in Kentucky. Each year this group of young people hosts a large conference around this theme.

"Whatever a man sows, that he will also reap"

(Galatians 6:7b).

Have you ever felt that your work was in vain? I have. The feeling doesn't usually last long, thank the Lord! It's good to have a reminder that our efforts are rewarded. We may not see the results immediately or even in our lifetime. But Colossians 3:23,24 says, "Whatever your task, work heartily, as serving the Lord and not men, knowing that from the Lord you will receive the inheritance of your reward; you are serving the Lord Christ."

Patient persistence pays off. Published authors receive rejection slip after rejection slip. Successful parenting requires long hours of patient labors of love. The scientist who finally makes a life-changing discovery has usually invested a lifetime in research. Jesus modeled the way to live so that we may receive the most in the present and in the life to come. He taught us about denying self, loving our enemies, turning the other cheek, going the second mile, and taking up a cross and following Him. Jesus told His disciples that He will return and "then he will repay every man for what he has done" (Matthew 16:27b). Work is rewarded. Paul put it this way, "Therefore, my beloved brethren, be steadfast, immovable, always abounding in the work of the Lord, knowing that in the Lord your labor is not in vain" (I Corinthians 15:58).

Will we be pleased when we receive the dividends of our life's investment? I pray that we will.

Dear Lord, please forgive me for the times I fail to serve You well. Strengthen me where I'm weak, because my heart longs to please and bless You. *Amen*

Which Seven Words?

I can do all things in him.
Philippians 4:13a

Someone has said that the seven most deadly words ever spoken in a church are: "We've never done it like this before." Closed-mindedness can be devastating. It doesn't require many of these statements to negate a dream and discourage the dreamer. I've often wondered why it is that so many people seem to have an automatic negative response to any new idea.

On the other hand, there are seven words that can change a church forever. These are: "I can do all things in him." This attitude is simply affirming faith in *God's* power, not ours. It's the kind of attitude we must have if we are to be the person and body of Christ we need to be.

"God did not give us a spirit of timidity but a spirit of power and love and self-control" (II Timothy 1:7).

All of us have limitations. Churches have limitations, too, but we serve a God with unlimited power and presence. The apostle Paul knew this. He was God-sufficient. He knew he could face anything because he walked with God.

During Paul's lifetime he experienced about every type of suffering possible, yet he knew his source of strength. In Romans 8:35 he said, "Who shall separate us from the love of Christ? Shall tribulation, or distress, or persecution, or famine, or nakedness, or peril, or sword?" He answers his own question in verses 37 and 38, "No, in all these thing we are more than conquerors through him who loved us. For I am sure that neither death, nor life, nor angels, nor principalities, nor things present, nor things to come, nor powers, nor height, nor depth, nor anything else in all creation, will be able to separate us from the love of God in Christ Jesus our Lord."

Which seven words will guide and control our lives and churches? I pray that we can believe, like Paul, that "I can do all things in him."

Lord, help us live by faith and not by fear. Replace our timidity with courage. Through Christ our conqueror. *Amen*

Germs and Jesus

Blessed are those who have not seen and yet believe.
John 20:29b

A friend of mine tells the story about a little boy who attended kinder-garten at a local church. One day his teacher told him to go wash his hands before snack time. He wanted to know why. The teacher explained that it was to get the germs off. He walked toward the bathroom, shaking his head and saying, "Germs and Jesus. Germs and Jesus. That's all I hear around here, and I've never seen either one of them."

Can we walk by faith and not by sight?

We would have to admit that there is an element of faith in washing our hands. We can't see the germs. Our hands can *look* clean, yet we're told we need to wash them anyway.

It takes faith to believe in Jesus. Like the little boy, we've never seen Jesus. And like Thomas, we want to see with eyes of sight, not eyes of faith.

There is an uncommon honesty in children, and Thomas had this same quality. He had no pretense about his doubts. Doubts like the ones Thomas had usually end in certainty. Thomas's doubts took him all the way to a conviction and a confession, "My Lord and my God!" (John 20:28).

Faith was not easy for the little kindergarten boy or for Thomas. Faith may not be easy for us either. But once Thomas was sure—once he had seen with his own eyes—he went to the ultimate limit in faith and obedience.

Jesus said that those who have not seen and yet believe are blessed. They are happy. Faith, not fear, is the key to happiness. Which one of these will guide my life today?

Dear God, I believe and yet I need help with my unbelief. I pray that You will strengthen my faith and obedience. I promise to give You the praise. In Jesus' name. *Amen*

Pride Goes Before Destruction

Pride goes before destruction, and a haughty spirit before a fall.
Proverbs 16:18

While attending an outdoor youth concert I experienced a painful fall. Instinctively, I looked up to see who had seen me take my tumble. A young man, intending to be humorous, said rather wryly, "You know, pride goes before a fall!" Later, I realized that he not only had failed at being funny, but he also had failed to quote Scripture correctly.

Ironically, I had been asked by this person to pray for the concert, and I had. Yet, he failed to even offer a helping hand to me. This unpleasant experience seldom comes to mind any more, but I am ever aware of the danger of pride. Pride can stand sentinel at the doors of our hearts to shut out compassion, honesty, humility, peace, and joy. James 4:6 says, "God opposes the proud, but gives grace to the humble."

When we place our lives beside the example of Christ, there is no room for pride.

Jesus set the example for humility. Philippians 2:8 says, "And being found in human form he humbled himself and became obedient unto death, even death on a cross." Jesus didn't desire his own way, but God's way. He desired to be a humble servant. Jesus had a word of wisdom for the proud: "Everyone who exalts himself will be humbled, but he who humbles himself will be exalted" (Luke 18:14b).

Is pride a part of our lives? I hope not. It has no place in a Christian's life. We need to live as Peter admonished the Christians in Asia Minor: "Clothe yourselves, all of you, with humility toward one another" (I Peter 5:5a). Did pride cause my fall? I don't think so, but the misquoted Scripture in response to it has surely caused me to be more conscious of the dangers of pride.

Dear Father, forgive me of any part of my nature that is unpleasing to You. Be merciful to me when I fail or when I fall, and help me to do the same for others. In Jesus' name. *Amen*

No Sleep

Behold, he who keeps Israel will neither slumber nor sleep.
Psalms 121:4

*M*ost of us have probably fallen asleep at times when we tried desperately to stay awake. It may have been during a worship service, sitting by the bedside of a sick person, or, God forbid, driving on the highway. I remember the embarrassment of falling asleep during a telephone conversation.

God's eye is on the sparrow, so I know He watches His children.

Weary from a difficult day of teaching kindergarten, I had just stretched out on the couch when the phone rang. Hearing the voice on the line, I knew this would be an hour-long conversation. I moved the phone by the couch, and at some point in the conversation I went to sleep. Minutes later I awakened and placed the phone back to my ear. Having no idea what had been said, I tried to join in the conversation by saying, "Uh huh." I still wonder what I agreed to that day!

The most vigilant of us can unintentionally fall asleep, but I'm thankful that God doesn't do that. He is not finite like us. He is infinite with no limitations—and no need for sleep. The psalmist rested in the fact that God never slumbers nor sleeps. We have the same assurance. God keeps a watchful eye on His creation. Regardless of where we are or what we are doing, His presence goes with us.

We, in our human limitations, are not completely dependable. Our hearts and minds may desire to be trustworthy, but even the most cautious of us are prone to fall asleep when our bodies are exhausted. I'm so thankful that our heavenly Father needs no sleep and keeps a watchful eye on us all. This fact can continually bring us comfort and peace.

Thank You, dear heavenly Father, for Your watchful care of Your creation. Help me to live each day in this assurance. In Jesus' name. *Amen*

What Should We Wear?

Put on the Lord Jesus Christ.
Romans 13:14a

*M*ost of us have said at one time or another, "I don't know what to wear today." Deciding on what to wear took on new meaning for me recently. I attended a program entitled "What Should We Wear?" At the beginning we were asked to walk by a series of tables and choose cards that listed "unbecoming apparel." There were cards that read pride, jealousy, anger, dissention, hate, etc. We were to choose the cards that described a part of ourselves that we needed to remove. We would later throw the cards in a trash can.

What people see in our lives today may determine their attitude toward Christ in the days ahead.

We then moved to another section of the room and chose for ourselves "becoming attire." Here we were offered love, joy, peace, kindness, goodness, faithfulness, and self-control. We kept these cards. It was a sobering experience for me to look at the parts of my "wardrobe" that are Christ-like and the parts that aren't.

It is said that when Augustine read the above verse, he set as his goal to put on the Lord Jesus Christ. The truth of God's Word lodged deeply in his heart. He de-robed himself of his old lifestyle by God's grace. Augustine took on a new look and a new outlook. So can we!

When we put on the Lord Jesus Christ, the old nature passes away. We are a new creation. II Corinthians 5:17 says, "Therefore, if any one is in Christ, he is a new creation; the old has passed away, behold, the new has come." With Him, we have a brand new wardrobe!

Dear Lord, clothe me in Your likeness so that others will see You in Me. Through Christ. *Amen*

Bought with a Price

You are not your own; you were bought with a price.
So glorify God in your body.
I Corinthians 6:19b,20a

Who or what influences our children's self-image? Is it parents, peers, movies, church, MTV, Larry Flint, or a myriad of other aspects of today's society? Junk values seem to reign in our American culture. Is anyone telling today's youth that they are of worth—infinite worth? Do they know that they have been bought with a price? Have they ever been told that Jesus gave His very life that they may have abundant life?

Our worth in Jesus' eyes is defined by the price He paid for our eternal life.

A high school in a neighboring town recently sponsored a program on drugs. It was discovered that 50 percent of the youth in that school are involved in using some kind of drugs. But the startling discovery was that peer pressure was not the main cause of their turning to drugs. Rather, they said the cause was lack of purpose in life; they felt that they had nothing for which to live. What brings this emptiness of soul to our young people?

Jesus says in John 10:10, "The thief comes only to steal and kill and destroy; I came that they may have life, and have it abundantly." If a person is convinced of his or her infinite value to God, that person will likely give occupancy in his or her heart to God.

I wonder how different the self-image of our children today would be if parents made the time to explain to them their worth: that God knit them together in their mother's womb (Psalms 139:13b); that they were bought with a price (I Corinthians 6:20); and that they belong to God (Acts 27:23). I believe it would make *all* the difference.

Loving Father, thank You so much for the investment You made in us through the gift of Your Son. Help us to share this good news with Your children, and especially with those in our own family. In Jesus' Name. *Amen*

Fill Your Own Shoes

Having gifts that differ according to the grace
given to us, let us use them.
Romans 12:6a

*H*ave you ever seen someone wear a piece of clothing and wish you had something like it? I have—more than once. I have a tendency to forget that the garment that looked good on someone else may not look good on me.

I remember admiring the beautiful, white leather, low-wedge slippers that a pretty, petite young girl wore in high school. They were just right with an open heel, an enclosed toe, and a nice, cut-out design all around. How I longed for a pair of those slippers!

I am the only person who should fill my shoes.

Then one day I walked into the local department store and there they were—right in my path and on sale for three dollars. It didn't really matter that the pair closest to my size was a little too narrow and short. I bought them anyway. I just knew I could make them work. They felt miserable, and they looked even worse on my feet. I never wore them.

I learned a valuable lesson from that experience. The shoes that are right for me may not be right for someone else, and vice versa. Each of us is different. We can't fill each other's shoes, nor should we try. God has blessed each of us with different body styles, different personalities, different likes and dislikes, and different gifts and graces. We need to enjoy being the person God made us to be. So we need to fill the shoes that feel comfortable on our own feet. We need to stop comparing our talents with someone else's and develop our own to our fullest potential.

The Lord has blessed each of us in special ways. Let us accept and use our gifts to His glory.

Father, You created each of us with a special purpose in life. Help me each day to please You in all that I am and in all that I do. In Jesus' name. *Amen*

Known from Afar

O Lord, thou hast searched me and known me...
thou discernest my thoughts from afar.
Psalms 139:1,2b

I have always wished I could walk gracefully. One day while walking down our lane from the school bus stop, I decided to try to walk more gracefully—more like the popular girls in my class. I remembered hearing someone say that we should walk as though a book were being balanced on our head. I lifted my shoulders, tilted my chin upward a little, and moved into a different pace.

God knows all about me—inside and out!

Straight down the lane I went, almost believing I was getting the hang of a new and better way to walk. I didn't notice mother out in the yard, so I was a little surprised at her greeting: "Why, Kate, it's *you*! I didn't recognize your walk as you came down the lane." Of course she knew it was me. She just knew I was trying to walk like someone else and didn't want to embarrass me.

I'll never forget that lesson. When we aren't ourselves, it's noticeable. Pretense is always obvious even from a distance. God not only knows all about our outward appearance—the Scripture says that even the hairs on our head are numbered (Matthew 10:30)—but He also knows our hearts. "Man looks on the outward appearance, but the Lord looks on the heart" (I Samuel 16:7b).

I could never fool my mother, and certainly I can never fool God. He made me. He has called me by my name. I am His (Isaiah 43:1). He knows if I'm walking my walk and talking my talk or if I'm trying to copy someone else.

Today—and always—I want to be my real self. Phoniness is recognizable and never attractive. I'm so thankful for that lesson learned a long time ago.

Loving Lord, thank You for accepting and loving us just as we are. Help me grow into Your likeness. In Jesus' name. *Amen*

"I Lub You So Much"

Greater love has no one than this, that he lay down his life for his friends.

John 15:13 (NIV)

I longed to hear our little granddaughter talk. Being autistic, she didn't begin to speak until around four years of age. I remember the first time Katie uttered the words, "I lub you!" Then it wasn't long before she said to me, "I lub you so much!" How these words blessed me!

God has been saying "I love you" since creation. Throughout the Old Testament God manifested His love to His people in many ways. In Isaiah 43:3 God says, "You are precious in my eyes, and honored, and I love you." Later when God sent his Son into the world, He was still saying, "I love you." But it was when He allowed Jesus to suffer and die on the cross,

God's "so much" love will bring so much joy.

taking on the sins of the whole world, that God said, "I love you *so* much!" John 3:16 says it: "For God so loved the world that He gave His only Son." There is no greater love than this.

It's difficult for me to fathom this kind of love. If I knew I had only one more opportunity to give witness to my faith, I would try my best to tell about God's love. I would try to explain how he loves us *so* much. I believe this is good news worth telling!

Have you experienced God's love in your life? If you haven't, you can by asking Jesus to come in to your heart today.

Dear God, I am so thankful that You loved us so much that You gave Your Son to die for us. Help us to share Your love with the world. In Jesus' name. *Amen*

Persona Dolls

Then God said, "Let us make man in our image, after our likeness....
Genesis 1:26a

Leafing through the toy catalog I came upon a doll that caught my attention. It's called the "Persona Doll." This doll can be constructed to reflect the same characteristics of its owner. If a child has lost a limb or has other visible marked features of impairment, the doll can be made in the child's image.

How does my life reflect God's image?

We're told that these dolls help children with disabilities accept and like themselves as they are.

This is a new and wonderful idea for a doll. Dolls have always appeared perfect. No flaws. No blemishes. No visible handicaps. Perfect hair, clothes, and skin tones. Yet, when a doll becomes worn or flawed, its owner doesn't reject it. On the contrary, the doll is loved and treasured even more with each passing day.

And hasn't perfection been a driving force in our society? We aren't satisfied with who we are and what we look like. If our hair is too curly, we want to straighten it. If it's too straight, we want to curl it. Some people use bleaching cream to lighten the skin. Others bake in the sun—even risk skin cancer—to darken the skin. The Chinese are credited for saying that Americans are as crazy as they can be. They boil tea to make it hot, put ice in it to make it cold, put sugar in it to make it sweet, and put lemon in it to make it sour.

We need to know who we are and more importantly, whose we are. Knowing that we are made in the image of God should help us to accept ourselves. God loves and accepts us. He bought us with a price. We are His. Therefore, we need to reflect the characteristics of our owner!

Creator God, I'm so thankful that You love us enough to give Your only Son for us. Help me to take on Your likeness and that of Jesus. In His name. *Amen*

Being Our Best

But to all who received him, who believed in his name,
he gave power to become children of God.

John 1:12

Most of us, at one time or another, have heard, "Do the very best that you can!" or, "Give it all you have," or, "You're doing great!" These are challenging and affirming words that I believe bring out the best in a person.

Ethel Waters is said to have made this statement, "God don't make no junk!" It's true that God created each of us unique in our own rights and with potential to be our best. He even provided for us a way through His Son, Jesus, to become His children! In his gospel, John names two requirements: receive Jesus and believe in His name.

William Barclay explains that to believe in His name means to receive the nature and characteristics of God and place our trust in Him. Being our best means putting our trust in God's Son and taking on His characteristics. Only a sinful world can make us feel like junk.[2] God doesn't make junk. He has created us with the potential to be the best of whatever we are.

As children of God, we're not junk; we're jewels, precious in His sight!

I remember when David gave his first speech in the fourth grade. I can see that little freckled-faced, red-headed boy, determined to do his best as he spoke on "I'm Just One." He closed that speech with the words of Douglas Malloch:

> "If you can't be a pine on the top of the hill, be a shrub in the valley, but be the best little shrub by the side of the hill. Be a bush if you can't be a tree. If you can't be a highway, just be a trail. If you can't be a sun, be a star. It isn't by size that you win or fail. Be the best of whatever you are."[3]

By receiving and believing in the One who made us, we can become His children. That makes us very special and should cause us to want to be our best.

Loving Creator, thank You for creating us and making a way for us to be Your children. Help us to be our best today—for Your honor and glory. In Jesus' name. *Amen*

As We Have Forgiven

Forgive us our debts, as we also have forgiven our debtors.
Matthew 6:12

"Our house has been burglarized!" I moaned as we pulled into our driveway. There were too many telltale signs: open garage door, open kitchen door, lights on inside in unusual places.

A neighbor called the police for us. Later, we followed the police through the house, overwhelmed with all sorts of feelings: anger, disgust, disbelief, pain, and shock that the sanctity of our home had been violated. Tears flowed as we walked from one ransacked room to another.

Healing begins when forgiveness begins.

Around 4:00 A.M., as waves of bitterness still swept over me, I heard a sound of singing coming from our twelve year old son's room. As we made our way toward the sound, stumbling over dresser drawers and their contents, we clearly heard the words to the hymn "What A Friend We Have in Jesus."[1] There it was—the comfort our family needed. Of course, we could take everything to God: our hurting hearts, the burglar's sin (and ours), and our exhausted bodies, minds, and spirits.

We could also take to Him our gratitude that none of us was harmed in the break-in. It was God who had directed me to require the children to go to the airport with us that night, following the revival service that we had all attended. It really hadn't made sense at the time. They had come to the revival in Debbie's old car in order to go straight home after the service to complete homework. We knew that our own car would be over-crowded with our family of four plus the evangelist and the two music leaders. But God, in His infinite mercy, kept us together and spared our children—maybe all four of us.

There in the jumble of David's room the words of the hymn echoed in our ears. The four of us embraced. "Well, we do have to forgive them, you know," David reminded us. He was right. If we are to be forgiven, we must forgive. I felt the bitterness begin to fade as we prayed for the ones who had broken into our home. A child had led us to forgiveness and peace.

Our Father, help us to remember your Son's ultimate example of forgiveness on the cross. Give us the grace to follow it. *Amen*

Almost Persuaded

Almost thou persuadest me to be a Christian.
Acts 26:28 (KJV)

*H*ow often in life are we "almost persuaded" in situations? Some of these decisions would lead to our betterment, others to our detriment. Some would affect us for a lifetime, others are less important.

In our Scripture, King Agrippa was almost persuaded to accept the Christ that Paul defended. While theologians differ on King Agrippa's sincerity, I believe he was at least impressed by Paul's witness—impressed, but not convinced.

In matters big and small, Christ holds the answer to them all.

I recall the revival during which I accepted Christ into my heart. All week I wanted to walk those few steps up to the altar in our little country church. Each day, at the close of the service, we sang "Almost Persuaded."[2] But it was not until Friday of that week that I moved forward and said "yes" to God.

We can be almost persuaded in life-changing decisions like becoming a Christian. We can also be almost persuaded in decisions that are perhaps of less consequence, but nevertheless important. For three years our son David promised his "little brother"—also a David—to fly him to Atlanta for a weekend if "Little David" maintained a C average in school.

For two years, young David sent his success record by way of his grade card, and he loved the trip that was his reward. However, one year young David ended the school year with one D+ on his grade card. He immediately implored David that the grade was a "high D"—almost a C. "Couldn't you just let me come, David?" he begged.

Our son was almost persuaded to bend the rules. After all, it had been a difficult year for young David. But he knew that if he bent the rule on small matters, the example would be set for bending the rule on big issues. He knew that a pattern for life could be set this way. He knew, too, that young David would eventually recover from the disappointment, and maybe he would have learned an important lesson in life.

Merciful Lord, help us to have the courage and wisdom to make the right decisions in life. In Jesus' name. *Amen*

A Way of Escape

No temptation has overtaken you that is not common to man. God is faithful, and he will not let you be tempted beyond your strength, but with the temptation will also provide the way of escape, that you may be able to endure it.

I Corinthians 10:13

Crossing Monteagle, a mountain in Tennessee, I noticed signs for trucks with brake problems that said "Runaway Ramp Ahead." After a series of signs announcing the distance to the runaway ramp, we came to it. Leading off from the left lane of the interstate highway was a roadbed filled with sand. Truckers whose brakes had failed could take advantage of this way of escape by burying their wheels in the deep sand.

"If thy law had not been my delight, I should have perished in my affliction" (Psalms 119:92).

Runaway ramps on mountains provide truckers a strategic and safe way of evading a serious accident and perhaps death. But what about persons who face dangerous temptation on the roads of life? What can a person do with runaway emotions such as uncontrolled anger, hate, and fear? How can the teenager, tempted on every hand to let his or her sexual feelings run away, find a way of escape?

When the brakes on an eighteen wheeler cease to function properly, the driver needs a way of escape. Persons whose lives are out of control need a way to escape and a way to endure. Paul says that God is faithful. He can be trusted to keep us from being tempted beyond our strength and, with every temptation, will provide an escape route.

But there's a requirement for both the truck driver and the person facing temptation: each has to decide to use the way of escape. If a truck driver fails to use the sand-filled incline, or we who are tempted fail to call upon our heavenly Father, our lives will continue the unchecked, downward plunge toward suffering and destruction.

For us, the signpost for the way of escape is in God's Word. For safe travel in this life, God's message needs to be written upon our hearts.

Father, help us to lay up Your Word in our hearts so that we are prepared to face the temptations and trials that come our way. Amen

The Urgent and the Important

Make good use of every opportunity you have.
Ephesians 5:16a (TEV)

*H*ave you ever said, "I need more hours in the day"? As a parent I certainly feel this way often. But if we would be honest with ourselves, we would admit that more hours in the day is not the answer; rather, it's being more careful how we spend the hours.

The most precious and treasured moments spent with our children were those times when we stopped everything and did something for the sheer fun of it. We baked a gingerbread man; climbed to the top of the highest hill in Louisville to watch an early morning launching of a balloon race; made a new doll dress; or just sat and talked until the wee hours of the morning.

Children never outgrow the need for the gift of our time.

I wish I had attended to the important more often. I wasn't always careful not to allow what seemed urgent to crowd out the important. What felt urgent might have been attending a routine women's meeting at the church. Or cleaning the house when this could have waited for another day. Or volunteering for some task at church or at school because I felt it was my duty.

At the birth of our first grandchild, I made a counted cross-stitch wall hanging with these words for our daughter:

> Cleaning and scrubbing
> Can wait 'til tomorrow,
> For babies grow up
> We've learned to our sorrow.
> So quiet down, cobwebs,
> Dust, go to sleep.
> I'm rocking my baby,
> And babies don't keep.
> —Author unknown

Loving Father, please remind me to attend to the important in life. In Jesus' name. *Amen*

A Strength Exchange

They who wait for the Lord shall renew their strength.
Isaiah 40:31a

While preparing to lead a retreat recently, I discovered a fresh meaning for this verse from Isaiah. Isaiah was writing to a people in exile who needed added strength for their journey. Their temple was in ruins. The land that God had given them was run over by hordes of pagans. They were beginning to doubt God's fairness, and were close to being embittered.

God's strength instead of our weakness—what an exchange!

Isaiah was saying, "If you're willing to be patient—if you are willing to wait on the Lord—your strength will be renewed." In Hebrew the word used for "renew" means to exchange strength. It means that God will exchange *His* strength and power for *our* weakness. I love that thought! When our strength is gone, then His is given. Later Paul reminded us of God's advice for us: "My power is made perfect in weakness." (II Corinthians 12:9a).

We may not experience the struggles and suffering of the exiled people, but none of us will escape some kind of struggle and suffering in life. Illness, death, financial loss, and stresses of all kinds are a part of our lives. But the God who has been faithful throughout history is still our faithful God today. He still gives strength exchanges! It would be well for us to remember Isaiah's promise: new strength can be ours if we're willing to wait upon the Lord.

Loving Father, we need Your strength for our journey—not just each day but each minute. Help us never to run ahead of You. *Amen*

You Can!

I can do all things in him who strengthens me.
Philippians 4:13

*D*uring a retreat, colorful paper leaves were distributed among the group. On each leaf were the words, "You can!" I've saved my leaf and keep it as a positive reminder of the faith that should be a part of my daily walk.

No one has promised us that overcoming will be easy. But history is filled with persons who have said, "I can!"—in spite of physical limitations, failure, and poverty. In spite of deafness, Ludwig von Beethoven composed some of the greatest symphonies the world knows today. Abraham Lincoln lost many elections before finally winning one. John Milton was blind but wrote some of our most beautiful literature. Loretta Lynn grew up in Butcher Hollow in Appalachia but became a renowned country music star.

You and I can live the victorious life through Christ who strengthens us.

Each of us knows our limitations. We deal with our own fears, insecurities, and doubts. We often let an "I can't" attitude hinder us from reaching the potential God has for us. But once we muster enough faith in a power greater than our own, the battle is won.

When we affirm this Scripture, "I can do all things in him who strengthens me," we have moved beyond ourselves and our weaknesses, hardships, and hindrances. It's then that we can courageously face life—and even death—because Christ's resurrection proclaimed, "I can!" once and for all. Through the Holy Spirit—provided for us by our risen Lord—nothing is impossible!

Heavenly Father, we thank You for the victory You have provided for us through Your Son, Jesus. Help us never to doubt Your power. *Amen*

Three Magic Words

The King will answer them, "Truly, I say to you, as you did it to one of the least of these my brethren, you did it to me."
Matthew 25:40

*M*y college psychology class decided to tour a local center for the profoundly disabled. I had visited the place many times, and it was never a pleasant experience. My heart always ached as I saw the devastation of these young lives.

I had been to the facility when our church group provided Christmas parties. During these visits, the children who were least handicapped were brought to the lobby and many responded to the singing and enjoyed the treats. But on this day we were going to visit *all* the children.

The message of love is heard not just through the ears, but also through the heart and soul.

One by one we walked by the patients. Our guide explained the particular nature of each child's disability and how long he or she had been at the facility. We turned a corner and I noticed a crib in the hallway. The guide stopped momentarily and warned us that there would be no response from this patient; we need not make the effort to communicate. I fell behind the group and was the last person to pass the crib. I could not believe my eyes as I looked upon the emaciated form of what looked to be an eight- or nine-year-old boy. He lay lifelessly staring at the ceiling.

Bending over the crib, I whispered to him, "I love you." As long as I live, I will remember the big, broad smile that spread across his face. No eye contact. No movement. No response except that angelic smile.

Running as quickly as possible, I managed to catch up with the class without their missing me. The words that our guide spoke during the remainder of the tour meant very little to me. For I had just learned the most important lesson I could ever learn: the power of three magic words, the power of love. And to this day, I find myself wondering how many of God's special children have been labeled "vegetable" or "hopeless" when they might respond to warmth and love if given a chance.

Dear God, forgive us when we label one of Your children "helpless" or "hopeless." Help us to share Your love, so that others may know happiness. In Jesus' name. *Amen*

Included Out

Let each of you look not only to his own interests,
but also to the interests of others.
Philippians 2:4

*Y*ou shut me out of your circle!" Neither I nor the young adult class I was teaching could believe what we were hearing from one of the class members. "I know you didn't mean to," she said. "You probably weren't even aware that you were shutting me out, but you did! I know that I come to class late sometimes, but none of you ever offered to open your circle when I entered the room—let alone offer me a chair!"

Shame and embarrassment came over all of us as we began to hear—really listen to—this young, divorced mother of two daughters. How could we have been so insensitive? We didn't want to admit that her accusation was true, but we could remember the many times she arrived after the class had started.

How often does our insensitivity shut persons, including Jesus, out of our hearts and lives?

We had the perfect setting for a classroom. We had the ideal resources and teaching materials. We made bright, colorful banners with catchy phrases like "Life is fragile…handle with prayer." We placed freshly potted plants in new macramé hangers. And always the aroma of freshly brewed coffee filled the room.

But when a newcomer or a latecomer arrived, we were so caught up in our own little world that we closed our circle to an aching heart. How thankful we were she had the courage to confront the situation

Apologies flowed freely during the moments that followed. We *had* been blind and insensitive. But, thankfully, we soon were able to chuckle about the whole incident, and, on subsequent Sundays, her appearance in the doorway brought an immediate circle expansion! Best of all, this dear young woman became a vital part of this supportive fellowship. She no longer felt included out! In fact, no one else ever felt included out of this Sunday school class either.

*L*ord, bind us together by Your love. Please help us keep from becoming so wrapped up in our own selves that we exclude You or one of Your precious children. *A*men

Kick the Rock Out

*Out of my distress I called on the Lord;
the Lord answered me and set me free.*

Psalms 118:5

*R*everend Roscoe Tarter, a United Methodist pastor (now deceased) in Kentucky, once told of an interesting experience during his early years in the ministry. Coming home from a busy day of visitation, his car came to a standstill atop a long, winding hill. Even worse than running out of gasoline, he had also ran out of money that day.

Regardless of the obstruction or interference, God can remove it.

Walking around the car and struggling with his dilemma, he noticed the left front tire fixed firmly behind a good-sized rock. Over and over a voice seemed to say, "Kick the rock out!" *I don't know what good it would do,* the young pastor reasoned. *I have no way to buy gasoline.* "Kick the rock out! Kick the rock out!" came the repeated command. *How can I kick the rock out when it's wedged firmly under the front tire?*

Again the clear instruction was given: "Kick the rock out!" With one firm blow from the toe of his shoe, the rock rolled out to the side of the road. Young Tarter jumped into the slowly moving vehicle and safely guided it into the filling station at the foot of the hill. He had momentum enough to bring it to a stop beside a gas pump.

Shortly, the familiar face of a parishioner appeared at his car window. Taking out an old faded bandana handkerchief, the man untied a knot and removed three crumpled dollar bills. He handed them to his pastor. "This is all I have," he said. "But something tells me to give this to you."

Most of us face obstacles in our lives every day. We "run out of steam" and become discouraged. We feel that our paths are blocked. What is blocking your path? What is hindering you in your faith? What holds you back from serving the Lord? Whatever the barrier may be, kick it out! By an act of the will, and with God's help, set yourself free to serve!

Dear Father, thank You for hearing our hearts in times of distress. Help us to listen to Your directions each day. In Jesus' name. *Amen*

octo ber

A Sieve for Our Words

Let no evil talk come out of your mouths, but only such as is good for edifying, as fits the occasion, that it may impart grace to those who hear.

Ephesians 4:29

I recall as a child watching my mother sift coarse corn meal. The corn was grown on our farm and ground at my uncle's mill. It contained particles unusable for cornbread, but with a little sifting, the finely ground part of the corn was ready and usable. The remainder was discarded.

We would do well to sift our words as well. We need to rid our talk of the harmful and hurtful parts. Do our words edify? Do they impart grace? Can you recall a time when you've said something and the minute the words were out, you knew they had wounded someone? Most of us, if we were honest, would have to answer "yes" to this last question.

Sticks and stones can break our bones... and words can hurt us, too.

How are we going to "sift out" those words that should never be uttered? An ancient bit of wisdom suggests that we can put our words through this test: Are they necessary? Are they true? Are they kind?

If we could practice this "word check" we would discover a sieve for what we say. We would have an instrument for separating our "coarse," hurtful words from the "fine," helpful words.

James said, "From the same mouth come blessing and cursing. My brethren, this ought not to be so" (James 3:10). Paul instructed the Christians at Colosae: "Let your speech always be gracious" (Colossians 4:6a). In Ephesians 4:29, Paul indicates that when we edify others with our words, we "impart grace to those who hear."

The world is hungry for kindness and truth. Will my words today cause someone to be encouraged or discouraged? That answer lies in how well I sift through my unnecessary, untrue, and unkind words to get to the words that edify, impart grace, and fit the occasion.

Dear Lord, help me to bridle my tongue. Forgive me for times I have uttered words that are unpleasing to You. In Jesus' name. *Amen*

God Knows Us

I know my own and my own know me.
John 10:14b

No one knows us like God knows us. Jeremiah reminds us that even before we were born God knew us and consecrated us (Jeremiah 1:5a). In Isaiah, God reminded the people that He had redeemed them, He had called them by name and then added, "You are mine" (Isaiah 43:1).

I want to know the One who knows me best.

Geneticists tell us that at the point of conception a completely new genetic code becomes a part of the new life in the womb. Each one of us has a DNA code unlike anyone else in the world. Even identical twins have differing fingerprints, footprints, and voice-prints.

It's mind-boggling to think about the numbers of people who have lived and are currently living on this planet. Yet our Creator God knew all of us even before we were formed. Surely this God who knows when a sparrow falls—and even knows our DNA code—wants only good for us.

God knows us. He knows our dreams and our longings. He knows our disappointments and our discouragement. But through it all, He wants us to fulfill the plan He has for us. Jeremiah 29:11 says, "For I know the plans I have for you, says the Lord, plans for welfare and not for evil, to give you a future and a hope." How good it would be if we could begin each new day asking God to reveal His plan for us—just for that day.

God knows us. He formed us. He consecrated us. He desires only good for us. Surely our lives should reflect His goodness.

Loving Father, thank You for knowing and loving us—even before we were born. Please reveal Your plan for my life today. *Amen*

A New Identity

Therefore, if anyone is in Christ, he is a new creation;
the old has passed away, behold, the new has come.
II Corinthians 5:17

*I*t's a comfort to know that Jesus sees us not only as we are, but also as what we can become. Jesus saw this kind of potential in Simon Peter. The name "Simon" means "reed"—weak, flexible, easily bent or broken. But when Simon confessed Jesus to be "the Christ, the Son of the living God," Jesus said, "You are Peter, and on this rock I will build my church" (Matthew 16:16,18).

Is my daily life reed-like or rock-like?

Peter had a new identity. He was changed from a weak, wavering reed to a strong, stable building stone—worthy of being a part of the foundation of the church! His new identity now held the strength to withstand the gates of hell.

Peter was a new creation in Christ. The old, reed-like person became a rock because of what Christ did in his life. There are changes in identity throughout the Old Testament as people encountered God. Sarai was changed to Sarah which means "princess"; she would become the mother of nations.[3] Abram was changed to Abraham; an "exalted father" became a "father of a multitude."[4] Jacob was re-named Israel; he was transformed from "he takes by the heel"[5] to "a prince of God."[6]

New creations in Christ are still occurring today. As people receive Christ and acknowledge His lordship they may not take a new name, but their very nature changes. The old passes away and the new comes. They look different. Their motives and priorities change. Their attitudes and ambitions are new and different. God gives a new identity.

Loving God, help us to become all that You created us to be. Continue to remake us into Your image each day through Christ our Lord. *Amen*

But God Stepped In

Peter was kept in prison; but earnest prayer for him was made to God by the church.

Acts 12:5

Peter was thrown into prison right after Herod killed James, the brother of John. Herod was on a roll when he saw how his violence pleased the Jews. He made sure that Peter was in safekeeping by assigning four squadrons of soldiers to guard him. But God stepped into the picture. God stepped in and changed the direction of events because of the earnest prayers of believers.

"The prayer of a righteous man has great power in its effect"

(James 5:16b).

The church became committed to praying for Peter's release, and things began to happen. An angel came to the cell where Peter lay bound between two sentries. Peter awoke and got up, and the chains fell off! Can you imagine the feelings Peter experienced, as he was literally set free from the chains that bound his hands?

God steps into our lives, too, to free us from whatever binds us. Earnest prayer is the key to our freedom. "Peter was kept in prison, but…" One little conjunction introduced the secret to Paul's escape: "…earnest prayer was made to God by the church."

From what bondage do we need release today? What about our families and loved ones—what binds them? What binds and holds back the work of the Lord in the church? What imprisons the power of the Holy Spirit? Is it greed, self-centeredness, jealousy, gossip, slander, lust, or a combination of the many ways that evil raises its ugly head?

As we commit ourselves to earnest, fervent prayer, God can, and will, step into our lives, into our families and churches. No chain can permanently bind the believer who prays in faith.

Merciful God, help me to remember that Your freeing power is at work in my life in proportion to my sincere asking for it in prayer. Through Christ. *Amen*

God Can Still Use Us

Jonah rose to flee to Tarshish from the presence of the Lord.
Jonah 1:3a

Have you ever felt like running away from a challenge? Is it easy for you to celebrate another person's good fortune? Can you feel joy when someone repents if that person is someone you dislike? If we answer these truthfully, we may not feel totally glad about our answers. Yet God can still use us—in spite of ourselves!

The prophet Jonah is an interesting character. Many of us can identify with him. God told Jonah to go to Ninevah, the capital city of the hated Assyrians, but Jonah rebelled. He wanted to run away to Tarshish—the opposite direction—to get away from God's presence.

In our return and repentance we are restored for usefulness in God's kingdom.

Jonah was not only rebellious, he was lethargic; he fell fast asleep during a storm while en route to Tarshish. He was prideful, too; he didn't want Ninevah to be spared. He said he'd rather die than see this happen (Jonah 4:3). He was long on judgment and short on mercy.

God's everlasting love stood over Jonah's hate. Jonah's petty selfishness, blind prejudice, and violent reactions were a perfect backdrop for God's gentleness. God knew He could still use Jonah.

Do we see ourselves in Jonah? Are we ever prideful, selfish, lethargic, prejudiced, disobedient? We need to know that God can still use us as He did Jonah.

God had the last word. He sent a storm and allowed a fish to swallow and then release Jonah. God will have the last word with us as well. We may run from Him and His call upon our lives, but God can and will draw us back unto Himself if we will only allow it to happen.

Dear God, thank You for Your love and mercy. Continue to draw us unto Yourself so that we can reach out to others. Through Christ. *Amen*

Resources Multiplied

He who supplies seed to the sower and bread for food will supply and multiply your resources and increase the harvest of your righteousness.

II Corinthians 9:10

Sometimes it's easy to excuse ourselves from responsibilities by saying we don't have the proper resources. Proper resources might include money, talent, time, or whatever we see as important for a task to be done. We may also use another excuse: we don't feel that what we do makes much difference anyway.

God not only supplies, He also multiplies!

I've used both of these excuses and have felt them more often than I've expressed them. But I have to remind myself often that God takes our fractions and multiplies them to become whole numbers.

In the sixth chapter of John, we see that the disciple Andrew found a way for God to multiply fractional resources. Andrew had probably overheard Jesus ask Phillip about where they would buy bread to feed the multitude. Phillip couldn't see any way of feeding the crowd because of the sheer cost of it, but Andrew did what he could. He brought to Jesus a little boy with a few resources—five fish and two loaves of bread. Realistically, there was no way this could feed the crowd of five thousand men, plus women and children. Andrew trusted the outcome to Jesus, and Jesus honored that trust.

We know the outcome of this trusting: there was enough to feed the whole crowd and twelve baskets left over! Little is much in Christ's hands. He takes what we offer Him, multiplies it, and brings the needed harvest.

Loving Father, thank You for accepting our fractional efforts and multiplying them until they become whole and effective. In Your Son's name. *Amen*

Birth and Rebirth

She does him good, and not harm, all the days of her life.
Proverbs 31:12

*I*t's not often that we know people who have assisted in both our physical birth and our spiritual rebirth. Flora Radford was just such a person in my life. I was born in rural Cumberland County, Kentucky, and there was no doctor available to assist with my birth. Miss Flora, as we kids called her, was living near us and assisted as midwife.

At the age of twelve I marched, along with some thirty other elementary age children, from the one-room school to the one-room Methodist church in my community. For many years the custom was for our school to attend the morning services of the annual revival.

Who can I encourage today to take a step toward Christ?

I knew in my heart that it was time for me to make my decision to accept Christ, but I found it very difficult to summon the courage to walk to the altar. I remember standing there hesitantly, longing to take that first step.

That day in October of 1949, the evangelist's closing story spoke to my heart. Reverend Lewis Woodward told of a young girl who was brave enough to leave home to live out her faith.

I found myself hoping the closing hymn would not end before I could muster the courage to walk the four steps to the altar. Then, I felt a gentle tap on my shoulder. Turning to the side and batting away the tears, I saw Miss Flora. "Don't you think it's time to make your decision?" she asked. Without a word, I made my way to the varnished step leading up to the pulpit area, which served as our church altar.

Miss Flora was a vital part of two of the most important events of my life: my birth and my rebirth. How grateful I will always be for her help not only with my entry into this world, but also into the world to come!

Father, thank You for those dear people who help us to have life in the now and also in the world to come. Help me to invite others to You. Through Christ. *Amen*

Freedom from Fear

For God hath not given us the spirit of fear;
but of power, and of love, and of a sound mind.

II Timothy 1:7 (KJV)

I believe we have to *intentionally* fight fear, as we would the plague. We have to set our wills as the psalmist said: "I fear no evil, for thou art with me" (Psalms 23:4). This presence—always with us through the Holy Spirit—is reason enough for us to be free from fear.

Satan uses fear to make us weak. God uses His Word to make us strong.

But we have to also be intentional about making use of this presence with us—in the small everyday fears, as well as the big ones. Sometimes those seemingly insignificant fears can continue to invade our thoughts, haunting us and hacking away at our joy. Regardless of the size or severity of our fears, the same truth about them prevails: God didn't give them to us. Rather, His gifts to us are power, love, and a sound mind.

It's normal and healthy to have concern at times. Most of us know what it is like to dread giving a speech, going for a job interview, facing surgery, traveling during bad weather, and so on. These concerns will probably prompt us to perform more wisely and safely. But *real fear* can be destructive. It is the enemy of happiness. It can immobilize us and make us miserable little by little.

My own experience has proven that God's Word is the most enduring source of comfort and help in times of being tempted to fear. My favorite verse is John 14:27, "Peace I leave with you; my peace I give to you; not as the world gives do I give to you. Let not your hearts be troubled, neither let them be afraid." Then there's John 16:33a, "In the world you have tribulation; but be of good cheer, I have overcome the world." And I John 4:18, "There is no fear in love, but perfect love casts out fear."

There are many ways of dealing with fear, but the greatest help for me in finding freedom from fear is to allow God's Word to minister to me—and to pray. Then I can affirm the psalmist who said, "I sought the Lord, and he answered me, and delivered me from all my fears" (Psalms 34:4).

Thank You, Father, that You free us from fear when we find our refuge in Your Word. Through Christ. *Amen*

Sheep Astray

All we like sheep have gone astray;
we have turned every one to his own way.
Isaiah 53:6a

I treasure my experience attending a one-room school as a child. Classroom resources may have been limited, but community pride and support of Howard's Bottom School were in plentiful supply. People filled the school room for the annual box supper fundraiser. Then when the time came to prepare for the big, county-wide school fair, parents worked hard to make costumes for the children. Our school often won first place in the competition. There was always a generous supply of help from a caring teacher.

Will I turn to my own way today, or will I be obedient to the Good Shepherd?

Recesses were special, too. Many times the entire eight grades played together. At other times, girls and boys divided to play a favorite game. On other days, all of us seemed to have a bit of wanderlust in us and off we'd go to explore.

On one particularly warm day, the whole group decided to follow the creek near our school. Every grapevine along the way needed trying out as a swing, and our jumping skills needed testing at the narrow places in the stream. On and on we followed the creek as it snaked its way toward the Cumberland River. Time seemed to stand still.

Suddenly, we awakened to reality. Faintly in the distance we heard the call of "Books! Booooks!" signaling the end of recess. Like a herd of sheep gone astray, we had gone too far and rushed back to the school.

Miss Dorothy was waiting. Her usual expression of kindness was now solemn and stern. I pled, "Please don't punish us. We are sorry. We didn't realize we had gone so far!" She studied my face for what seemed like an eternity; our hearts pounded within us as we waited for the verdict. Finally, like a general commanding a small army, she said, "Get in that school, get to work, and don't you go that far away from this school again!" We didn't! And what an important lesson we learned that day!

Loving Father, thank You for seeking us when we go astray. Thank You for forgiving us when we return and for expecting and enabling us to lead new lives of obedience. *Amen*

Unwrite My Name

*As far as the east is from the west, so far does
he remove our transgressions from us.*

Psalms 103:12

$\mathcal{M}$ike was a bright, personable little kindergartner. He seldom had to be corrected, but, on this particular spring day, his vivacious spirit got the upper hand. His name was placed on the chalkboard for the first time that year. Mike's name was the fourth written on the board—under the three who nearly always got their names on the chalkboard.

Will my life reflect today that I have been forgiven?

Throughout the morning Mike glanced at his name on the board; he couldn't shake the fact that it had happened. The usual twinkle in his beautiful brown eyes was now replaced with a somber look. It was heartbreaking and humiliating for him to think about his friends running freely at playtime while he spent his five-minute "time out" standing by the teacher.

Finally, the whole situation got the best of Mike. He eased from his seat and walked slowly toward me. I noticed his eyes were swimming in tears. His pride quickly batted the tears away as he neared my desk. He asked softly, "Miss Thomas, Miss Thomas…would you *please* unwrite my name?"

In my heart, I wanted to go immediately and erase Mike's name, but my head told me that I shouldn't—not yet. After all, he had broken class rules, rules that he had helped formulate at the beginning of the school year. I knew, too, that I had to treat the four children alike. I asked Mike to return to his table and explained to him and the other three that good behavior the remainder of the morning would erase their names—this time.

The bargain worked. But, it occurred to me: Jesus doesn't delay "unwriting" our names when we come to Him asking for forgiveness. If we come to Him with a sincere, repentant heart, His forgiveness is instantaneous. And I believe, in both human forgiveness and divine forgiveness, we are to go and "sin no more." (John 5:14b). I knew that Mike would try very hard to do just that! Would that we might do the same.

Thank You, loving Father, for forgiving our sins. Help me to always have a forgiving spirit. In Jesus' name. *Amen*

We Need a Pattern

I have given you an example, that you also should do as I have done to you.

John 13:15

*T*he window swags on display at the fabric store didn't look difficult to make. I carefully drew a sketch, measured, cut, sewed, and was ready to hang the new window treatment. To my surprise and dismay, the swags did not fit the window. Worse than that, there was no way to adjust them to make them fit. Lost time, money, and energy—all because I had not followed a pattern.

Am I taking seriously my opportunity to represent Christ to those around me?

In reflecting on this experience I thought of my need for a pattern for living. I can *think* I know how to live out each day. I can carefully plan, even sketch out these plans, hour by hour. I can work hard at creating a good life for myself and my family. But unless I follow the example given by Jesus, my efforts won't produce a meaningful life.

We need to ask ourselves: Am I following Christ's example? Is my life a good pattern for someone to follow? Does my example help or hinder the person who may be watching me? Paul said in I Corinthians 11:1, "You should follow my example, just as I follow Christ's" (TLB).

The only way we can be a worthy example for someone is by following Christ's example for our lives.

Dear God, I want to live in the way that pleases and honors You. Help me each day to follow the example of Jesus. *Amen*

Our Stabilizer

He calms the storm and stills the waves.

Psalms 107:29 (TLB)

I was recently a passenger in a late model car that would stabilize and balance its load upon being placed in gear. This was an interesting experience for me. I could feel, hear, and even see this stabilizing and balancing of the body of the car.

I was going through a frustrating time at this point in my life. I felt rocked about by circumstances beyond my control and burdened by a heavy load. As I spent time in prayer, asking God for His strength and peace to be with me, I again felt the effect of a stabilizing force. But this time, it happened within me, not around me. My body began to relax as tension ebbed away. I felt a power beyond my own settling me, balancing my load, giving me the peace and stability I needed.

If I draw near to God, He will draw near to me and be my stabilizer.

Just as a vehicle, through electronic and mechanical wizardry, can become balanced and stabilized, so can we! Through the presence and power of the Holy Spirit at work in our lives, our storms can be calmed and the waves that sweep over us can be stilled.

Our Master can utter one word into our hearts—"peace"—and we know it's enough. None of us desire the stormy times or the heavy, unbalanced loads on our shoulders. But I can and should be reminded that I don't have to remain in my discouragement. The Holy Spirit is near and ready to bring stability and balance to my life. As with the car, I just need to access the power available to me.

O Holy Spirit, dwell in me. Empower me. Balance me. Keep me stabilized in You, my only source of power and peace. In Jesus' name. *Amen*

Brokenness and Blessing

The Lord is near to the brokenhearted, and saves the crushed in spirit.
Psalms 34:18

The China tea set was in a thousand pieces when it arrived in the mail. I was heartbroken. My brother, Windell, who was serving a term in the Navy, had mailed the dishes to me from Japan. Now all I could see in the box was bits of oriental flowers and Japanese writing characters on the broken remains.

I sifted through the pieces and discovered one little cup in perfect condition. What a thrill! At least now I could envision what the tea set should look like. I found myself wanting to glue the pieces back together, but I knew it would be impossible.

God's mending power is greater than the world's breaking power.

One little cup. Amid all the broken pieces, one blessing. I have often thought of this experience as an analogy of life. Most of us, at one time or another, experience brokenness and pain. Sometimes we may feel that our lives are so disconnected and damaged that we question whether healing and mending can ever happen.

But, in the midst of the brokenness of our lives, there are still cups of blessings to be found. We still have reasonable health, a family who loves us, and friends. We have a purpose in life, and, most important of all, our Lord is with us!

Regardless of how difficult life may become, there are cups of blessings worth calling to mind. We may not be able to trust the postal service to deliver unbroken dishes, but we can trust the promises of our Lord. He is near to the brokenhearted. He does save the crushed in spirit. Paul said it so well, "We are afflicted in every way, but not crushed; perplexed, but not driven to despair; persecuted, but not forsaken; struck down, but not destroyed" (II Corinthians 4:8,9). Thanks be to God for His constant cups of blessing!

Dear Father, You are the healer of all our hurts. Help us to remember to trust Your promises in our pain. Through Christ our Lord. *Amen*

Early Bonding

*Before I formed you in the womb I knew you,
and before you were born I consecrated you.*
Jeremiah 1:5a

The sacrificial love of family can never compare with the sacrificial love of Jesus.

"There's something else I want to tell you about, Kate," my oldest brother said on the cassette tape. My ears perked up as I listened to the six hours of oral history that had been recorded by my niece Judy, my brother's oldest daughter. Windell had just told of my being critically ill as an infant, describing my weight loss and chalky white skin. The "something else" was how he rocked me under the old elm tree in our back yard.

I was touched as I envisioned my twelve-year-old brother patiently rocking his sick baby sister, hour by hour, day by day. I imagined the gratitude Mother must have felt to be given the time to take care of the basic chores in raising five children on a small farm with few modern conveniences.

Those weeks of being held and rocked by my brother was an early bonding time. I have always felt a special closeness to Windell, but I was sixty years old before I knew the sacrifice he had made for me. Jeremiah tells us that God loved us even before we were formed and consecrated us before we were born. He also reminds us that the Lord says, "I have loved you with an everlasting love" (Jeremiah 31:3a). The bonding with God comes even earlier than the bonding with family.

God loved us even before we were aware of Him. Missionaries have shared accounts of converts to Christianity who, having never heard the gospel before, said that in the depths of their soul they knew there was a higher being. That's early bonding! Sometimes it takes a long time to realize it, understand it, and accept it. Bonding with loved ones on earth enriches our lives, but accepting Christ and bonding with Him leads us to life eternal.

Dear heavenly Father, thank You for Your love brought to us through Your Son, Jesus. Thank You for the love of family. Help me to love others in return. Through Christ our Lord. *Amen*

Guarding the Tree

The Lord is faithful; he will strengthen you and guard you from evil.
II Thessalonians 3:3

*D*uring a recent visit to our childhood home, my two sisters, my brother, and I found ourselves reminiscing about our childhood. We envisioned how the seven of us sat around the kitchen table. We recalled gathering eggs and carrying in firewood at the end of the day. We could picture Mother's beautiful vegetable garden and could almost smell the sweet scent of honeysuckle growing in the lane.

God's angels are in charge of us, to guard us in all our ways (see Psalms 91:11).

The barn that was once filled with the sound of animals was now silent. Windows to our old home were now boarded up. Fruit trees were gone and most shade trees were either dead or broken by the elements of nature.

We laughed at memories of fun times. We cried some, too, because these were only memories—never to be lived again. But one experience that day will remain with me always. My brother pointed to a big tree in the front pasture field. It was the only tree around, standing stately and proud. He explained that one day our dad was mowing sagebrush and sawbriars off that field, and he and my other brother knew the tree, only a scrub then, was about to be mown. They knew that they would have to stand guard to protect it. With Windell on one side and Allen on the other side, they stood bravely guarding the sapling from the "evil" blade of the mower. Daddy mowed all around them that day, never touching the little tree or his young sons. Today, the tree stands full-grown and beautiful.

When spring arrives again this year at our childhood home, many trees will not show new life. But one special tree in the front pasture field will once again be green and healthy, a tribute to two little boys who were faithful to guard its life.

Our faithful Lord guards His children from the sources of evil that would destroy us. He wants each of us to grow strong and vital in our faith and live out the purpose for which He placed us on this earth.

Heavenly Father, thank You for Your care and protection. In Jesus' name. *Amen*

My Hidden Treasure

For where your treasure is, there will your heart be also.
Matthew 6:21

A whole carton of chewing gum—all for me! I couldn't believe my eyes. For a nine-year-old farm girl in the 1940s, this was a small gold mine. My brother Windell, who was in the Navy, had mailed me a real treasure.

I made that gum last a long time, too. Not because I didn't like it, but because I rationed it. I found a special place to keep it: way back on a shelf in the closet under the dining room stairs. And, to be honest, my heart was right there with my treasure. I would check on it often, making sure that neither mice nor man had been around it.

What earthly treasure claims my heart's devotions?

I've often thought about my treasure of chewing gum. It was childish of me to treasure it so. As I've grown older, I've tried to put away childish ways. Or have I? Does my heart sometimes focus on "treasures" that have no real meaning in my life? Do I always clearly discern the difference between a need and a want? What sacrifices am I willing to make to live simply so that others may simply live?

I need to be reminded every day of this verse of Scripture: "Take heed, and beware of all covetousness; for a man's life does not consist in the abundance of his possessions" (Luke 12:15). My treasure of chewing gum didn't last forever, but I trust that the lesson I learned will.

Heavenly Father, forgive me when I place a priority on the things of this world. I want my heart to be where You are, for You are our greatest treasure. In Jesus' name. *Amen*

Truth and Consequences

You will know the truth, and the truth will make you free.
John 8:32

Truth hits home many times, often in ways we do not welcome. When I was about twelve years old, my friend and I decided we would write each other "honest notes." In these we would feel free to point out each other's faults and suggest ways we thought the other could improve. Although it sounded like such a good idea, it proved to be a little painful.

I could hardly wait for my first letter. Our "mailbox" was a fence post with a split at the top. We had noticed it many times before, because it helped anchor the gate between our adjoining farms. Skipping down the pasture field, I couldn't get to the "post box" fast enough to send my first letter. In it I praised my friend's good qualities, but I also pointed out some areas for improvement—as we had agreed to do. After all, these were to be truthful notes.

Truth is more easily heard when spoken in love.

After a few hours I checked to see if my note had been removed. It had, but no note was left for me. Several days passed without a note from my friend.

Finally, one day I found my first note! Tearing into it excitedly, I began to read. "I hope this won't hurt your feelings, but you are a little too fat." I was stunned. I guess I hadn't expected this much honesty! At least I had said some positive things about her. Maybe this wasn't such a good idea after all.

Trudging back up the hill and past the barn toward our house, I began to do some honest reflecting. I really *did* have a true friend. Her criticism was true, and she had spoken this truth to me in love. Jesus told His disciple friends that knowing the truth would make them free.

Though my friend's note to me was painful at first—as any constructive criticism can be—it was also a freeing experience. It helped me see my faults as a twelve-year-old, and has helped me since that time to more easily accept constructive criticism.

Dear God, help me to more perfectly love You, because You are the way, the truth, and the life. Through Jesus. *Amen*

Horizontal Days

Great is thy faithfulness.
Lamentations 3:23b

*H*ave you ever experienced a horizontal day—a day when discouragement hangs heavily over you? Most of us have had these times when we feel we aren't getting anywhere. We're trudging two steps forward and one step backward. We feel we aren't making any real progress toward our goals and dreams.

Even horizontal days are special days if we remember that God is with us.

On my way home one day I noticed an interesting sight. It seemed to depict for me a horizontal day. Smoke coming out of a chimney wasn't going anywhere. It was hardly moving at all. Rather, it seemed to stretch out in a long, gray horizontal line over the housetop. *That's me,* I thought. *That's how I feel— strung out and not really going anywhere.*

Ordinary, uneventful, horizontal days. Just like the smoke. Gray. Inert. Stagnant. Still. Many of my days are like this. Events seem commonplace. But an important lesson I've learned over the years is this: God is in the horizontal days, too! His presence is dependable every day; He is with me even if I'm not aware of His presence.

Jesus must have had some horizontal days, too. His days as a young carpenter probably didn't hold a lot of excitement. Even after He announced His call to ministry, there was still the daily trudging of the dusty roads. But Jesus never walked alone; God was with Him. He said in John 14:11, "Believe me that I am in the Father and the Father in me." He walks our dusty roads, too. He is with me, even if I'm not aware of His presence. God's faithfulness satisfies the heart that longs to see more purpose in the journey. Knowing this helps us face the ordinary, uneventful, horizontal days of life. Great is God's faithfulness! It's new every morning!

Loving God, we need reminders of Your faithfulness. Thank You for sending them to us every day. Through Christ. *Amen*

Faith and Fear

I sought the Lord, and he answered me,
and delivered me from all my fears.

Psalms 34:4

I keep a file of news clippings and ideas for writing. Recently, I noticed that my file on "faith" was right in front of the file on "fear." Fear and faith are two master emotions. The psalmist, David, is talking about both of those in our Scripture passage today.

Evangelist Billy Sunday once said that when fear knocked at his door, faith answered, and there was nobody there. Faith dispels fear. The Bible tell us, more than three hundred times, to "fear not." Jesus would not have taught this if it were not possible to live without fear.

When fear knocks at my heart's door today, I want faith to answer.

How do we rid our lives of fear and begin to walk by faith? I believe it is a matter of the will. In a closing worship service some time ago, people were asked to name situations in their lives that were difficult. Following each statement, the audience resounded in unison: "Have no fear!" We have to *decide* that fear will not rule our lives.

Fear can squeeze the joy out of life, but we don't have to allow this to happen. We don't have to allow fear to warp our perspective. We don't have to allow fear to hold our thoughts hostage. We don't have to allow fear to rob us of our relationships with God.

Isaiah 41:10 says, "Fear not, for I am with you…" and that's really enough. Fear is not of God. "God did not give us a spirit of timidity [fear] but a spirit of power and love and self-control" (II Timothy 1:7). Paul talks about "the measure of faith which God has assigned" (Romans 12:3b). With God's gift of faith we can exert our wills to work against fear each day of our lives.

Faithful Father, I thank You for the victory of life over death, of salvation over sin, and of faith over fear. I thank You for the sacrifice of Your precious Son to make it so. Help me to walk by faith each day. In Jesus' name. *Amen*

Danger Signs

Be sober, be watchful. Your adversary the devil prowls around like a roaring lion, seeking some one to devour.

I Peter 5:8

In our part of Kentucky there are "deer crossing" signs everywhere. Deer are beautiful creatures, but they have the potential to destroy life if they run into the path of motorists. Along with being alert, motorists can attach to their vehicles an instrument that causes high frequency sounds sufficient to scare deer.

We must never let the seeming attractiveness of the devil deceive us into destruction.

Today's Scripture tells us to watch for an even greater threat to our well-being. The writer of Hebrews labels the devil as an adversary, an opponent or enemy. The analogy "like a lion" follows with the stark reminder that he seeks someone to devour.

Some people deny or diminish the reality of evil in our world. Others go to the other extreme by seeing Satan in every problem in life. This has to be sorted out. I believe that God's sovereignty supercedes all the powers of evil, but Satan still has a sphere of influence. This is the reason for the scriptural admonition to "Submit yourselves therefore to God. Resist the devil and he will flee from you" (James 4:7). We need danger signs along the way. We need a way to scare the devil away.

It seems to me that in our society today, we tend to water down evil—and sometimes even glamorize it. The grayness of right and wrong has become imbedded into our society. Sin is rampant. Pornography has become a multibillion-dollar industry in America. Brokenness is all about us.

Perhaps it's time to heed the danger signs and decide that we're done with the devil-induced decadence of our day. Satan is a defeated power, but he still prowls about. We who have entrusted our lives to Christ need not live in fear, but we need to be alert to signs of the "devil crossings" in our pathways.

Dear Lord, help me today to heed the warnings in Your Word about the wiles of the evil one. Protect and guide our pathways by Your sovereign grace. *Amen*

Through the Clutter

All things should be done decently and in order.
I Corinthians 14:40

$\mathcal{I}$ looked down at the water in the cove behind our parsonage and saw a strange sight. The leaf cover on the water seemed to be opening up, and a perfect inverted cone pattern was forming. Something was moving through the clutter of leaves and clearing them away! Upon closer inspection I could see the ducks swimming side by side toward the lake.

As I watched the clutter clear, I reflected on my own life. How often do I allow clutter to collect? Distracting thoughts, unimportant activities, failure to answer mail promptly, schedules overcrowded, lack of self-discipline—all of these and more can cause clutter in my life.

Order or disorder in our lives—the choice is ours.

What can I do to clean away the clutter? There comes a time when I must put things in order if they are to be "done decently" as Paul said. I need to plow through, sort out, throw away, catch up, organize, and set priorities if I want my life to be in flow with God's will.

I remember that as a college student, my dorm room received its best cleaning the night before a test. I couldn't seem to settle down to studying with my room cluttered. Maybe it was a form of procrastination, but I believe that bringing order to my room helped me to order my mind as well. I learned that to delay the ordering of my room only meant less study time later, and less study time normally meant a lower grade on the exam.

So it is with life. If our life needs putting in order, delay only adds to the problem. The psalmist said, "I hasten and do not delay to keep thy commandments" (Psalms 119:60). Jesus said in John 9:4, "We must work the works of him who sent me, while it is day; night comes, when no man can work."

Today, will my life be lived in an orderly manner in the midst of the world's clutter?

Dear Lord, help me to live in a responsible way so that my life will bring You honor and glory. *Amen*

Grace to the Humble

*Clothe yourselves, all of you, with humility toward one another,
for "God opposes the proud, but gives grace to the humble."*
I Peter 5:5b

ootwashing seemed a bit foreign to me. Yet I continued to feel led to close the retreat with a footwashing service. I talked with my co-leader, Greg Hatfield, and he encouraged me to go on with the idea. He said, "If you feel God is leading you to have a footwashing service, I say go for it!"

Humility often begins on our knees.

I slept very little that night. Doubts dogged me. Would these young adults receive this example of servanthood set by Jesus? Or, would they think I had totally flipped out? Would the Lord give me the grace to get down on my creaky knees and wash the first feet?

We did close the retreat with the footwashing service, and what a meaningful experience it was! Tears flowed as words of affirmation were spoken. One by one every person received not only words of kindness, but deeds of kindness as well. God graciously supplied grace to the humble that day.

Jesus "girded himself with a towel" (John 13:4a) and became a servant for His disciples. Peter was remembering this when he said in our text, "Clothe yourselves…with humility." He admonished the Christians at Rome, "I bid everyone among you not to think of himself more highly than he ought to think" (Romans 12:3a).

Thinking of oneself more highly than we ought to think can shape us into a callused person. It can create an attitude of self-centeredness that is in direct contrast to the servant life of Christ. Jesus cared for others. He came to give life—the abundant life. He came to hear hearts and heal hurts. He was so moved with compassion for a lost world that he was willing to die for it.

After Jesus finished washing the disciples' feet, He said, "For I have given you an example, that you also should do as I have done" (John 13:15). How willing are we to be servants today? We are humble in God's eyes when we serve like his Son.

Lord, I pray that You will give me the grace to be Your humble servant. In Jesus' name I pray. *Amen*

Riding Out the Tide

The Lord sits enthroned over the flood,
the Lord sits enthroned as a king forever.

Psalms 29:10

*O*ver the years as we have visited St. Simons Island, Georgia, I have become fascinated with the little marsh hen. She has an amazing wisdom for building her nest. She builds it to adapt to the ebb and flow of the tide. She weaves her nest around the tall grasses of the wet marshland in such a way that it will rise or fall with the flow of the tide. And so the nest and all that it contains are always safe.

Surely there are lessons for us from the little marsh hen. There are high tides and low tides in our lives. There are floods, storms, and dangers. If we are to weather these times triumphantly, we, too, must make preparation. Our homes and our lives must be secure, yet flexible. They must be anchored, yet adaptable.

We can ride out the tide when we are confident in the One who is in control.

Change is inevitable. Someone has said that we cannot put our foot in the same river twice. The water is never still. Life is never motionless. It moves on. We can either weave our lives in a way that they can be managed successfully or we can let life overwhelm us. The manner in which our anchor is fastened is important. But our faith in the One who is "over the flood" is even more important.

The psalmist David knew about distress. He knew about life's high tides and low tides. But he also knew about deliverance because he knew the Lord who is "enthroned over the flood…forever." The little marsh hen prepares her nest in such a way that it stays anchored as it rises and lowers with the tides. So, too, must we prepare our homes and our individual lives to stay afloat through life's highs and lows. That can happen as God becomes our anchor. That can happen because His faithfulness is new every morning!

Merciful Lord, thank You for watching over us through the ebb and flow of our lives. Help us to stay anchored to You. *Amen*

The Devil's Snares

Give no opportunity to the devil.
Ephesians 4:27

Our son David came home one day after substitute teaching looking very discouraged. Normally, he entered the front door whistling and singing, but not that day. There was not even a "Where's everybody?" Signs of a difficult day were all about him: drooping shoulders and a tired, taut expression on his face. "Well, how was your day?" I asked, trying to avoid any sound of concern.

Because of Christ, Satan is a defeated power.

"Unbelievable!" was his answer as he pulled a crumpled notebook page from his pocket. "You won't believe what's on this!" On the crumpled page were all sorts of satanic symbols: the inverted cross, the flaming pitchfork, the 666, and a number of other drawings. Chills ran over me. I stared in disbelief. The sheet of paper had been taken from a freshman boy in one of the classes of a respected neighborhood high school.

We had heard of the stories that were circulating about devil worship and the occult groups active in our area and across the Ohio River in Indiana. But, somehow, we felt our lives were insulated from these isolated incidents.

It was Holy Week, which seemed to magnify the student's mockery. During the time we were remembering our Lord's cruel death on Calvary for our sins, a fourteen-year-old boy was mocking and blaspheming Him. When David tried to talk to him he would only shrug his shoulders.

While none of us would knowingly involve ourselves in devil worship or dabble in the occult, how often do we participate in gossip, slander, cheating, envy? Sin is sin, and the devil is active. He is a defeated power, but evil is rampant in our world about us. Those of us who know Christ's power to redeem and restore lives must tell others. James 4:7 promises that if we resist the devil, he will flee from us. Let us believe this, and, more importantly, let us teach it to our children.

Father, thank You for Your victory over sin at Calvary. Help us to live so that resurrection power is evidenced in our lives. Through Christ, our risen Lord. *Amen*

Guard the Truth

Guard the truth that has been entrusted to you by the Holy Spirit who dwells within us.
II Timothy 1:14

*I*n an attempt to manipulate the pastor, a parishioner recorded three pages of false accusations against him. This person would not sign her name, but managed to circulate the paper at a staff-parish relations committee meeting. Later, when confronted about the false statements, she denied having written them. But when asked, "Can you honestly say, knowing that God is your witness, that you did not write these accusations?" she hesitatingly answered, "Well, my husband helped me."

"...let everyone speak the truth with his neighbor..." (Ephesians 4:25).

Does having assistance in committing a wrong make one less guilty? Whatever happened to good, old-fashioned integrity? Is truth becoming an obsolete word? Paul was warning Timothy to guard truth, to be strong in Christian character.

William Barclay says, "In every church there are certain people who have to be guarded against."[1] It is sad that we have to guard ourselves against those who are not trustworthy within the body of Christ—and especially those who knowingly speak untruths.

The Holy Spirit has entrusted truth to us, so we must guard it. Truth is necessary for living out our faith. It's a part of our armor: "Stand therefore, having girded your loins with truth" (Ephesians 6:14a). Truth sets us free: "You will know the truth, and the truth will make you free" (John 8:32).

Jesus embodied truth. He was "full of grace and truth" (John 1:14b). He came into the world to "bear witness to the truth" (John 18:37b). He said, "I am the way, and the truth, and the life: no one comes to the Father, but by me" (John 14:6). Jesus wanted his followers to know truth. He prayed, "Sanctify them in truth; thy word is truth" (John 17:17).

When we hear statements that are untrue, should we remain silent? I believe not. When we no longer stand for truth, we no longer stand for Christ. We need to guard truth.

Merciful Lord, help me to live truth, speak truth, and guard truth. In the name of the One who is truth. *Amen*

Having Done All, Stand

*Therefore take the whole armor of God, that you may be able to
withstand in the evil day, and having done all, to stand.*
Ephesians 6:13

*M*ost of us have experienced times when we've done our best to be fair and honest in a situation, yet misunderstanding, rejection, or even ridicule come back to us as the response. When we have exhausted all avenues for communication and harmony, maybe we need to take a look at Paul's advice to the Christians at Ephesus: put on God's armor, and stand. He repeats this admonition several times.

In this world we will have tribulation; but be of good cheer for Christ has already taken His stand for us at Calvary (see John 16:33).

This advice came home to us when David ran for student government president in college. He campaigned unabashedly on Christian principles and won the primary election two to one. The three other candidates issued allegations that David broke election rules. He went on to win in the general election, resulting in an even greater outcry from his opponents. A university committee investigated the election, found no wrongdoing, and the election stood. Still more accusations came from the opponents and another investigation cleared David again. This second committee was challenged, so the opponents were allowed to suggest names for a third committee to investigate. This group, too, acquitted David.

During this time threats and insults were daily occurrences for David. On one occasion, verbal assaults were hurled at us while we visited him. There seemed no end to the harassment, and we finally realized the time had come to stand. Wally called the dean's office and said that if the controversy was not cleared up within twenty-four hours he would bring a busload of character witnesses plus a lawyer. The matter was cleared—by the deadline—and David served faithfully as student government president that year. Sometimes, having done all, we have to stand!

Dear God, help me to take on Your armor, do all that I can, and then have the courage to stand. In Jesus' name. *Amen*

What's in Your Hand?

The Lord said to him, "What is that in your hand?"
Exodus 4:2a

Some of us may question what services we have to offer to our Lord. It is easy to name someone else who could do the job better or who has more talents to offer. What we sometimes fail to do is factor in how God will help us.

Moses was finding excuses when God told him to go to the people of Israel. Moses quickly told God that he would be neither heard nor believed. Plus, he was simply not an eloquent speaker. But God came back with an answer for Moses, saying, "I will be with your mouth and teach you what you shall speak" (Exodus 4:12).

Jesus can take our little bit and make it much.

Jesus needed to feed five thousand people and found a way to do this in the hands of one little boy. Because that little boy was willing to share what he had in his hands, he was written up in the gospels and has blessed untold millions by his example.

Jesus saw a certain widow cast two mites into an offering plate. It wasn't much, but she was willing to share what she had in her hands. Jesus thought her gift was most generous, even saying she gave more than anyone else.

What's in your hand? It may not be much in your opinion, but when blessed and used by God it is multiplied. William Barclay says that Jesus does not demand of us that which we do not possess. He just says, "Come as you are, however ill-equipped; bring to me what you have, however little, and I will use it greatly in my service."[2]

I want to always be willing to let God use what I have in my hand. Then the God who created my hand in the first place and blessed me with all that I possess can bless and use whatever I give.

Dear Lord, all that I am is Yours. Thank You for accepting my meager gifts, and me, and using everything for Your glory. In Jesus' name. *Amen*

An "If" and a Promise

If you abide in me, and my words abide in you,
ask whatever you will, and it shall be done for you.

John 15:7

The many "ifs" attached to promises in the Bible fascinate me, and I have to admit that at times I have struggled with the whole idea of requirements for God's blessings. This has somehow seemed almost contradictory to the theology of grace—God's unearned and undeserved love for us. However, Scripture makes it quite clear that with the promises come requirements:

Will God's precious promises be proven in my life today?

Here are some examples (all emphases mine):

• For answered prayer: "And whatever you ask in prayer, you will receive, *if* you have faith" (Matthew 21:22).
• For forgiveness: "For *if* you forgive men their trespasses, your heavenly Father also will forgive you" (Matthew 6:14).
• For truth: "*If* you continue in my word, you are truly my disciples, and you will know the truth, and the truth will make you free" (John 8:31b).
• For His presence: "Jesus answered him, '*If* a man loves me, he will keep my word, and my Father will love him'" (John 14:23a).
• For the healing of our land: "*If* my people who are called by my name humble themselves, and pray and seek my face, and turn from their wicked ways, then I will hear from heaven, and will forgive their sin and heal their land" (II Chronicles 7:14).
• For souls to be won to Christ: "And I, *if* I be lifted up from the earth, will draw all men unto me" (John 12:32 KJV).

Jesus spoke clearly about our need to obey His commandments. In John 14:15 He said it in nine simple words: "*If* you love me, you will keep my commandments" (emphasis added). Obedience and disobedience have consequences. Obedience brings blessings; disobedience brings difficulty and disaster. Consider these words of Jesus:

- "*If* you do not forgive men their trespasses, neither will your father forgive your trespasses " (Matthew 6:15 emphasis added).
- "*If* a man does not abide in me, he is cast forth as a branch and withers" (John 15:6a emphasis added).

Our own parents probably functioned with ifs and promises, as have those of us who are parents. With our heavenly Father *and* our own earthly parents, we can rest in the fact that love inspires the requirement and the response!

Loving Father, my heart's deep desire is to live a life that pleases You. Forgive me when I fail to be obedient. In Jesus' name. *Amen*

The Power of Touch

She said to herself, "If I only touch his garment,
I shall be made well."
Matthew 9:21

During my mother's radiation treatments for lung cancer, she lived with Wally and me. Often, members of our church dropped by to encourage and pray for her. On one occasion I felt a strong urge to suggest that a person lay hands on Mother as he prayed, but I wasn't sure how Mother would feel so I said nothing. Many times I have regretted my silence.

When Christ touches our lives we become whole persons.

Jesus knew the power of touch. Touching was often a part of His acts of healing. He touched the hand of Peter's mother-in-law, and the fever left her (Matthew 8:15). He healed the woman with the hemorrhage after she touched the hem of His garment (Matthew 9:21-22). The men of Gennesaret brought all the sick of that region, and "as many as touched it [hem of His garment] were made well" (Matthew 14:36). Jesus touched the two blind men on the road outside Jericho and immediately they received their sight and followed Him (Matthew 20:34). Through touch Jesus healed a man of deafness and a speech impediment in the region of Decapolis (Mark 7:33). Luke, the physician, tells of Jesus healing a man "full of leprosy" by touching him (Luke 5:12,13).

Parents in Jesus' day knew the blessing brought by the Lord's touch. Luke tells of infants being brought to Him "that He might touch them" (Luke 18:15). Mark gives a similar account of Jesus blessing the children: "He took them in His arms and blessed them laying His hands upon them" (Mark 10:16). Wherever Jesus went, people sought the power and blessing that resulted from the power of His touch.

We need need the healing touch of the Lord for all healing—physical, emotional, and spiritual. We also need to be His hands touching others—through the warmth of a handshake or an encouraging and comforting pat on a shoulder.

Sadly, though, in today's society, more and more caution is required. A touch can be misinterpreted. Also, we need to remember that some people, for various reasons, prefer not to be touched. But, I do believe that the healing power of God's love and care can be channeled through us as our lives touch those around us.

Father, give us wisdom for the ways our lives can touch others—and the courage to carry them out. In Jesus' name. *Amen*

Calling on the Lord

And it shall be whoever calls on the name of the Lord shall be saved.
Acts 2:21

*E*n route to Kentucky from Oklahoma, my niece Judy was suddenly hit by a person driving under the influence of alcohol. Judy recalls only one thing that occurred before her car whipped around and crossed the median. She remembers calling on the Lord by saying one word: "Jesus."

Calling on Jesus was sufficient that day. He spared her life. He was right there beside her as traffic clogged the interstate highway in both directions.

Jesus was with Judy even before she called His name: He was present through His Spirit. What a blessed comfort this is. Through the Holy Spirit, God goes before us, stands beside us, and follows after us!

"Our help is in the name of the Lord" (Psalms 124:8a).

The psalmist said, "Whither shall I go from thy Spirit? Or whither shall I flee from thy presence?" (Psalms 139:7).

Our omnipresent God is always with us. Haggai 2:4 says, "My Spirit abides among you; fear not." We can call on the name of the Lord anytime and anywhere. One word, when that word is "Jesus," is sufficient. Hallowed be the name of the Lord.

Thank You, Lord, for Your faithfulness when we call upon Your holy name. Continue to sustain us by Your mercy and grace. In Jesus' name. *Amen*

The Power of God's Word

For the word of God is living and active,
sharper than any two-edged sword.
Hebrews 4:12

In the hymn, "A Mighty Fortress Is Our God," Martin Luther says that one word will cause Satan to fall.[2] This truth is what Paul was talking about in describing the "armor of God" (Ephesians 6:10-17). The sword of the Spirit is God's Word; it is powerful, and we need to know it!

How much of God's Word have I hidden in my heart?

God's Word is the weapon Jesus used against the devil during the forty days and nights of temptation in the wilderness. Jesus was hungry, so the devil tried to tempt Him to turn stones to bread. He answered the devil by quoting Deuteronomy 8:3, "Man does not live by bread alone." Again and again Jesus confronted and conquered the tempter by quoting God's Word. Matthew 4:11 says that after Jesus quoted Scripture, "then the devil left him." God's Word is living and active and sharper than a two-edged sword. It completely rends asunder the devil's power.

John 17:17b says, "Thy word is truth." His Word is freeing. It pierces through pretense. "You will know the truth, and the truth will make you free" (John 8:32).

God's Word has the power to illumine our paths. It is a lamp and a guide; it dispels darkness and gloom. Psalm 119:105 says, "Thy word is a lamp to my feet and a light to my path."

God's Word comforts; it soothes and heals the broken heart like nothing else can. This comfort is lasting: "The grass withers, the flower fades; but the word of our God will stand for ever" (Isaiah 40:8). Surely God's Word is worthy of a permanent place in our hearts and lives.

Loving Father, I am so thankful for those who have sacrificed so much in order that we today can read Your written Word. Help me never to take this blessing for granted. *Amen*

The Heaviest Load

For every matter has its time and way,
although man's trouble lies heavy upon him.
Ecclesiastes 8:6

What is life's heaviest load? What continues to weigh us down and gnaw at our insides? It is probably an experience that hurt us and which we haven't fully forgiven. This poem by Ted Snell is an important reminder:

"The Heaviest Load You Can Bear"

So you're bitter and all disillusioned
And you think you've been hoodwinked and had!
Look around! There are others less lucky;
And you'll find that it isn't so bad.

Is there someone you trusted and shouldn't?
Forgive it. Forget it. Go on.
Maybe vengeance is sweet for the taking
But it's bitter remembered anon.

I'm not one for the preaching of sermons:
To live and let live; that is all.
Not to judge or condone or condemn them.
When the music has gone, leave the hall!

And I've learned from each bitter experience
Not to hate or despise or compare.
If you live with a chip on your shoulder
It's the heaviest weight you can bear.[4]

The troubles that lie heavy on us can be cast upon the Lord.

Most of us have at one time or another felt disappointed in people who have let us down. But there is no future in hating, judging, despairing, and resenting. The load becomes too heavy to bear. God will see to the judging and vengeance. He said, "Vengeance is mine, I will repay" (Romans 12:19). That removes our heaviest weight! Thanks be to God for carrying our burdensome load.

Loving Lord, forgive us when we forget to let You carry our loads. Thank You for modeling forgiveness on the cross. *Amen*

In Time of Need

Let us then with confidence draw near to the throne of grace, that we may receive mercy and find grace to help in time of need.

Hebrews 4:16

A few months ago I went to Louisville for a breast biopsy. Upon returning, I felt a need to be alone with God awhile, and I came to my little study nook in the guest bedroom. An unfinished devotional was lying on my desk. The title and Scripture was all I had written thus far. It was no coincidence that the title was "In Time of Need."

"Wait for the Lord; be strong and let your heart take courage" (Psalms 27:14).

Today as I finish the devotional, I recall so many times that God intervened when I needed Him. I remember how God parted the Red Sea long enough for the Israelites to arrive safely on the opposite shore. I think about how He sealed the mouths of the lions and spared Daniel's life. How He sent an angel to protect Shadrach, Meshach, and Abednego from the fiery furnace. How he broke into human history to come to earth in the form of Jesus to be our Savior and Lord.

Jesus stepped into situations wherever there was a need. He supplied wine for a wedding feast. He cared for little children. He calmed the fears of His disciples in the midst of a storm. He taught them how to better cast their nets. He called a little man out of a tree to have lunch with him. He fed the hungry and healed the sick, the lame, the blind, the demon-possessed, and the lepers. He even raised the dead from the grave!

Jesus was always present in times of need, and He still is. Before He left us to return to the Father, He provided for us a helper—the Holy Spirit. His mercy and grace are sufficient, of this I am confident. He can be trusted. Thanks be to God for coming to earth and remaining through His Spirit in times of need.

Thank You, loving Father, for being with me in my time of need, and for the good report from the biopsy. In Jesus' name. *Amen*

The Futility of Separation

Apart from me you can do nothing.
John 15:5b

*A*s I write today's devotional, I'm sitting before an open fire. Although the idea isn't original with me, I am reminded of a Christian's likeness to a coal of fire. If an ember is removed from a bed of glowing coals, ash will soon form and cover it. As long as the ember is a part of the fire, it both receives and gives warmth. Once it's severed from the source of warmth, the ember loses its glow and usefulness.

Is my life bearing fruit or is it lifeless and cold?

It seems to me that Jesus reveals the truth to us in His analogy of the vine and the branches. As long as we remain a part of the fellowship of Christian believers, we are alive and we are bearing fruit. But apart from Christ and His body on earth, the church, we lose our vitality and purpose like the ember separated from the fire.

Before Jesus went to the cross, He talked about the vine and branches. He urged the disciples to stay close to Him or else they would do nothing. Their lives would be fruitless. Like the coal removed from the fire, we don't cease to exist if we separate ourselves from the fellowship of believers; we just become cold and lifeless—present, but void of warmth and usefulness. Jesus said, "Apart from me you can do nothing." Separated from the Source, life loses its meaning and purpose. Connected to Jesus, we are empowered to live out His purpose.

Dear God, I want to always remain close to You so that my life will be fruitful. In Jesus' name. *Amen*

Flight Control

Jesus spoke to them, saying, "I am the light of the world, he who follows me will not walk in darkness, but will have the light of life."

John 8:12

I am told that landing a plane is more dangerous and difficult than the take-off. When I fly I always take comfort in the fact that the flight control tower takes over when a pilot can no longer see his way clearly. When he isn't able to follow the flight plan, he must rely on the nerve center of the airport—the flight control tower. It is then that the air-traffic controllers, who are skilled in the use of radio, radar, signal lights, and special instruments, use their quick judgment to bring the struggling plane to safety.

God's guidance comes to us as we surrender the controls of our life to Him.

So it is with us. When we lose our way and walk in darkness, Jesus provides us with the Light of life. This can't happen, though, as long as we grope in darkness, trusting our own "flight plan" for life. God's guidance comes to us as we surrender—totally surrender—the controls of our life to Him.

Air-traffic controllers are dependable people; otherwise, they would not be in such a responsible position. But flight control towers can become temporarily dysfunctional from storms, fires, and natural disasters. In contrast, our heavenly Father neither slumbers nor sleeps. He is our ever present guide through the Holy Spirit. Jesus said in John 8:12, "I am the light of the world." He also said in John 14:6, "I am the way." I want Him to be in control of my life. Then I'll know that He will bring me safely home.

Loving Father, I ask You to show me Your way every day through the Holy Spirit. *Amen*

Searching in the Wrong Places

They sought him among their kinsfolk and acquaintances; and when they did not find him, they returned to Jerusalem, seeking him.
Luke 2:44,45

Most of us have misplaced or lost items of value at one time or another, but few of us have experienced being separated from a child in the way spoken of in the above Scripture. Recently I walked out of our church with a young couple as their two young children playfully ran toward their car. Suddenly, in utter dismay, the father cried out, "Where's the baby? Oh, no, we've left him in the nursery!" Their infant hadn't quite become a part of the routine for them yet.

Happiness evades us when we search for it in the wrong places.

Probably Mary and Joseph weren't used to Jesus accompanying them to the Passover. Neither Jesus' separation from His parents nor the young parents walking out of the church without their baby was due to carelessness. But there was one difference between the two situations: the young parents knew where to find their baby, but Jesus' parents did not. They searched for awhile among kinsfolk and acquaintances. But they looked in the wrong places.

Not long ago I lost an earring. Normally, losing an earring would not be so significant. But this earring was of a pair that was a silver anniversary gift from Wally, and it held much sentimental value for me. I was so disappointed and, at the same time, a little embarrassed that I allowed myself to become so attached to material things.

In the bathroom that evening I suddenly heard the earring hit the tile floor. There it lay, safe and sound! It had been caught in my clothing all afternoon. Similarly, the "lost" Jesus had been close to His heavenly Father all the while—in His "Father's house," as Luke 2:49 puts it. Like Joseph and Mary, I had looked in the wrong places. Maybe the earring will serve as a reminder that the most important thing in life is staying close to my heavenly Father.

Father, forgive us when we search in the wrong places for what we feel is important. Help us to remember that You are the source of all real happiness. In Jesus' name. *Amen*

Thank Him in Advance

For we walk by faith, not by sight.
II Corinthians 5:7

*O*ne day I was praying about a special need in our family and felt God speak a tough challenge to me. He clearly impressed on my mind these words: "Can you thank me in advance?" I pondered these words. *That's too hard—to thank God for something when you don't have a clue that it's going to happen.*

If we saw the answers to our needs before we prayed, we would never need to pray.

The thought would not stop coming into my mind. Finally, I made an entry in my journal and said, "Yes, Lord. This is but one more hard lesson in faith."

I'm not given to songwriting, and there have been very few times in my life that God inspired a song in my heart. But on that day, I took pen in hand and began writing. These words, along with a tune, began to flow from my heart:

Can you thank me in advance
For the work I'm going to do?
Can you thank me in advance
That I'm going to see you through?
Can you thank me?

O thou blessed Trinity,
Though the future I can't see
In my faith I should be strong
Knowing You can do no wrong.
I can thank you…in advance!

Since that day, I have often sung this song. Thanking God in advance doesn't seem so unreasonable now. After all, that's what faith is: "The assurance of things hoped for, the conviction of things not seen" (Hebrews 11:1a).

Whatever you need today, trust God for it. And thank Him in advance.

Dear God, You are trustworthy. Because I can trust You I will walk by faith today. Through Christ my Lord. *Amen*

Surrendered Savings

*For they all contributed out of their abundance; but she out of her
poverty has put in everything she had, her whole living.*
Mark 12:44

A missionary from Africa spoke in our church, sharing with our congregation the dire need in his homeland for a simple building in which to worship. Hearing of this need just as we moved into our beautiful and comfortable new sanctuary caused many of us to look at our priorities. Worship under a tree in Africa, contrasted with our padded pews in Louisville, began to tug at our complacent hearts.

Do we give out of our abundance or our poverty?

Waiting for the time for the service to begin, Wally and the Rhodesian pastor heard a gentle knock on the study door. Nancy had brought her love gift. Smiling, she began, "Brother Thomas, I've been thinking about this pastor's need in Southern Rhodesia. I have withdrawn all of my savings to help start a fund for that new building!"

Knowing that Nancy could ill afford such a sacrificial gift, Wally hesitated to take the gift and assured her that no one expected her to give that much. She insisted that she had given much thought to the need, and the look of joy on her face confirmed her decision.

Nancy's sacrificial gift prompted others to give out of their abundance. Christmas Club savings were shared. Others gave from their tithe accounts which had become over-sized. But no one gave as much as Nancy.

During the weeks and months that followed, pictures were mailed to our congregation from southern Rhodesia as the new church was built. Somewhere today there stands an edifice where God's people worship—all because one dear lady surrendered her savings to the glory of God. And great will be her reward in heaven!

O God, You have so richly blessed us. Help us to realize that all we have comes from You so we can be cheerful givers. In Jesus' name. *Amen*

Gratitude–A Language of the Heart

For out of the abundance of the heart the mouth speaks.
Matthew 12:34b

A few years ago, my family and I visited Amsterdam. We were warned of the pickpockets, beggars, prostitutes, and general decadence of that city. We had also seen the beautiful pictures of the fields of tulips and daffodils for which Holland is famous, and visiting them was our daughter Debbie's lifelong dream.

What abundance of the heart will my words reflect today?

Weary from crossing the English Channel, we were anxious to locate our hotel before dark. A thirty-minute ride on a crowded city bus took us to the general area, but, from there, no one seemed to know for sure where we should go—and we knew least of all.

As our bus pulled away, we had a sinking feeling that we were lost in the middle of a deteriorating neighborhood. No hotel sign was in sight. Dropping our suitcases in the middle of the sidewalk, our eyes searched in every direction for some evidence of our hotel.

Then an elderly lady turned a corner and came in our direction. She must have sensed our apprehension, because she slowed up as she looked toward us. We asked her if she knew the location of our hotel, and she pointed down the street. Finally, we spotted the hotel sign in the distance.

We could not understand the woman's Dutch, and she couldn't understand our English. But she knew we were lost, and she understood the name of the hotel. She also understood two other words that I had learned: "thank you," in Dutch. I repeated them over and over and the woman's face burst into a broad grin. She embraced me, jabbering profusely all the while. I believe we communicated through our hearts in that moment, rather than through my feeble attempt to say thank you in Dutch.

I'm sure we'll never see the woman again, but that experience has made me more aware of the universality of the language of gratitude. Gratitude comes from the heart, and, although I spoke her language poorly, this dear woman heard my heart.

Father, help me to have a heart of gratitude so that, wherever I may be, my heart and mouth will express it. *Amen*

Light and Life

In him was life, and the life was the light of men.
John 1:4

A local television station recently presented a series on near-death experiences entitled "The Nearly Departed." People were given the opportunity to share about times in their lives when they had been near death. I watched with keen interest as one by one these people reaffirmed my conviction of life after death and what awaits us as Christians.

Many persons mentioned "light" as a part of their near-death experience. One person described the light as "shining like the afternoon sun." Another said, "What is waiting for us in the beyond is much better." And another said that we don't have to "worry about stockpiling a lot of money or things." Still another said, "This experience has made me less fearful of death." One person heard a voice say, "Don't be afraid." Some mentioned that they experienced no pain. The consensus was that there is purpose in life. As one person commented, "There's more at the end of this life."

I can go forward unafraid—through life and through death—because of the One who goes with me.

These experiences of persons who have been near death remind us that death is very much a part of life. But for Christians, death is only a door to something better. Jesus promised in John 3:16, "For God so loved the world that he gave his only Son, that whoever believes in him should not perish but have eternal life." Later, in John 10:28, Jesus reaffirms that promise: "And I give them eternal life, and they shall never perish, and no one shall snatch them out of my hand."

A friend once said, "I don't fear death—I just don't want to feel it." Suffering usually precedes death, but Paul even discounts suffering. He said, "I consider the sufferings of this present time are not worth comparing with the glory that is to be revealed to us" (Romans 8:18).

Yes, death is real. It is inevitable. But our Lord has removed its sting. He not only provides light along the way, but life eternal at the end of the way.

Merciful God, thank You for preparing a way and a place for us so that we can be with You. Through Jesus, our Lord. *Amen*

Living Thanks

Give thanks in all circumstances;
for this is the will of God in Christ Jesus for you.

I Thessalonians 5:18

*P*aul was instructing the Christians at Thessalonica to give thanks *in* all circumstances, not *for* all circumstances. Sometimes, circumstances are such that make it difficult to muster feelings of gratitude.

Such was the case of the parents who called Wally at two o'clock in the morning. They were two thousand miles from home and had just received word that their son had taken his life. I saw the deep grief and pain on Wally's face as he searched to find the right words to comfort these dear friends. Then he began to pray for them, linking hearts across our country with the great God of the universe—our only real source of comfort.

During all circumstances of life, we can always be thankful that He is with us.

Wally preached the funeral in a little rural church in Tennessee. Being the Wednesday before Thanksgiving, it was awkward to find adequate words to encourage the family to go on with life. Standing in front of the church, the mother shared about how she dreaded "getting through the holidays." She said, "I've tried to think of what we have to be thankful for. And, you know, we do have many blessings for which we can still thank Him."

This dear mother knew not just about *giving* thanks, but also *living* thanks; she knew the meaning of thanking God in all circumstances of life. How often we fail to count our blessings. Yet, this aching heart could experience gratitude even in the midst of her loss and pain. I believe God honors a thankful heart, and knows the pain it holds.

Thank You, Lord, for Your presence with us every day of our lives, through the good times as well as the bad. I pray that my life will reflect my gratitude. *Amen*

The Plastic Heart

Let not your hearts be troubled, neither let them be afraid.
John 14:27b

It was an unusually dark and gloomy day the Wednesday before Thanksgiving. Falling temperatures, coupled with continuous rain, caused concern, especially since each of our children would be driving home in old, worn-out cars.

I moved through the day of substitute teaching, praying continuously for Debbie and David's safety. As often as possible, in a room full of active first-graders, I centered my thoughts on my favorite verse of Scripture: "Let not your hearts be troubled, neither let them be afraid." Peace would come, yet it was always short-lived.

I want to be ready to share the comfort of God's Word with others.

The noise level seemed to rise with each passing minute. Suddenly, little hyperactive Jacob bounded from his desk and came skipping up to mine. His dark eyes sparkled like diamonds. My first impulse was to send him right back to his seat, but, before I could say anything, he commanded, "Hold out your hands!" I obeyed. "Close your eyes!" came his second command.

Suddenly, I felt a small, smooth piece of plastic in the palm of my hand. I opened my eyes to see a red plastic heart. Thanking him sincerely, I gestured for him to return to his seat. "Well, read it!" he insisted. Seeing nothing on the topside, I turned it over. The words before me penetrated to the very core of my being: "Let not your hearts be troubled, neither let them be afraid."

Pulling Jacob close to me, I confessed, "Jacob, you will never know how much this means to me today." Jacob beamed, and skipped back to his seat. The message on that little plastic heart will forever be imprinted on my own heart.

Merciful Father, forgive my foolish fears. Thank you for our children's safe journey home. Give me the simple, child-like faith of Jacob. Through the One who came to bring peace, I pray. *Amen*

An Attitude Check

Let each of you look not only to his own interests,
but also to the interests of others.

Philippians 2:4

A friend of ours looks upon each day as a gift from God. He says, "I wake up and say to myself 'Self, this is going to be a good day.'" Each day *can* be good if our attitude is good. I believe the apostle Paul was dealing with attitudes when he advised the church at Philippi to get beyond themselves and look to the needs of others. Paul knew that concentrating on self means elimination of others.

Are my interests for myself today or have I included others?

The following poem illustrates well the power of our attitude:

What We Are

Two cripples entered a church one day
Crippled—but each in a different way.
One had a body strong and whole,
But it sheltered a warped and twisted soul.
The other walked with a halting gait,
But his soul was "tall and fair and straight."
They shared a pew. They shared a book.
But on each face was a different look.
One was alight with hope and joy
And faith that nothing could destroy.

The other joined not in prayer or hymn,
No smile relaxed his features grim.
His neighbor had wronged him, his heart was sore.
He thought of himself and nothing more.
The words that were read from the Holy Book
Struck deafened ears and a forlorn look.
To one came comfort—his soul was fed.
The other gained nothing from what was said.
Two cripples left the church that day,

Crippled—but each in a different way.
A twisted foot did one body mar,
But the twisted soul was sadder far.
                    —Author Unknown

Perhaps it would be good for us to read the poem again and check our own attitude.

Father, forgive us when we allow our attitudes to cripple us and others. Help us to see beyond our own needs, as modeled through Your Son, Jesus. *Amen*

A New Creation

Therefore, if anyone is in Christ, he is a new creation:
the old has passed away, behold, the new has come.
II Corinthians 5:17

I can still smell the fresh cedar as my dad patiently whittled. I loved watching the curls form as his knife blade trimmed them one by one then let them fall into the metal pan on his lap. An artist in his own way, my dad spent many hours in his later years carving and whittling wood.

Is my life becoming what my heavenly Father envisions it to be?

From a rough chunk of wood he created birds and animals, bowls and pitchers, spoons and forks, and numerous other items. The highlight of his year would be the local Arts and Crafts Fair when he had the opportunity to display his creations. Often people complimented and encouraged him, and at least once he took the blue ribbon for his work.

It always amazed me that Daddy could take a piece of wood, envision what it could become, and slowly make his dream a reality. The purpose of his carving, whittling, and finishing was to create something new and beautiful. But, in order for this to happen, he had to use a wood like cedar, poplar, or butternut walnut that could be shaped by a human hand. Hard woods like oak or hickory would not work.

I've often thought how akin my dad's ability to form beautiful creations with his hands is to my heavenly Father's work in our lives. As with Daddy, the Lord needs material that can be shaped—people with hearts that are soft and can be touched and changed. He created humankind in the beginning bearing His own image. He continues to re-make us, as we allow Him, into His new creations. As with my dad, I believe our heavenly Father smiles with deep pride in His precious re-creations.

I want to remain moldable. Even when the carving process becomes painful at times, I want Him to continue to form me more and more into His likeness.

Lord, as You shape me into Your image, help me to be patient. I pray that my heart would always remain soft and moldable so my life may bless others. *Amen*

Leave Him with Me

I trust in thee, O Lord, I say, "Thou art my God."
My times are in thy hand.
Psalms 31:14,15a

Twice within two weeks I felt strongly impressed with these four words: "Leave him with me." Each time, the thought would come when I was praying for a specific family member. I realized that God was asking me to surrender this person *totally* to His care and keeping. I wish I could say that I obeyed the first time—or at least the second time. But in all honesty, I only took a baby step in that direction. Over a long period of time, I have been able to leave this person with God more and more.

Take your burdens to the Lord and leave them with Him.

Hearing Jan Johnson speak recently has helped me move a little farther in surrendering my needs to God. Jan is a mother, an author, a pastor's wife, and a frequent seminar and retreat speaker. She suggests that we simply pray, "Into Thy hands." She says, "Yes, it's simple, but what a relief to grow into a relationship with God where we don't have to go on and on explaining everything. We can rest in the confidence God already knows and understands."[5]

What a difference this could make in our life each day if we would pray this prayer: "Into Thy hands." Then the small as well as large concerns would be placed where they should be—in God's hands. The psalmist said, "My times are in thy hand." And we can say, "My family is in Thy hands." With this kind of simple surrender we can know peace. We can know joy. We can know acceptance of the things that are beyond our power to change.

What do you need to place in God's hands and leave with Him today? I Peter 5:7 says, "Cast all your anxieties on him, for he cares about you." Let God fight the battles for you; "the battle is not yours but God's" (II Chronicles 20:15).

Dear God, when the load becomes too heavy to bear alone, help me remember to leave it with You. In Jesus' name. *Amen*

Endurance

For you have need of endurance, so that you may do the will of God and receive what is promised.

Hebrews 10:36

"The Tortoise and the Hare" from *Aesop's Fables* always reminds me that endurance precedes the victory. The hare, knowing how slowly the tortoise would move in their race, decided that he had time for a nap along the way. But the old tortoise, weary as he was, persevered to the end. The hare enjoyed the nap, but the endurance of the tortoise enabled him to win the race.[6]

Victory can be ours in anything, if we depend on God for everything.

The kind of endurance required of Christians as we run the race of life is not so simple. Paul's advice in Romans 5 says that this kind of endurance is produced by suffering and results in character—and character produces hope. Most of us would be glad to be persons of endurance, character, and hope, but we would choose to avoid the suffering.

The wise counsel in Hebrews for the Jewish Christians was, "You have need of endurance." They were facing affliction and mistreatment as they tried to do God's will. While none of us will likely experience the suffering and persecution of the early Christians, we are not exempt from the trials and temptations of our day. We, too, have need for endurance—*daily*. Perhaps in our lifetime we will know suffering and adversity because of our faith. If this occurs, we can know that God will magnify His presence at our point of greatest need.

By His example, Jesus taught endurance—to the end. He became weary and experienced the need to go apart for awhile, but He never lost sight of His mission in this world. Jesus endured to the end. So must we.

Father, help us not to grow weary in well-doing, for we know that Your promise is sure for those who endure. In Jesus' name. *Amen*

Our Confidence

Such is the confidence we have through Christ toward God.
II Corinthians 3:4

I came upon a meaningful poem recently:

Adverbs
May I seek to live this day
Quietly, easily,
Leaning on Your mighty strength
Trustfully, restfully,
Meeting others in the path
Peacefully, joyously,
    waiting for Your will's unfolding
Patiently, serenely,
Facing what tomorrow brings
Confidently, courageously.
    —Author Unknown

Confidence in God gives us confidence for life.

It is possible to live life victoriously. We can have a confidence that only comes through Christ. We may not be able to live every day as described in this poem, but I do believe that our God will supply all our needs. Resting in this confidence goes a long way to help us be secure.

We can be secure because we are anchored in Christ. Hebrews 4:16 says, "Let us then with confidence draw near to the throne of grace, that we may receive mercy and find grace to help in time of need." Peter said, "Through him you have confidence in God, who raised him from the dead and gave him glory, so that your faith and hope are in God" (I Peter 1:21).

The world can disappoint us. Life can disappoint us. Even our own families can disappoint us. But we can take heart if our confidence is beyond family, friends, life's circumstances, and conditions in the world. Place your confidence in Christ. You won't be disappointed in Him!

God, thank You that we can face life confidently when we wait for Your will. In Jesus' name. *Amen*

True to Our Word

Let what you say be simply "yes" or "no";
anything more than this comes from evil.
Matthew 5:37

On a church marquee I saw these words: "After all is said and done, there's a lot more said than done." Have you ever heard it said of a person, "They're all talk"? Do we sometimes make commitments that we fail to fulfill? Do we sometimes make promises with no intention of keeping them?

No oath should be needed for us to be trusted.

Jesus clearly warns us against making careless commitments: "I tell you on the day of judgement men will render account for every careless word they utter; for by your words you will be justified, and by your words you will be condemned" (Matthew 12:36,37). In Proverbs we read, "Even a fool who keeps silent is considered wise" (Proverbs 17:28a). The psalmist knew about the sins of the tongue: "I will guard my ways, that I may not sin with my tongue" (Psalms 39:1). James warns, "From the same mouth come blessing and cursing. My brethren, this ought not to be so" (James 3:10).

No, this ought not to be so with Christians, but who has never uttered a careless word? Our talk should be pure. Our "yes" needs to mean "yes," and our "no" needs to mean "no." I've heard my parents say that our word should be our bond, and it's true. When we make a voice commitment, our sincerity should not be in question. All promises are sacred for they are made in God's presence and hearing.

There should not be one standard of language inside the church and a different one outside the church. The validity of our promise should be guarantee enough that we are telling the truth.

> We need a solution to verbal pollution,
> Broken promises only bring pain
> We must today mean what we say,
> Or no one's trust will we gain.

Gracious God, help us be true to our word. Through the One who is the way, the truth, and the life. *Amen*

Give God the Glory

Let your light so shine before men, that they may see your good works and give glory to your Father who is in heaven.
Matthew 5:16

Have you ever known someone who stole another person's idea but gladly accepted the credit for it? In one particular church where Wally served as pastor, this was a common occurrence. In planning sessions, good ideas would emerge, be accepted, and included in the proposed short- or long-range goals for the church. Then at the following administrative board meeting, often someone would report the idea as his or her own, expecting and receiving the credit.

Whatever our good works may be, the glory belongs to God.

The truth is that God alone deserves the credit and glory. Good ideas, like good deeds, need to draw attention to God and not to us. As Christians we should not dwell on what we have thought up or accomplished, but rather we should dwell on what God has enabled us to do. Our Scripture verse today clearly defines who is to receive the glory.

George Washington Carver is said to have come across a peanut, held it up, and asked God what the purpose for the peanut was. As the story goes, Mr. Carver believed that God showed him over three hundred uses for peanuts. Later he was asked to testify before a senate committee about where he learned these things about the peanut. Mr. Carver replied that he learned them from the Bible. He was asked if the Bible speaks of peanuts, and Mr. Carver is said to have explained that the Bible speaks of the God who created everything. George Washington Carver gave God the credit for showing him what could be done with a peanut.

I guess it's only natural to want to receive a little of earth's applause now and then, but if we do God's work His way we'll be sure that He gets the glory.

Loving Lord, You are the source of any wisdom we may have and the enabling power for all we do. Help me to remember always that You alone deserve the honor, glory, and praise. *Amen*

Jesus Said, "Rest Awhile"

He said to them, "Come away by yourselves to a lonely place, and rest awhile."
Mark 6:31

*I*n this Scripture, Jesus was saying to the disciples, "You need a break!" He knew they were tired and weary of crowds. Too often when I've read this chapter I have been caught up in the story of the feeding of the five thousand and paid too little attention to Jesus' command to simply go apart and rest.

There needs to be a balance between Christian doing and Christian being.

Jesus knew from experience the importance—even necessity—of going apart to be with God to be able to come back and minister to the people. He wanted His disciples to learn this important lesson, and I believe He wants us to do the same. When I fail to take—or *make*—the time to be still and rest both body and mind, I soon find myself running on empty. God has assured us that "in quietness and in trust shall be your strength" (Isaiah 30:15b). Psalms 46:10 says, "Be still, and know that I am God." Jesus said, "Come to me, all who labor and are heavy laden, and I will give you rest" (Matthew 11:28).

After God finished His work of creation, He "rested on the seventh day" (Genesis 2:2). This day of rest was important enough for Him to write it into a tablet of stone, "Remember the Sabbath day, to keep it holy" (Exodus 20:8). This commandment has almost been forsaken in our land. It's common now to see tractors in the fields, lawns being mowed, construction work in progress, activities scheduled, and more and more businesses open during the traditional hours for Sunday morning worship.

I believe that God modeled a rhythm between work and rest. Jesus modeled spending time alone with God and spending time ministering to people. The same One who told us to "go into all the world" (Mark 16:15) also said "come away by yourselves…and rest awhile" (Mark 6:31). Perhaps before we move into the busy Christmas season, it would be good for us to find a way to rest awhile.

Heavenly Father, You are the source of our strength. Help us to realize that resting awhile is also serving You. In the name of our example, Jesus Christ. *Amen*

Secret Service

Beware of practicing your piety before men in order to be seen by them.
Matthew 6:1a

*O*ne of our parishioners gave generously of her worldly possessions to worthwhile causes. The only problem was that she wanted everyone to know of her generosity. She practiced her piety before people in order to be seen by them.

Jesus said that if we give alms to demonstrate our generosity, we will get some admiration from people, but that's all. He said that if we pray in a way to flaunt our piety, we may get a reputation for being extremely devout, but that's all. Likewise, if we fast in such a way that everyone knows we are fasting, that's all the reward we'll receive.

Eternal reward is much more important than earthly praise.

It's *secret* service that pleases the Lord. He doesn't want His followers to serve in order to be seen. But those who secretly serve and seek no reward will receive their reward in full from the heavenly Father. He doesn't want us to give in order to glorify self. This kind of giving or serving is an act—it comes from the head and not from the heart.

Jesus sees serving in secret with no thought of reward as laying up treasures in heaven. The Christian who serves with humility will be exalted later. Jesus said in Luke 18:14b, "For every one who exalts himself will be humbled, but he who humbles himself will be exalted."

Serving others must be the instinctive overflow of a heart filled with Christ's love. Christ is not as interested in our deeds as He is in our hearts that prompt us to deeds.

Lord, forgive me for times that I haven't served in the right spirit. Help me to be emptied of selfish pride and filled with Your selfless love. *Amen*

Gifting or Giving

*If I give away all I have, and if I deliver my body
to be burned, but have not love, I gain nothing.*
I Corinthians 13:3

*A*s the Christmas season approaches, I must ask myself, "Will I be gifting or giving this year?" Someone once said that when we give money, we can earn more money. When we give clothing, we can buy more clothing. When we give food, we can either grow more or go to the supermarket and buy more.

Real giving comes from the heart, not the pocketbook.

But when we give someone our time—minutes, hours, days—we give our very life. We can never replace time.

A gift is a donation—a present. But giving requires the sacrifice of time, that irreplaceable blessing from God. Giving means taking the time to write a note of encouragement to someone. It's mowing the lawn for a sick neighbor or sitting by the bedside of a friend in the hospital. Giving is inviting an international student to the family Thanksgiving dinner. Giving is motivated and prompted by *agape* love. Giving without being motivated by love is meaningless.

Giving is not dropping a token gift in the Salvation Army kettle, the beggar's cup, or the church offering plate. It's walking to the front door of a rundown shack and offering to help repair the broken window.

All about us are opportunities to give of ourselves—our time and energy, not just monetary gifts. May we always remember the One who gave His all for our eternal life and, in turn, may we give a portion of our earthy life to others.

Father, help me to remember the greatest gift of all—Your Son's giving of Himself on the cross for us. In His name. *Amen*

For Moses, For Katie

I will be with your mouth and teach you what you shall speak.
Exodus 4:12

Throughout this book I have shared how God has been with Katie and our family as we have struggled with autism. Before completing the book, I want to give you an update on her. Five years have passed since Katie's diagnosis. God has been so faithful. His mercies have truly been new every morning for Katie and all of us.

Katie has made significant progress during these five years. She is now in the third grade and is being mainstreamed into a regular class more each year. She's reading well, and her teacher has twice called her a "model student." On award's day last May she was given an "Academic Award for Language Arts Excellence."

God is the same yesterday, today, and in all our tomorrows.

God is with Katie as she slowly but surely develops language skills. Like Moses, Katie needs help. God promised Moses that He would be with his mouth and teach him what he should speak. We've claimed not only this Scripture verse for Katie, but also Romans 8:26, which promises that the Spirit helps us in our weakness and intercedes for us.

God deserves all the glory for Katie's progress. Fifty persons throughout the world pray for Katie daily, and we are so indebted to them. II Corinthians 1:11 talks about "the blessing granted us in answer to many prayers." Prayers for Katie have been heard and answered. Katie's mother and a host of loving, helpful people have put feet and hands and hearts to these prayers.

God is so good. Katie, with God's help, will come to know how God has enabled her as He did Moses so long ago. Thanks be to our loving heavenly Father whose presence with us is new every morning!

Loving God, we praise You for Your power that is made perfect in our weakness. Continue to lead us always through Your Spirit. In Jesus' name. *Amen*

More Than We Can Imagine

Now to him who by the power at work within us is able to do far more abundantly than all we can ask or think, to him be the glory in the church and in Christ Jesus to all generations, for ever and ever. Amen.

Ephesians 3:20,21

When David was five years old, we invited about twenty little friends to his birthday party. At gift opening time the children encircled his chair, watching excitedly. About mid-way through opening the packages, David suddenly threw both hands in the air, and bellowed out, "TOO MUCH PRESENTS!" He was overwhelmed by so many gifts of love, for they were more than he could imagine. At least he was honest, but I was a bit embarrassed.

Eternity won't be sufficient time to thank God for His great gift of Jesus.

God blesses us every day more than we can understand. When I think of the ineffable gift of eternal life through Christ's death and resurrection, I am overwhelmed. When I recall how God spared our whole family in an automobile accident, it's beyond my comprehension. When I think of the countless ways God has directed and sustained us over these many years I can only say with Paul, "Thanks be to God for his inexpressible gift!" (II Corinthians 9:15).

The extent of God's love is limitless. It is more than we can fathom. John, in the prologue to his gospel, put it this way, "And from his fullness have we all received, grace upon grace" (John 1:16). We have received gift upon gift, blessing upon blessing. David was overwhelmed by the birthday presents from his friends; the gifts bestowed on us by the greatest Friend of all are truly more than we can ask or think.

Heavenly Father, when I think of all You have done for us through Your Son Jesus, it is beyond imagination. Thank You for the gift of Your love, which makes our joy complete. Through Christ our Lord. *Amen*

God's Way

This God—his way is perfect.
Psalms 18:30a

A teenager promised her mother to straighten her room—as soon as she could find it. Orderliness has a lot to do with what we accomplish each day. I try to have a list of goals for almost every day. I don't always accomplish them, but having a plan seems to help.

Orderliness was set into God's plan for our world. The sun rises in the morning and sets in the evening. Flowers blossom at their appointed time. Jobs begin and end at certain times. Life follows a schedule. God's way was to bring order out of chaos as He created the world.

Our lives need to have order, but ordering our ways doesn't come easy. It requires self-discipline. It requires an act of the will. It requires doing things God's way. Doing things in an organized, systematic way helps us use our time—God's time—wisely. We need the wise counsel of the Holy Spirit to order our lives according to God's way. In our Scripture passage for today, the psalmist David said, "This God—his way is perfect." He also said, "Make me to know thy ways, O Lord; teach me thy paths" (Psalm 25:4). Proverbs 3:6 teaches, "In all your ways acknowledge him, and he will make straight you paths."

Ordering our ways will not only benefit us, but also enable us to better minister to others.

Our ways are not always God's ways. We can plan, but the Lord must direct us. Jesus is the Way. He said, "I am the way, and the truth, and the life" (John 14:6). We reflect Him when we live orderly lives. I Corinthians 14:33 says, "For God is not a God of confusion but of peace."

So, today when I face a big task, will I approach it in an orderly way? Will I ask the Holy Spirit to show me *God's* way? I trust so. I want my life to please the Lord.

Lord, I want my ways to be Your ways. Forgive me when I selfishly follow my own heart's desires. In Jesus' name. *Amen*

Stay Planted

This is why I left you in Crete, that you might
amend what was defective.
Titus 1:5

*B*ishop Robert Morgan visited the Mediterranean Island of Crete, and discovered that the name "Titus" was on the cornerstones of several buildings. Paul had left Titus in Crete because he could trust Titus to "stay planted." He gave Titus a great task and called him his "true child in a common faith" (Titus 1:4).

Am I trusting God's plan for my life today?

Crete was an island of many cities and Paul wanted the churches there to follow Titus's model. Paul wrote to Titus, "Show yourself in all respects a model of good deeds" (Titus 2:7a). Paul knew Titus would be faithful and effective in helping the Christians amend whatever was defective in the churches.

Titus stayed planted in Crete. Cornerstones remain today as a testimony to his perseverance and commitment. I believe that we, too, are called to stay with a task in the church until it's complete. We may be tempted to throw in the towel during trying times, but we may need to "stay in Crete." Trials and tragedies can tempt us to stop trusting, but the God who calls us will equip and sustain us. James 5:11 says, "Behold, we call those happy who were steadfast." The writer to the Hebrews reminds us that we "have need of endurance, so that you may do the will for God and receive what is promised" (Hebrews 10:36).

In the ministry it seems that pastors sometimes decide prematurely it's time to move on to another church. It may be that they are right in the middle of Crete, and exactly where God would have them serve. Like Titus, God may be entrusting us to make a difference in our own neighborhood. We may never have our name placed on a cornerstone of a building, but we can be remembered for trusting God's plan of planting us wherever our Crete may be.

Heavenly Father, give us wisdom to know Your will for our life and the courage to live it out—wherever You plant us. In Jesus' name. *Amen*

Holy Day or Holiday

There was no room for them in the inn.
Luke 2:7b

*E*very year as Christmas approaches, I make a new commitment to make Christmas a holy day and not just a holiday. Every year I hang an ornament that says "Happy Birthday, Jesus." I place the ornament under a framed poster that says "Jesus Is the Reason for the Season." On my refrigerator I put Christmas magnets around the four corners of a cartoon that has appeared in *The Courier Journal* for several years. It's a depiction of Jesus in the midst of a mound of gifts with a shopper carefully checking his list. The caption reads, "Let's see…have I forgotten anyone?"

Will our schedules and hearts become so overcrowded that we will again shut out the Son of God?

Our various crèches are carefully placed throughout the house, along with other reminders that we're preparing for more than a holiday. I try to begin addressing Christmas cards a little earlier each year. Gifts are purchased all year long. But inevitably, the Christmas crunch catches me. I just can't seem to prepare ahead enough to avoid it. My heart truly longs for more room in our celebrations for the Christ who deserves our all.

This year I've made a commitment to leave off whatever is necessary in order to include the most important. If the day set aside to honor our Savior's birth is nothing more than a commercialized holiday, then the "No Vacancy" sign hangs over our hearts and homes.

There is room in my heart and home for Jesus. I will see to it that it remains that way. Otherwise, I'm helping to carry on the rejection by the innkeeper long ago.

Dear Jesus, please forgive us for allowing the holy day of Your birth to become a holiday. Come into our hearts again today. *Amen*

Brag on Jesus

Therefore, as it is written, "Let him who boasts, boast in the Lord."
I Corinthians 1:31

Marshall R. Owen, a United Methodist pastor for over half a century, was a man of great wisdom. One particular saying he had is good advice for all of us: "When you run out of anything to talk about, just brag on Jesus."

Though he probably meant these words primarily for fellow pastors, it would be well if each of us practiced them. Children seem to have an instinctive nature to want to boast or brag. "My truck is stronger than yours!" "My doll is the prettiest!" "My dad has a better job than yours." "I can beat you to the car!" On and on children can brag about their possessions or parents or whatever else that comes in handy. But Paul advises us in I Corinthians 13:11 that when we are older we should give up childish ways.

"Let the words of my mouth and the meditation of my heart be acceptable in thy sight…" (Psalms 19:14).

Bragging about our Lord is a different matter. It's always appropriate. The Bible encourages it. I Corinthians 1:31 admonishes us to "boast in the Lord." Psalms 44:8 says, "In God we have boasted continually, and we will give thanks to thy name forever." I Peter 2:9 says, "Declare the wonderful deeds of him who called you out of darkness into his marvelous light."

How different our lives and our families would be if our thoughts were centered on the goodness and blessings of God. How different the spirit of our churches would be if our energies were directed more toward the greatness and faithfulness of God. Idle gossip would have no place in conversations. Fear would fade away. Discouragement would disappear. Negative attitudes would be replaced by the positive power of God. Christmas would be Christ-centered.

When we don't know what to talk about, it would be well for us to simply brag on Jesus. He is worthy of our praise.

Dear God, You are the author and finisher of our faith. A lifetime would not be long enough to brag on Your Son, Jesus. In His name I pray. *Amen*

Anger–The Devil's Opportunity

*Do not let the sun go down on your anger,
and give no opportunity to the devil.*
Ephesians 4:26b,27

Someone has said that losing your temper is no way to get rid of it. I suppose that most of us have said words or acted in ways we regretted later. Paul was speaking of anger as being the devil's opportunity. It's the perfect door through which the devil can enter, and the longer that door is left open, the greater the power Satan will gain in our thoughts. The longer anger lingers, the more bitter a person grows.

Am I willing to ask God to help me with my anger today?

Anger is not always bad. Anger at sin, injustice, and evil in the world is a dynamic force for good. Without anger at the wrongs in our society, who would rise in defense of the suffering? But selfish and uncontrolled anger has no place in the Christian life. There were times when Jesus was angry. He was angry when the scribes and Pharisees were watching to see if he would heal the man with the withered hand on the Sabbath (Mark 3:5). He was angry when he drove the moneychangers out of the Temple courts because of their unfair practices (John 2:13-17). Christ's anger was at sin, injustice, and evil.

Paul said, "Be angry but do not sin" (Ephesians 4:26a). He warns us to guard this door of anger through which the devil gains an opportunity to enter our life. Here are some safe guards:

- "Let every man be quick to hear, slow to speak, slow to anger" (James 1:19).
- "Take every thought captive to obey Christ." (II Corinthians 10:5b).
- "Cast all your anxieties on him, for he cares about you" (I Peter 5:7).

The Christmas season can be a stressful time for families. Let's commit to guarding against giving the devil opportunity through anger.

Dear God, guard us today from giving opportunity to the devil. Help us to remember that with every temptation to sin You provide a way out. In Jesus' name. *Amen*

Passion Without Compassion

The Lord is compassionate and merciful.
James 5:11b

*H*ave you ever known someone who is driven with passion for a worthy cause and yet lacks compassion for those around him or her? A senior pastor had a passion to see the youth group in his church flourish and grow in numbers. There is nothing wrong with that, but his passion for growth in his youth group was negated by his lack of compassion for the youth minister. Behind the scenes the youth pastor was doing well to keep his head above water. He was struggling with financial problems, his study load in seminary and some other matters. The result was that he lost heart. Some compassion from his senior pastor would have blessed him so much. Maybe it would have increased his own compassion for the youth group.

Robert Frost said, "There never was a heart truly great and generous that was not also tender and compassionate."[2]

William Barclay says, "No amount of talk of Christian love will take the place of a kindly action to a man in need."[1] I John 3:18 says, "Little children, let us not love in word or speech but in deed and truth." Matthew tells about Jesus seeing the great crowds and having compassion on them. Jesus had a great passion for people, but it was His compassion for them that caused Him to act in their behalf.

Regardless of how strongly we may feel about a worthy cause, we must temper our actions with compassion. Otherwise our efforts will fall short of the mark. During this Christmas season may we not only have a passion for the needy in our world, but also have hearts of compassion as we do something to help them. Unless we have enough compassion to vicariously walk in another person's shoes, our passion is not likely to take on compassion.

Gracious God, give us hearts full of compassion following the example of Jesus. In His name. *Amen*

Paths of Kindness

Be kind to one another.
Ephesians 4:32a

An early December snowfall came as a surprise, followed by another surprise: We looked outside to see a perfect path scooped out of the snow from our house to the neighbor's house across the street. Jane Marie, our teenage neighbor, created a path of kindness that morning.

The path of kindness not only connected us to our mailbox and our neighbor's home, but also allowed visitors to walk our driveway safely. The greatest blessing of the cleared path came when another neighbor, a cancer patient, arrived with fourteen members of her family to sing carols to us. How thankful we were that this family had a safe path to our door because of another's kindness.

What would happen if every Christian on this globe created a path of kindness to someone?

Our Lord set the example for paths of kindness. He came to earth to tell us about and show us the Father's love, goodness, and grace. In Titus 3:4, Paul talks about "when the goodness and loving kindness of God our Savior appeared." The goodness and loving kindness that came to earth through Jesus are still making a difference in our world through people like Jane Marie.

Paul was advising the church at Ephesus to look to the needs of others and not inward at themselves. The world today needs Christians to reach out in loving deeds of kindness. We need to make safe paths of kindness that reach out to our family and neighbors. We should create paths of kindness for the unbeliever to travel until he or she meets the source of all love and kindness, Jesus our Savior and Lord.

Dear Father, help me find ways to share Your love and kindness so that others will meet You on their life journeys. Through Christ I pray. *Amen*

Jesus Close to Your Heart

Let the peace of Christ rule in your hearts.
Colossians 3:15a

*D*ebbie called one day to tell us about her visit to the gynecologist. The doctor suggested a cone biopsy to remove a small spot on her cervix. She assured us that the procedure is a fairly simple one and that the doctor was confident the biopsy would give a good report.

> *How wonderful it would be if all of us held Christ in our hearts—at Christmas and throughout the year.*

I was pleased that Debbie seemed at peace about the visit with the doctor. Normally she tends to worry about the unknown, especially about medical issues. Closing the telephone call, Debbie said, "I have one more thing to tell you." She explained that as she left that morning for the return visit to the doctor, she picked up the small baby Jesus figurine from her nativity set. "I put it in my purse so Jesus would be close all day," she said softly.

Debbie read her devotional books en route to Louisville, and during her prayer time she held the Jesus figurine close to her heart. She has always held Christ dearly in her heart, as Paul advised in I Peter 3:15. Now she was experiencing the peace that Christ brings when He rules in our hearts.

Debbie concluded that conversation by saying, "I may just keep the Jesus figurine in my purse always!" "That would be fine," I said, "But you know He's with you whether or not you have a figurine of Him in your purse."

"Yes, I know," she answered confidently. "He's always in my heart."

Heavenly Father, thank You for the peace that Your presence brings to our hearts. Help us to stay close to You always. In Jesus' name. *Amen*

Christmas Distractions

Turn my eyes from looking at vanities, and give me life in thy ways.
Psalms 119:37

During December I always place a child's nativity set in Katie's room at our house. I enjoy putting the youthful figurines on the little table by the desk.

Something interesting caught my eye today. Everything seemed in place. Young Mary and Joseph looked down at baby Jesus. The shepherd boy and lambs were in place as were the three boyish wise men. One change had occurred. Two of the wise men were facing Jesus, but one was looking backward. He appeared distracted from his mission of sharing his gift with the newborn Savior.

I want to stay focused on the One whose eyes are ever on His children.

To this day I'm not sure how one wise man turned around, but it has served as a meaningful reminder to me that I, too, can become distracted. I sometimes lose sight of the real purpose of our Advent journey: the Christ child. I sometimes turn my eyes—at least for a time—from the real reason we celebrate Christmas.

Let us consciously guard against the distractions that take our focus off of Jesus. As our Scripture says, let us turn our "eyes from looking at vanities." This Christmas, let us bring to Him again the gifts of our hearts and lives. Then we will experience the joy of His birth anew in our lives.

Dear God, free us from the distractions all around us. Help us to center our lives on Your Son, our Savior and Lord. *Amen*

Stained Joy

Yours shall be everlasting joy.
Isaiah 61:7b

A Christmas banner flows in the wind just outside our front window. Sitting at my desk during my devotional time today, I noticed something different about the banner. The colors from the letters in the word "JOY" are streaking down the white background of the banner, discoloring most of the lower half.

Today I want Jesus to fill me with His pure and lasting joy.

Our "JOY" Christmas banner is stained. Sobering thoughts crossed my mind: *Is my own joy stained? Is the joy of this holy season pure and unblemished in my heart today? Or is the banner waving outside an indication of the atmosphere of our home inside?*

I must deal with these questions: *Am I focusing on the event in history that angels announced with such joy? Or am I focusing on all the physical preparations of greeting cards, shopping, decorating, wrapping, cooking and the endless list of what we think is necessary during the days before Christmas? Am I concentrating more on the celebration of Christ's coming than Christ Himself?*

I hope not. I pray that the true joy of Christmas breaks through stained banners, busy schedules, and stuffed stomachs.

Loving Father, forgive me for allowing Your joy to become stained in my life. Cleanse me and restore the joy of Your Salvation. In Jesus' name. *Amen*

From Chaos to Calm

Let me hear what God the Lord will speak,
for he will speak peace to his people.
Psalms 85:8a

The Christmas season has become a time of chaos for many people. There's tension over stretched budgets, schedules too full, and many other distractions.

The disciples were frantic during the storm at sea. They were in the midst of chaos. Then Jesus asked them about their faith and rebuked the winds. A great calm came over the troubled sea and troubled disciples. They moved from chaos to calm.

God will speak peace to our hearts if we will be still and listen.

As I look back on other chaotic times in my life, it has been God's Word that has brought calming and lasting comfort. Your life may be in the midst of a storm right now. I encourage you to get away to a quiet place and go to God's Word for comfort. Here are some verses that will move you from chaos to calm: John 14:27; Psalm 23; Isaiah 26:3; Philippians 4:7,13,19; Psalms 4:8; and Romans 8:28.

Wherever we are in life, Jesus can bring calmness to our chaos. As today's Scripture promises, God will speak peace to His people. Let's focus on the Prince of Peace as we move through the hectic days of this Christmas season.

Dear God, thank You for calming the chaos in our lives. Help me to remember that You are a very present help in trouble. In Jesus' name. *Amen*

Jesus Is the Reason

Every good endowment and every perfect gift is from above.
James 1:17a

I left the twenty-two shell ornaments with the clerk to be personalized—one for each of our church staff. It felt good to have that decision and purchase made while it was till June.

Two days later I picked up the completed ornaments, but I waited until December to look at them. They were beautiful! The red hearts were trimmed in an edge of gold with each person's name inscribed on them in gold and black. Holly leaves and berries added the finishing touch, and on the back was a simple "K and W, 1991."

The heart of God, Jesus, was our bonus gift of love freely given.

These will be perfect on the white tablecloth for the Christmas dinner, I thought.. I counted to double-check the number, then counted a third time. There were twenty-three ornaments instead of twenty-two. I soon discovered why the twenty-third ornament was added. It was just like the others—with gold trim, holly, and a gold and black inscription—but this one had a message inscribed instead of the name. It read, "Jesus is the reason."

The sweet clerk in the Christmas shop had added a bonus ornament—without charge—as a reminder of the profound truth that underlies all Christmas preparation: Jesus *is* the reason. He is the reason for everything we do in preparation for Christmas. Jesus is the ultimate gift to all human kind—the sacrifice of God's only begotten Son on Calvary. That gift is the reason we know about love and the reason we give our gifts.

Jesus is the reason we have churches and staffs and staff Christmas dinners. He's the reason we want to share a token of our love and appreciation with our staff. He's the reason a total stranger added to an order a small, red heart ornament saying simply "Jesus is the reason." Thank you, Beth, for your timely reminder.

Dear Father, thank You for Your precious gift of love. Help us to remember the real reason for celebrating Christmas during every month and not just in December. In Jesus' name. *Amen*

The Refining Process

He knows the way I take; when He has tried me,
I shall come forth as gold.

Job 23:10

*A*s I drove along the highway, I heard these words introduce a commercial: "Hark the herald angels sing, how I love to get gold things." I was saddened and repulsed by another effort to commercialize Christmas.

I began to think of "gold things" and why we love to get them. Gold is valuable and scarce. It's a beautiful metal that has been refined by a heat process.

Refined gold can be shaped into various forms and put to many uses. It is resilient and easy to work with. It is resistant to rust and other chemical changes, giving it protection from the world around it. A good craftsman can form a work of lasting beauty from gold.

Today's refining process is a part of tomorrow's higher purpose.

Job felt that he had been in a refining furnace. He said, "When he has tried me, I shall come forth as gold." Many of us can identify, at least to some degree, with Job. Life has a way of providing furnaces of suffering and struggle: times that can refine us for a higher purpose. I Peter 1:6,7 says, "In this you rejoice, though now for a little while you may have to suffer various trials, so that the genuineness of your faith, more precious than gold which though perishable is tested by fire, may redound to praise and glory and honor at the revelation of Jesus Christ."

After the refining process, if we keep our faith in God as Job did, we'll be remolded. We'll be reshaped into more of His likeness. We'll be more resilient and more willing to follow the Master craftsman's plan. Our lives will be more resistant to the temptations and tarnishes of sin. And, like gold, our lives will be made useful and beautiful.

Gold was one of the treasures brought to the baby Jesus by the wise men. Gold, king of metals, was a gift fit for the King. How much it must gladden the heart of God for our heart, refined and yielded, to be offered to Him as a gift.

Dear God, help me to put my complete trust in You. Remold and refine me after Your will. Let my life be a pleasing gift to You. Through Christ I pray. *Amen*

Sorrow for Us, Joy for the Lord

Precious in the sight of the Lord is the death of his saints.
Psalms 116:15

What a welcome sound it is to hear a son or daughter fling open the door and shout, "Mom! Dad! I'm home!" There is no joy quite like that of welcoming a loved one home. I believe this experience is but a small taste of the rejoicing in heaven at the homecoming of one of God's children.

The grief we experience in giving up our loved ones becomes heaven's joy in receiving them.

In contrast to the deep joy of welcoming a family member home is the sorrow that surrounds us at the death of a loved one. I can still feel the keen sense of loss when my parents died. Their death left such a void. I remember describing my feeling of being "less loved." Giving up our loved ones is sorrow for us, but if they have accepted Christ it is joy for them.

None of us really know what heaven will be like, but the Scripture describes it well enough for us to know that it will have many rooms—a place for all believers (John 14:2). It will be a place where there will be no more pain or death, no more tears (Revelation 21:4), and filled with joy (Luke 15:10).

Norman Vincent Peale wrote that before Thomas Edison died, he said, "It is beautiful over there."[3] We know that Mr. Edison didn't report anything he couldn't prove.

God's Word says, "Weeping may tarry for the night, but joy comes with the morning" (Psalms 30:5b). Right now you may be experiencing the night's weeping; holidays for many can be a sad and painful time. In our humanness, we weep when death touches our families and friends, but in our faith we can be sure of the joy that is theirs in heaven.

Thanks be to the One who promised to prepare a place for all who believe in Him. Joy *will* come in the morning!

Loving God, You are so good. You comfort us in our sorrow on earth and rejoice with us in heaven. Thank You for being with us—in life as in death. In Jesus' name. *Amen*

The Power of an Imprint

Unless I see in his hands the print of the nails, and place my finger in the mark of the nails, and place my hand in his side, I will not believe.
John 20:25b

I remember my first doubts about existence of Santa Claus. I really didn't want anyone to know about my doubts. My brother Allen must have known my thoughts, because one Christmas morning he proudly announced so that I would hear, "Well, we have the proof on old Santa now. There are reindeer tracks all over the back yard!" I quickly wrapped up and ran out to see for myself. And, sure enough, under the old elm tree there were dozens of the most authentic looking deer tracks I had ever seen!

"Blessed are those who have not seen and yet believe" (John 20:29a).

I reached down and carefully touched the imprints in the soft ground. They looked so authentic, and I wanted so much to believe that Santa was real—that there was a good-natured, jolly old man who once a year shared joy with children all over the world.

I've often wondered how long Allen worked to make all those "reindeer" tracks, and how he managed to make them look so real. But his efforts paid off that Christmas, buying some time for my believing in Santa Claus.

The disciple Thomas struggled with doubts. He was a natural pessimist, but he loved Jesus. And Jesus knew his heart. Jesus knew that, in order for Thomas to believe that He was the resurrected Lord, He would have to grant Thomas's request to see and touch the imprint of the nails and sword. And it worked! Touching the imprints was a powerful experience for Thomas. His heart overflowed in love and devotion as he said, "My Lord and my God!" (John 20:28).

Do we struggle with doubts? Do we need proof today of who Jesus really is? The best proof is the power of the imprint of Christ on a believer's life. When a person accepts Jesus as Savior and Lord, the change is visible. The distinguishing characteristics of the fruits of the Spirit are firmly imprinted. The power of this imprint renews our faith and we can say with Thomas, "My Lord and my God!"

Dear God, help us in our doubting times. Thank You for the power of Your imprint upon our hearts and lives. I pray that others can see it clearly and come to faith. *Amen*

A Sweet Aroma

We are the aroma of Christ.
II Corinthians 2:15a

*O*ne special memory our children have of going to their grandmother's house was the sweet aroma from her kitchen. As soon as we entered the kitchen door, that wonderful smell of home cooking wafted by our nostrils. Usually all four of us would make our way to the range to see what was cooking.

Even after my mother's death, we felt comforted by the sweet aroma that seemed to linger in her home.

What is it in my life that would draw others to this Christ whose birth we are about to celebrate?

God has blessed us with five special senses. Our sense of smell tells us of a certain perfume someone is wearing. It warns us of a fire or food scorching. We can pick up on the ammonia in mop water, or honeysuckle growing down a country lane, or coffee brewing in the early morning.

Paul talks about Christians being the aroma of Christ. What aroma does our spirit impart? Each of us invokes an image, an impression, a certain response. Is it pleasant? Desirable? Does it cause others to want to know Christ? Is there something in my life that would make someone as eager to open his or her heart's door to Christ as our children were to open the door to Grandma's kitchen? I hope so. Paul said we should be "imitators of God, as beloved children. And walk in love, as Christ loved us and gave himself up for us, a fragrant offering and sacrifice to God" (Ephesians 5:1,2).

Dear God, I pray that others will see the sweet likeness of Your Son in my daily walk. Forgive me when I fail to reflect Your love. In Jesus' name. *Amen*

Christmas All Year

I am with you always, to the close of the age.
Matthew 28:20b

At the beginning of Advent one year, I filled each shelf of our lighted curio cabinet with symbols of Christmas. On the first shelf were angels depicting the annunciation and guiding the shepherds to the Christ child. On the second shelf were a number of crèches, Mary and Jesus figurines, and the three wise men. The third shelf held the figurines of Mary and Joseph's flight into Egypt, Christ the Good Shepherd, the cross, a pièta, and a crystal butterfly in an open glass box representing the resurrection.

The Christmas message is for every day of every year—for always.

The lower shelf was filled with churches, a figurine of a little boy playing a violin, and a globe ornament encircled with a red ribbon imprinted with John 3:16:"For God so loved the world that he gave his only Son, that whoever believes in him should not perish but have everlasting life."

After Christmas that year I started to pack the items away. Wally reminded me that those four shelves in the curio cabinet depicted clearly the birth of Christ, His life, death and, resurrection, as well as the birth of His church. "Why put it away?" he asked. "These are scenes we need to have before us all year long!"

It made sense. Jesus came. The angels announced His coming. He lived thirty-three years upon this earth, changing the whole course of history. He was crucified, dead, and buried. Thanks be to God, the tomb could not hold Him. Our resurrected Lord is with us still through the Holy Spirit!

Now His body on earth, the church, carries His message of redemption to the uttermost parts of this world. This baby Jesus who became our Savior and Lord is with us always, through the Holy Spirit, to the close of the age.

Yes, I will leave the story of Christmas in the lighted curio all year—and hold it in my heart forever. Thanks be to God.

Gracious and loving Father, thank You for sending Your Son, Jesus, to be our Savior and Lord. I pray that Your Spirit will dwell in our hearts forever. In Christ's name. *Amen*

My Heart–A Bethlehem

The place is too narrow for me; make room for me to dwell in.
Isaiah 49:20b

*M*y heart can be a Bethlehem! This is a fresh and exciting thought for me during this Christmas season. Luke 2:7 tells us that Jesus was laid in a manger—in a cattle stall—because there was no room for Him and His family in the inn. What about the space in our hearts? Is there room for Christ to dwell in us? What about my gift giving? Is He at the heart of it? Does He have a place along with our family and friends?

Making room in our hearts for Jesus can happen today!

Is my heart a Bethlehem this Christmas? I want it to be. I want to be sure I've allowed plenty of room for Him when He comes knocking at my heart's door. Christ is searching for a home in our hearts just as much today as Mary and Joseph searched for a room in the inn two thousand years ago. They would not force themselves on the innkeeper, although Mary's need merited a room. Neither will our Lord force entry into our hearts. The key to His entry is in *our* hands. If the space is "too narrow," as Isaiah put it, then He will abide outside. He will patiently wait for us to make room for Him.

Joseph and Mary looked for a room in Bethlehem in which the King of kings could be born. Today Jesus looks for room in our hearts where He can be King of our lives. Do we have room for Him? Can we receive Him, welcome Him, and allow Him to stay—not just during this Christmas season, but always?

Precious Lord, come into every part of my heart and remain with me always, I pray. *Amen*

Handkerchiefs

You have tasted the kindness of the Lord.
I Peter 2:3

There's something about a lady's handkerchief that brings warm memories to my mind. Perhaps it's because I so often saw my mother place a clean, neatly folded handkerchief in her purse before she dressed for a special occasion. Maybe it's because I was given a "handkerchief shower" on my last day in the rural school I attended. That gesture of kindness somehow softened the adjustment to the strange surroundings of a big county high school.

Through simple acts of love, we give and receive the kindness of our Lord.

But my most treasured memory of receiving a handkerchief goes back to the first circuit Wally pastored. It came from Mrs. Bessie Simmons. "Miss Bessie," as she was called, was a quiet, gentle lady. She didn't have an abundance of the world's goods, but she had "tasted the kindness of the Lord."

One day a letter came to me from Miss Bessie. It was addressed in pencil, and the small white envelope had smudges all over it. I opened the envelope to find a simple note wrapped around an old handkerchief. The note read, "Kay, I don't have much to give you for Christmas, but I want you to have this handkerchief."

How I treasured Miss Bessie's gift! It wasn't a fine linen handkerchief trimmed in imported lace. It wasn't even a polyester and cotton one. It was an old all-cotton handkerchief with tattered corners, and the large pink roses on it were faded badly. But it was clean, pressed, and folded. I'm sure it had caught many drops of sweat from Miss Bessie's brow and many tears from her eyes. I cherished this special handkerchief along with the ones from my school friends.

Then one night in 1975, all the handkerchiefs were stolen during a break-in at our home. I have often wondered what happened to these handkerchiefs. Were they thrown away in disgust? Did they rot in some landfill? I'll never know. But this I do know—no one can steal their meaning from my heart and their blessing upon my life.

Heavenly Father, thank You so much for the kind and loving persons You have allowed into our lives. We know You better because of them. *Amen*

Three Wise Men and an Angel

*He gives power to the faint, and to him who
has no might he increases strength.*
Isaiah 40:29

*M*ike was a dapper and handsome young man in our church. He radiated a sunny smile in spite of multiple sclerosis that confined him to a wheelchair.

As Christmas approached one particular year, Mike exuberated joy and excitement about the special Christmas gift he was having made for us. A few days before Christmas, the telephone rang. It was Mike calling to tell us to look for him soon at our front door.

*What gift of love will
I deliver during this
Christmas season?*

When I answered the door a few minutes later, I fully expected to see Mike in his wheelchair as usual. Imagine my surprise and joy to see a beaming young man standing proudly before me—alone and holding the Christmas gift! No crutches! No wheelchair! No one standing beside him as he handed me his gift of love.

"Mike!" I exclaimed "Is this really you?" Smiling broadly, he confidently replied, "I was determined to deliver this gift on my own two feet!" Then in the shadows near the end of the porch I saw a beaming, supportive mother. With her eyes riveted on her courageous son, she stood holding the crutches—ready to be by his side in an instant.

Mike was soon ready for his crutches again and stepped inside our door. I took his gift and lifted the white tissue paper from the box. Carefully placed inside were three beautiful gold papier mâché wise men and an angel. Their beauty was truly a work of art, but not nearly as beautiful as this young man's courage and love.

Each year at Christmas, one of our most meaningful moments is when we carefully unwrap the contents of the box marked "Mike's gift." The angel graces the treetop, and the three wise men have special spots on our entry hall table. These special Christmas figures will ever be a reminder of a wise and courageous young man who came bearing his gift of love—and of an angel who kept watch nearby.

Loving Father, thank You for Your wonderful gift of love brought to us through Your Son, Jesus. Help me to bring all my energies to bear on sharing Your love. *Amen*

"Joy All Over Me!"

*These things I have spoken to you, that my joy may
be in you, and that your joy may be full.*
John 15:11

Becca continued to giggle as my kindergarten class stood in line waiting for the dismissal bell. Being a rather reserved little girl, this sudden outburst of laughter baffled me. I didn't want to stifle her happy feelings and, yet, it takes only a little giggling from one child to throw the other twenty-four into total disruption. Adding to the spirit of the group was the fact that Christmas was around the corner.

Full joy overflows!

Shortly, I noticed a new dimension to the giggles. Now Becca was twitching to and fro and rubbing her arms. *She must be breaking out with chicken pox*, I reasoned.

Hoping that ignoring her actions would be the best approach, I turned to button a child's coat. Becca's laughter became louder and louder, and she loved the attention this was bringing from her peers.

I walked over to her and quietly whispered, "Becca, are you all right?" With sparkling eyes and a big, broad smile she replied, "Oh, yes, Miss Thomas. I'm fine!"

"But why are you rubbing your arms?" I asked. "Do they itch?"

"No-o-o, Miss Thomas, I've just got joy all over me!"

I can still see her now—big blue eyes looking into mine with the childlike faith that her teacher would understand. I hugged her close to me as deep joy came over me, too! The sheer, uninhibited joy of a precious five-year-old approaching the season of joy had spilled over on us all, and all of us laughed with Becca.

Why not feel joy? I asked myself as I straightened the room a few minutes later. Christmas *is* joy! Christ came to bring it! The angel announced it to the shepherds: "I bring you good news of a great joy" (Luke 2:10). Jesus brought joy as He came into this world so long ago, and that joy continues to fill our hearts today!

Father, thank You for giving us joy through Jesus. May our lives be so filled with this joy that our faces show it. Through Christ our Savior and Lord. *Amen*

Come to Me

Come to me, all who labor and are heavy laden, and I will give you rest.
Matthew 11:28

When the knock came to the church office door, it could hardly have come at a worse time. Wally had been up most of the previous night ministering to a bereaved family, and he had gone back to the office to attend to some urgent matters.

When we minister to the least, we serve the Highest.

The knock came again—this time more persistently. Reluctantly opening the door, Wally looked into the tired eyes of a weary transient. It was a common occurrence for these people to stop by the churches in Munfordville, Kentucky, on the busy 31-W highway. "I'm sorry, sir, but I was just leaving," Wally explained, hoping this would be a sufficient response. He couldn't quite muster enough patience or energy to deal with one more need, especially when he saw what looked like a dozen little faces peering through windows of the battered old van parked outside.

Sadly, the man stepped back and muttered softly, "I didn't know where to turn. My children and wife are hungry. When I saw the sign over your front door saying 'Come to Me' I thought I might find some help here."

The short of this story is that this family *did* find help and love. They ended up living in Munfordville two years. They were provided a small, but adequate home, some used furnishings, and a used car. The children excelled in school. Yes, there were difficult times—bouts with head lice, illnesses (physical and mental), and many adjustments on their part as well as the community. But, today, if the people of First United Methodist Church were asked to recall a meaningful Christmas, many would say it was "the year we helped make Christmas special for the Patera family." We received some of the "least of these" that year and, in so doing, received Christ into our midst.

Loving Father, help us to never miss an opportunity to share Your love. Make us more sensitive to the needs of others. Through Christ we pray. *Amen*

The Empty Chair

May the God of hope fill you with all joy and peace in believing,
so that by the power of the Holy Spirit you may abound in hope.
Romans 15:13

Our family dreaded the first Christmas following Mother's death. Yet, we were hoping to find a certain sense of comfort and support from each other.

Everyone assumed their usual job in preparing for the special meal. My sister brought Mother's jam cake with English walnuts and hard candy dotting the top of the caramel icing. The old, half-burned candles were placed in their usual spots. Even the Christmas tree blinked in its usual manner.

In fact, everything seemed as close to normal as one could expect. Daddy sat in his usual spot on the couch after the meal, waiting for the younger children to hand out the packages. But it was noticeable that something was missing from his spirit. Then it seemed that all of us became aware at the same time that no one was sitting in Mother's chair. It wasn't because we didn't need it. All chairs were in use and several family members were sitting on the floor. The old green towels, placed on the chair for protection, would have been removed that night had Mother been living. But no one wanted to change the way she left it. No one could fill that chair that night except Mother.

Our empty hearts can become filled again through the presence of the Holy Spirit.

As we began our traditional Christmas devotional, it seemed appropriate for us to focus on the empty chair. The violin sounded forth the notes of Christmas carols, and a sense of Mother's presence seemed all about us. Tears flowed freely, and we knew in our hearts that we would celebrate an eternal Christmas together one day. In the midst of the sadness of the empty chair, our hearts were full of joy and peace which our Lord came to earth to bring. Our focus moved from the empty chair to an empty tomb, and the hope our resurrected Lord came to bring!

Thank You, dear Father, for the sweet memories of our loved ones and for the comfort and hope You bring us. Through Christ. *Amen*

Not Out of My Way

They departed to their own country by another way.
Matthew 2:12b

*S*hortly after Christmas, Wally and I stopped by a fast food restaurant for a quick bite to eat. As I settled comfortably into a booth, my eyes became riveted on an elderly man standing near the opposite door. With shoulders stooped in his oversized, tattered clothes, he seemed to be waiting for someone. He kept pulling the gray overcoat tightly over his chest, as though dreading to go out in the cold night air. His feet shuffled nervously as he gazed at the floor.

How often do I let someone else reach out to help in my place?

Matthew 25:40 played itself over and over in my mind and heart: "As you did it to one of the least of these my brethren, you did it to me." My appetite seemed to leave me as I began to try to reason and rationalize. We could offer to buy him some supper, but he's probably already eaten since he's obviously ready to leave. Maybe we could offer him a ride home, but he may not have a home. So, where would we take him?

Just then a young father and his family started to leave the restaurant. "Do you need a ride?" I heard the young man ask. "You're probably not going my way," the old man replied, still looking at the floor. "It's not out of my way," came the gentle reply. The old man lifted his head for the first time. Again, the young father said, "It's not out of my way at all. We'll be glad to take you home."

Today's Scripture verse says that the wise men went home another way after visiting the Christ child. They did this to avoid the danger of Herod. No doubt, this wise young man had spent time with the same Christ, and he, too, was going home another way. He had not brought a gift to Jesus that night. Instead, he was giving the gift of Christ's love.

As I watched them disappear into the darkness, I thanked God that there are still people who care, and I determined that night to try in the days ahead to go out of my way to offer Christ's love.

Loving Father, forgive me for the times I fail to share Your love. Help me be aware of people in need, and reach out to them so they will know that someone cares. In Jesus' name. *Amen*

We Have Seen His Star

For we have seen his star in the East, and have come to worship him.
Matthew 2:2

On the drive from Campbellsville to Horse Cave, Kentucky, I began to notice large lighted stars on the front lawns of homes along the way. Christmas was in the air! A light snow was falling and we were going to meet our children and their spouses to see "A Christmas Carol." Joy welled up in my heart as each new star pierced the night's darkness.

I began to count them out loud. Seventeen. Eighteen. Nineteen! I commented to Wally, "You know, I just believe each one of these stars is a statement of faith by these people." Twenty. Twenty-one. Twenty-one homes along that dark country road had surely seen His star, and were wanting to share it with passersby. A verse from Isaiah came to mind, "The people who walked in darkness have seen a great light" (Isaiah 9:2a).

When His light illumines our lives, it will be natural for us to worship Jesus.

Scripture tells us that wise men from the East saw His star. These men knew of the orderliness of the universe, but, on this special night, it must have appeared to them that the very God of the universe broke into His own order and announced something special.

Many suggestions have been made over the years to explain this heavenly brilliance which the Magi followed. In any case, it was the profession of these wise men to watch the heavens. And on this particular night, they saw *His* star and set out to find and worship the child born King of the Jews.

Today, in the afterglow of Christmas, I ask myself: Do I expect God to break through to *my* world? It somehow seems easier to look for Him in December when there's a feeling of expectancy all about us. When the dreary days of January come crushing in on me, I want to remember with the psalmist that "The Lord my God lightens my darkness" (Psalms 18:28b). I have seen His stars, and I, too, want to worship Him.

Loving God, thank You for sending Your son, Jesus, to be light for our world. Please help me to walk in Your light and help me to be light to others. In Jesus' name. *Amen*

Christmas Love Continued

We will devote ourselves to prayer.
Acts 6:4

Unable to fall asleep, I returned to the den around midnight. Sitting there in semi-darkness, I noticed the wicker basket of Christmas cards by my chair. Each year after the rush of Christmas is over, I like to reread each card and pray for its sender. Three weeks had passed since Christmas, and it was time to put the cards away.

What a difference it would make if Christmas love continued every day of our lives!

I pulled a few cards from the basket and began to read them. The first card was from a family who was in the throes of a divorce. The next one was from a widow friend who needed our prayers. Then I opened the card from an older couple who, though experiencing special needs, had remembered us recently with a special kindness.

On and on I read and prayed into the early morning hours. One card was from a friend battling cancer. Another one had been hand delivered by a young family. But the card that really touched my heart had three signatures—one of which belonged to a friend who had passed away during the past week. My opportunity to pray for that friend was past.

I realized anew the need to devote myself to prayer as the writer of Acts admonished. Christ gave us the ultimate gift of love at Calvary. Because of His love, we are enabled to share love. We often send messages of love and good will at Christmas. I want to find ways to share God's love and encouragement *all* year and take the time to pray each day for family and friends.

Loving Father, help me to reach out in love and prayer each day of the year. In Jesus' name. *Amen*

Hindrances

He sought to see who Jesus was, but could not, on account of the crowd,
because he was small of stature.

Luke 19:3

Zacchaeus, the hated tax collector, heard that Jesus welcomed people like him—even sinners. He wanted to see Jesus, but could not because he was too short. So Zacchaeus decided that neither his small stature nor the crowd of people would block him from seeing this One about whom he had heard so much. Up to his lookout point in the sycamore tree he climbed!

There is nothing that can come into my life to hinder me from being with Jesus.

Zacchaeus didn't allow the hindrance of his height to keep him from Jesus, and his reward was much more than a glimpse. He was given a whole day with Jesus in his own home! Even more, he gained a new and wonderful friend. When Zacchaeus met Jesus, he became a changed person. As a changed person, he sought to right the wrongs of his past.

What about me? Do I find ways to spend time with Jesus regardless of life's hindrances? Do I let a crowded schedule choke out my devotional time? What about my attitude? Can I really enjoy the presence of the Holy Spirit in my life if I'm nursing an old wound or dwelling on some negative thought? Do I allow some physical "flaw" in my looks to affect how I perceive God's love for me?

I believe God sees our heart just as He saw the heart of Zacchaeus. Jesus knew that the heart of Zacchaeus longed to see Him. He knew that Zacchaeus made the effort to overcome the hindrance so he could do so. And when we put forth the effort to come to Jesus, He will come into our hearts and homes. Then we will want to make right the wrongs we've committed. Then we will be ready to move into the New Year ahead.

Loving God, thank You for sending Jesus my way and for helping me find the way to see Him and know Him. *Amen*

The Lord Is My Good Shepherd

The Lord is my shepherd, I shall not want.
Psalms 23:1

Someone once shared with me the following thought: *It is absurd to believe the Lord is our Shepherd and still worry*. This person suggested that we say, "The Lord is my Shepherd, so today I need to worry about _____." Filling in the blank we can hear the ring of inconsistency in this statement.

Does my life today reflect my faith in the Good Shepherd?

I've thought of this truth often as I've been tempted to worry. It is senseless for me to think or say, "The Lord is my Shepherd, so I need to worry about the future"—or any other aspect of my life. Either He is my Shepherd or He isn't. If He is my Shepherd, then I must do my part to take care of my body. If I'm concerned about our finances, then I must do my part in managing them well. On and on we could go.

But Jesus is not just any shepherd. He Himself said, "I am the good shepherd" (John 10:11a). A *good* shepherd has a personal relationship with his sheep. He knows them well—even their names. Jesus said, "I know my own, and my own know me" (John 10:14b). A *good* shepherd loves and cares for his sheep. Jesus said, "The good shepherd lays down his life for the sheep" (John 10:11b). We know that even today shepherds will lay their bodies across the door of the sheepfold at night to protect the sheep, even at the risk of their lives. If a thief or wild animal attempts to enter the sheepfold, he must first encounter the shepherd.

Knowing this about our Good Shepherd, we can well understand why David said, "I shall not want." Our Good Shepherd gave His very life for us, so it does seem a bit foolish to believe this and still worry. Rather, we can say with Paul, "For I know whom I have believed, and I am sure that he is able to guard until that Day what has been entrusted to me" (II Timothy 1:12b).

As we move into the New Year ahead, let us know that our Lord, the Good Shepherd, loves, protects, guides, and guards us along the way.

Dear Lord, I believe You are who You said You are. Help me to live today free of worry, fear, or doubt. In Jesus' name. *Amen*

God's Great and Wonderful Deeds

Great and wonderful are thy deeds, O Lord God the Almighty.
Revelation 15:3b

Have you ever tried to describe the indescribable? That's how the writer of the gospel of John must have felt when he concluded the book saying, "But there are also many other things which Jesus did; were everyone of them to be written, I suppose that the world itself could not contain the books that would be written" (John 21:25). The deeds of our Lord are truly great and wonderful. They are limitless! Books cannot fully explain them. Human beings cannot fully describe them.

God's great and wonderful deeds are too many to be contained in this book!

That's how I feel as I reflect on God's blessings in my life. He gave me good parents, a wonderful husband, and two beautiful children (and their families). Our lives have not been without heartache and struggle, but our God has supplied every need.

Like the psalmist my heart declares, "How great are thy works, O Lord!" (Psalms 92:5). "The Lord is faithful in all his words and gracious in all his deeds (Psalms 145:13b). I want to always be mindful of God's goodness. "He has caused his wonderful works to be remembered" (Psalms 111:4a), and I'm so thankful for this.

I understand a little bit of what the writer of John was feeling at the book's end. Words *are* inadequate to describe all that God has done. He touches us daily with His faithfulness. His love never ceases. His mercies are new every morning! Thanks be to God!

Dear God, when words or book pages fail us, we rejoice in knowing that You understand our hearts. Come in and abide with us forever, I pray, in Jesus' name. *Amen*

ENDNOTES

January

1. Perine, Lawrence. *Literature, Structure, Sound, and Sense.* (New York: Harcourt, Brace, and Javonovich, 1974), pp.691-692.
2. Peck, Scott. *The Road Less Traveled.* (New York: Simon and Schuster, 1978), p.15.
3. Sittser, Gerald L. *A Grace Disguised.* (Michigan: Zondervan Publishing House, 1995), p.68.
4. Russell, A. J., ed. *God Calling.* (Ohio: Barbour and Company, 1988), p.126.
5. Bolander, Donald O. *The New Webster's Quotation Dictionary.* (USA: Lexicon Publications, 1987), p.8.
6. Russell, A. J., ed. *God Calling.* (New Jersey: Fleming N. Revell, 1984), pp.118-119.
7. Ibid., p. 85.
8. Ibid., p. 85.
9. Swindoll, Charles. *Living Above the Level of Mediocrity.* (Dallas: Word Publishing, 1976), p.126.

February

1. Bernard, George. "Old Rugged Cross," *The United Methodist Hymnal.* (Nashville: The United Methodist Publishing House, 1989), p.504.
2. Williams, Margery. *The Velveteen Rabbit.* (New York: Grosset and Dunlap, 1993), p.5.
3. Cousins, Norman. *Head First The Biology of Hope and the Healing Power of the Human Spirit.* (New York: Penguin Books, 1989), p.122.
4. Ibid., p.126.
5. Bates, Katherine Lee. "America the Beautiful," The *United Methodist Hymnal.* (Nashville: The United Methodist Publishing House, 1989), p.696.
6. Black, James M. "When the Roll Is Called Up Yonder," *Mission Praise.* (United Kingdom: Marshall Morgan and Scott, 1983), p.268.
7. Money, Royce. *Building Stronger Families.* (Illinois: Victor Books, 1986), pp.67-70.

March

1. Guralnik, David B., ed. *Webster's New World Dictionary.* (New York: Simon and Schuster, 1982), pp.1566-1567.
2. Lucado, Max. *On the Anvil.* (Illinois: Tyndall House, 1985), p.52.
3. Hoffman, Elisha A. "Leaning on the Everlasting Arms," *The United Methodist Hymnal.* (Nashville: The United Methodist Publishing House, 1989), p.133.
4. Barclay, William. *The Gospel of Matthew*, Volume 2. (Scotland: The St. Andrew Press, 1958), p.296.

April

1. Author Unknown. "Were You There," *The Cokesbury Worship Hymnal.* (Nashville: Abingdon Press, 1979), p.255.
2. Barclay, William. *The Gospel of John*, Volume 1. (Philadelphia: The Westminster Press, 1975), p.137.
3. Ibid., p.138.
4. Campolo, Tony. *It's Friday, But Sunday's Comin'.* (Texas: Word Books, 1984) p.118.
5. Intercessors of America, "National Reports," Volume 22, Number 2. (Virginia: February 1995), p.4.

M a y

1. Miller, J. R. *In Green Pastures.* (New Jersey: Nelson, 1969), p.67.
2. Ken, Thomas. "Doxology," *The Cokesbury Worship Hymnal.* (Nashville: Abingdon Press, 1979), p.2.
3. Bocander, David O. *The New Webster's Quotations.* (USA: Lexicon Publications, Inc., 1987), p.159.
4. Bonhoeffer, Dietrich. *Life Together.* John Doberstein, translator. (New York: Harper and Row, 1954), p. 99.
5. Gabriel, Charles H. "My Savior's Love," *The Cokesbury Worship Hymnal.* (Nashville: Abingdon Press, 1979), p.163.

J u n e

1. Ogilvie, Lloyd J. *The Greatest Counselor in the World.* (Michigan: Servant Publications, 1994), p.115.
2. Mohr, Joseph. "Silent Night! Holy Night!," *The Cokesbury Worship Hymnal.* (Nashville: Abingdon Press, 1979), p.212.

J u l y

1. Cousins, Norman. *Head First The Biology of Hope and the Healing Power of the Human Spirit.* (New York: Penguin Books, 1989), p.106.
2. Barclay, William. *The Gospel of Mark.* (Philadephia: The Westminster Press, 1975), p.155.
3. Guralnik, David B., ed., *Webster's New World Dictionary.* (New York: Simon and Schuster, 1982), p.1373.

S e p t e m b e r

1. Atwood, J. K. "The Unclouded Day," *The Cokesbury Worship Hymnal.* (Nashville: Abingdon Press, 1979), p.207.
2. Barclay, William. *The Gospel of John*, Volume 1. (Philadelphia: The Westminster Press, 1975), p.63.
3. Mallock, Douglas. *Be the Best of Whatever You Are.* (Chicago: The Scott Dowd Company, 1926).

O c t o b e r

1. Scriven, Joseph M. "What a Friend We Have in Jesus," *The Cokesbury Worship Hymnal.* (Nashville: Abingdon Press, 1979), p.124.
2. Bliss, P.P. "Almost Persuaded," *The Cokesbury Worship Hymnal.* (Nashville: Abingdon Press, 1979), p.152.
3. Bowie, Walter Russell. *Interpreter's Bible,* Volume 1. (Nashville: Abingdon Press, 1939), p.615.
4. Ibid., p.609.
5. Ibid., p.665.
6. Ibid., p.725.

N o v e m b e r

1. Barclay, William. *The Gospel of Matthew*, Volume 2. (Philadelphia: The Westminster Press, 1975), p.102.
2. Ibid.
3. Luther, Martin. "A Mighty Fortress Is Our God," *The Cokesbury Worship Hymnal.* (Nashville: Abingdon Press, 1979), p.82.
4. Snell, Ted. Source unknown.
5. Johnson, Jan. *Enjoying the Presence of God.* (Colorado: Navpress, 1993), pp.23-24.
6. Untermeyer, Louis. "The Hare and the Tortoise," *Aesop's Fables.* (New York: Golden Press, 1965), pp.83-85.

D e c e m b e r

1. Barclay, William. *The Letters of John and Jude.* (Philadephia: The Westminster Press, 1976), p.84.
2. Boultinghouse, Philis. *Hugs for Sisters.* (Louisana: Howard Publishing Company, 2000), p.39.
3. Peale, Norman Vincent. *Plus—The Magazine of Positive Thinking.* (New York: The Peale Center for Christian Living, 1995), p.10.

TOPICAL INDEX

TITLE INDEX

NEW EVERY MORNING
ORDER FORM

Postal orders: Kate Thomas
185 Piping Rock Road
Brandenburg, KY 40108

Telephone and fax orders: 270-422-4897

Book Price: $14.99
plus 6% sales tax (.90 per book) for Kentucky residents

Shipping: $3.00 for the first book and $1.00 for each additional book to cover shipping and handling within US, Canada, and Mexico. International orders add $6.00 for the first book and $2.00 for each additional book.

Please send *New Every Morning* **to:**

Name: _____

Address: _____

City: _____ State: _____

Zip: _____

Telephone: (_____) _____

_____ books @ $14.99 each   _____

Kentucky sales tax (.90 per book)   _____

Shipping ($3.00 per book)   _____
$1.00 each additional book   _____

Total   _____

(Or contact your local bookstore)